INDUSTRIAL RELATIONS IN POSTWAR JAPAN

UNIVERSITY OF ILLINOIS PRESS, URBANA, 1958

INDUSTRIAL RELATIONS IN POSTWAR JAPAN

BY SOLOMON B. LEVINE

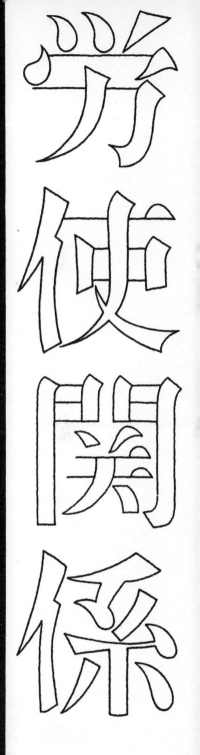

Second Printing, 1960

© 1958 by The Board of Trustees of the University of Illinois
Library of Congress Catalog Card No. 58-6997

MANUFACTURED IN THE UNITED STATES OF AMERICA

Foreword

The social and cultural interaction between America and other nations of the Western world has long been recognized. Until quite recently, however, the countries of Asia have seemed remote and of largely academic interest. World War II changed all this. During the war, millions of Americans came to realize in a highly personalized fashion that, incredible as it might seem, a tiny cluster of Pacific islands, known collectively as Japan, had somehow emerged as one of the great industrial powers of the world. After the war came the complex problems of carrying out an occupation which had as its major objective the reconciliation of the ideas of the East and the West.

In this book one of the few American scholars who possesses the rare combination of industrial relations expertise and knowledge of the Japanese language and culture passes on the fruits of his intensive studies in postwar Japan. What he has to say is important for a number of reasons. Japan is beyond any doubt more advanced industrially than other nations of Asia, but its history embraces the social and economic problems which other Asian nations are now facing and will continue to face. The way in which those other nations industrialize will be of immense interest to the rest of the world. Of particular importance is the relationship between the worker and the manager because it poses in microcosm the ideological problem which divides the world. Finally, the book contributes to that growing body of knowledge of industrial relations systems in the various countries of the world. These studies increase one's understanding of his own system and make possible analyses of similarities and differences under other systems. Out of all this may yet come a theory broad enough to encompass developments in widely different contexts.

America now finds itself in a position of leadership in the free world. In that connection it might be well to pause and remember that the American commitment to industrial self-government was in large measure a reflection of the conviction of its leaders that democracy in the plant contributed to democracy in government. This suggests that the study of industrial relations systems elsewhere may be more than ordinarily revealing of values which prevail in those countries. We live in a time when we must understand those values. This book is a significant contribution toward that end.

R. W. FLEMING, *Director*
INSTITUTE OF LABOR
AND INDUSTRIAL RELATIONS
UNIVERSITY OF ILLINOIS

Preface

At no time has our need for a careful appraisal of the impact of the West upon non-Western societies been as great as it is today. In order to be sure of our ground in the conflict of ideologies now raging throughout the world, it is urgent that we understand as thoroughly as possible why our values succeed or fail to gain acceptance among these peoples. Neglect of this task could lead to blundering efforts in the cold war struggle and perhaps to permanent relegation of democracy to a minority position in a major portion of the globe.

The experience of postwar Japan undoubtedly has been Exhibit A in the attempt to transpose the Western value system to the turbulent and dynamic Orient. Here, the occupying powers, chiefly the United States, undertook an immense and deliberate effort to restructure in their own ideological image the social, political, and economic arrangements of a nation which had already achieved an advanced stage of industrialization with a set of cultural values uncongenial to the tenets of democracy. As a social experiment, the occupation of Japan was without parallel in world history. To root out autocratic traditions, so deeply and tenaciously imbedded in this economically developed society, called for thoroughgoing scrutiny of nearly every aspect of Japanese life, great care in implanting democratic practices, and tireless guidance that these practices might flourish and spread. In the almost seven years of occupation, the investment for these purposes was enormous both in money and in human energy. Telescoped in such a short period were programs for social changes that had taken at least a century or two to develop elsewhere. Thus, what has emerged from this experience assumes special significance for the free world, for postwar Japan has been a major crucible in testing the appeal of Western ideology to a non-Western people.

Yet, even though the occupation ended more than six years ago, lack of careful follow-up investigation has left the results unclear. Of one thing we may be sure: the occupation served to release, or at least to implant, powerful social forces likely to produce durable changes in the Japanese nation. But our knowledge of what directions these changes are taking remains cursory and uneven. It is paradoxical indeed that, having assumed the primary responsibility for launching the New Japan and still possessing sizable economic and military commitments in that country, we of the free West have achieved little more than a superficial understanding of what has evolved in many facets of postwar Japan.

The purpose of this book is to report on one especially neglected but important phase of Japan's postwar rearrangements—her system of industrial relations. Broadly speaking, we may define industrial relations as the respective roles of management, labor, and government in the processes which relate workers to employers, workers to workers, and workers to work. Where industrialization occurs, the system of industrial relations becomes a main channel for the socio-cultural dynamics of a nation; that is, changes in industrial relations are likely to reflect major political, social, and economic trends. In view of the spectacular attempts by the occupation to reform Japanese industrial relations, this portion of Japan's recent experience warrants close attention for an adequate interpretation of contemporary developments in that nation.

It is useful at this point to indicate the viewpoint upon which this study rests. Unfortunately, we do not possess as yet a well-developed framework for the purpose of analyzing systems of industrial relations in differing national settings. Far more empirical and historical research and comparative analysis than we now have will be necessary before we can proceed with confidence in this task. Accordingly, the concepts used here are at best tentative in nature, and this study is offered as a contribution toward developing the needed general framework. To begin with, I have rejected the notion that industrialization everywhere follows a common pattern; rather, I have assumed that the historical process of industrialization is somewhat unique to the country under examination. This approach further assumes that factors which contribute to industrialization vary in form and content from culture to culture, and that, as a result, the systems which relate the parties who participate in the industrial process to one another and to those outside the process are also likely to differ significantly. In other words, it is not useful in this view to look to any one country as *the* model for industrialization and to measure the industrial relations systems of other nations against what has developed in the chosen model.[1] Thus, for example, while a labor movement seems to be a universal response to industrialization, its goals, functions, and structure may be quite dissimilar from country to country. To conclude that failure of a labor movement to conform to a particular model represents a "distortion" eventually to be corrected is to slight fundamental differences in the character of industrialism and the nature of cultural value systems. These two major variables are reference points to which the interpretation here will turn frequently.[2]

There have been relatively few conscious attempts in the field of industrial relations to undertake full studies based on the type of common framework suggested above. Although the works of Perlman[3] and Galenson,[4] among others, have been highly instructive, even these have usually been limited to analyzing the role of trade-unions in modern industrial societies instead of dealing squarely with whole systems of industrial relations. For this purpose, postwar Japan provides a useful case because, compressed within a very short period of time, the attempt to restructure the

[1] See Clark Kerr and Abraham Siegel, "The Structuring of the Labor Force in Industrial Society: New Dimensions and New Questions," *Industrial and Labor Relations Review*, VIII (January, 1955).

[2] Although a central interest of this study is to determine to what extent the restructuring of Japanese industrial relations has come to approach democratic Western (principally American) systems, it would be highly surprising to find that the type of industrial relations which has evolved in the experience of liberal capitalistic economies could be fully transposed to an environment whose characteristics have been of a very different sort. Moreover, it is not the intention of this study to evaluate the recent Japanese developments in terms of standards provided in American or any other Western democratic experience. American interests are likely to be served better by learning to understand why Oriental people behave the way they do within their own environmental contexts than by rushing in with bland pronouncements of what they should or should not be doing by standards related to another set of historical circumstances.

[3] Selig Perlman, *A Theory of the Labor Movement* (New York: Augustus M. Kelley, 1949), and "A Theory of the Labor Movement" (February, 1949), mimeographed.

[4] Walter Galenson (ed.), *Comparative Labor Movements* (New York: Prentice-Hall, 1952).

"web of rule" [5] governing manager and managed in industry came sharply to grips with a whole set of arrangements that had been developing for over half a century. The very starkness of the Japanese situation thus may be of considerable usefulness for suggesting significant questions about industrial relations in other countries.

Within the limited space of a short work, however, it is possible to cover only the main threads of Japan's postwar industrial relations. I have given little attention to many aspects which should be expanded in future research. I am also aware of other limitations of this study. Accurate observation and evaluation of events were difficult because many relevant materials were inaccessible and the historical perspective has been necessarily short. Yet, because of the urgency to build up our knowledge of the subject matter, I felt that it would be wiser to make available what is known in major outline, even at the expense of richness in detail and at the risk of some misinterpretations. There is value in raising questions as well as in answering them.

In the first chapter, I have dealt only briefly with the historical and environmental context of present-day industrial relations in Japan. The focus is largely on the principal characteristics of the contemporary Japanese economy, the process of Japan's industrialization, and the reforms undertaken by the occupation. I have introduced, where appropriate, additional analysis of these and other background factors in the succeeding chapters.

Chapters II, III, and IV take up the institutions of management and organized labor. For both, I have attempted to trace their evolution and present status. Because of the vital role entrepreneurship has played in Japan's modern economic development, I have tried to show in Chapter II the relationship between the managerial system in Japanese industry and the policies, attitudes, and approaches of employers toward their workers. Lack of detailed empirical data has prevented any but a generalized, impressionistic treatment of this subject. However, even at this level of analysis, the implications of the Japanese managerial system for industrialization and for the pattern of industrial relations are clear. The discussion relating to trade-unions is more specific than that relating to management because better records were available. Chapter III examines

---

[5] Kerr and Siegel, pp. 163-64.

in considerable detail the prewar origins and postwar growth of Japanese labor unions, and Chapter IV, the structure, functions, and ideologies of this movement.

Chapters V and VI deal with the interrelationship of employers and trade-unions, the former in terms of private collective bargaining and the latter in terms of the role of government. While it is difficult to discuss the two separately because of the pivotal position of the central government in the Japanese economy, I have analyzed them apart in order to assess the degree to which private collective bargaining actually has emerged and to clarify the areas where government affects bargaining relationships and directly sets terms and conditions of industrial employment. I have not attempted an analysis of the influences upon the formation of public policy toward industrial relations. This, I felt, would better be treated in a separate study of Japan's postwar political system.[6]

A final chapter summarizes the character of industrial relations in postwar Japan and offers observations on its future course. On the latter point, I have had to stray far afield into broad areas of world economics and politics in order to evaluate the position of the Japanese workingman—a hazardous undertaking at best.

In preparing this study, I have incurred many debts of gratitude to various groups and individuals. It is difficult to name all who furnished me with aid and guidance in undertaking this work. Without the generous support provided by the Ford Foundation and the United States Educational Commission in Japan (Fulbright Commission) and the grant of a sabbatical leave by the University of Illinois in 1953-54, it would not have been possible for me to spend a year in Japan for the collection of data and personal observation. I wish to acknowledge my indebtedness to these institutions, none of which, however, is responsible for statements of fact or opinion contained in this volume.

A substantial portion of the material included in the study de-

---

[6] Especially useful analyses are found in Harold S. Quigley and John E. Turner, *The New Japan: Government and Politics* (Minneapolis: University of Minnesota Press, 1956), and Allan B. Cole, *Japanese Society and Politics: The Impact of Social Stratification and Mobility on Politics*, Boston University Studies in Political Science, No. 1 (Boston: The Graduate School of Boston University, June, 1956). Other recent studies include Nobutaka Ike, *Japanese Politics: An Introductory Survey* (New York: Alfred A. Knopf, 1957), and Chitoshi Yanaga, *Japanese People and Politics* (New York: John Wiley and Sons, 1956).

rives from interviews and documents supplied to me by many Japanese informants. I am especially grateful to the Central Labor Relations Commission of Japan, to Hitotsubashi University, and to Dr. Ichiro Nakayama, present chairman of the Commission and recent president of the University, for providing me with resource materials and facilities while I was in Japan. I also wish to pay thanks to the two major trade-union centers of Japan, Sōhyō and Zenrō Kaigi, whose officials were extremely helpful in making available useful materials; to the Japanese Federation of Employers' Associations (Nikkeiren), also of inestimable help in this respect; and to various Japanese government agencies, especially the Ministry of Labor and the Ministry of Foreign Affairs.

I owe special debts to Professor Kazuo Okochi and Professor Mikio Sumiya and their colleagues in the Economics Department of the University of Tokyo; to Professor Shichiro Matsui of Doshisha University; to Professor Makoto Sakurabayashi of Sophia University, Tokyo; to Professors Keizo Fujibayashi and Hisashi Kawada of Keio University; and to Mr. Toyotaro Takemura, former liaison officer for the Central Labor Relations Commission. Without the wise counsel of these and many others too numerous to mention by name, no doubt I would have groped along less fruitful paths of inquiry.

Professor Iwao Ayusawa of the International Christian University of Tokyo, Mr. William Holland, Secretary-General, Institute of Pacific Relations, Professor Robert A. Scalapino of the University of California, Professor Sumiya, and my colleagues, Professors Robben W. Fleming, Milton Derber, William H. McPherson, and Bernard Karsh, spent many laborious hours reading the manuscript and offering invaluable criticisms and suggestions. I am also grateful to Mr. Hideaki Okamoto, formerly a graduate student in the Institute of Labor and Industrial Relations, University of Illinois, for his assistance. Only I, however, must be blamed for whatever errors of fact or interpretation have crept into this presentation.

For extremely helpful editorial improvements, I wish to thank Mrs. Barbara Dennis, also of the Institute, whose expertness transformed the manuscript into readable English. I also wish to thank the editors of The Journal of Asian Studies (formerly The Far Eastern Quarterly) for permission to draw from a previously published article. In the footnotes and in the selected bibliography, I have followed the style of The Journal in citing works of Japanese authors which originally appeared in Japanese and have not been translated into English. In the text that follows, Japanese names follow conventional Japanese usage.

Finally, I am especially grateful to my wife, Elizabeth Jane, and our children—Janet, Samuel, and Michael—who in sharing the experience of living in Japan for a year made the undertaking of this research even more pleasurable.

Contents

I

ECONOMIC SETTING,

INDUSTRIALIZATION, AND

OCCUPATION REFORMS

Japan's rapid, almost phenomenal, conversion from backward agrarianism to advanced industrialization often has been cited as unique among national economic developments. Although the process of this transformation has not been fully described as yet, the directions which it took and their implications for Japanese economic and political life have been carefully explored and reported.[1] It is clear that the changes wrought have provided an environmental setting for industrial relations wholly unlike that of Western nations.

This chapter provides a brief background for those to follow, first by examining the present Japanese economy for salient aspects which have emerged from the transformation—characteristics of the labor force and of the industrial structure, levels and distribution of income, and Japan's dependence upon international trade. It then outlines the nature of the underlying institutions that accompanied Japan's industrialization, and it concludes with a review of occupation reforms that dealt with these institutions and how these policies were applied during the seven years of occupation control.

LABOR FORCE

Knowledge of labor force size and distribution is a prerequisite to any discussion of a nation's system of industrial relations. To measure these, one must begin with population.

---

[1] See, for example, William W. Lockwood, *The Economic Development of Japan, Growth and Structural Change, 1868-1938* (Princeton: Princeton University Press, 1954), and Robert A. Scalapino, *Democracy and the Party Movement in Prewar Japan, The Failure of the First Attempt* (Berkeley: University of California Press, 1953).

From 1700 until the final decades of the nineteenth century, when Japan's industrialization first took shape, the population of the four home islands of Hokkaido, Honshu, Shikoku, and Kyushu had remained highly stable at less than 35 million. It more than doubled in the next fifty years. By 1920 it had climbed to more than 55 million. At the time of the outbreak of the Pacific war in 1941, the population was 72 million. It stabilized during the war years, but after V-J Day it began to rise again at a rate even more spectacular than before. An increase in birth rates, a decrease in death rates, and the repatriation of several million Japanese from overseas pushed the population to almost 84 million by 1950.

The rate of increase has not slackened. Recent estimates place Japan's population at more than 90 million. Despite a drop in birth rates below the American level, the population of Japan is expected to reach at least 95 million by 1965, 105 million by 1980, and 107 million by 1990. At that point it is expected to decline slowly to a minimum figure of 100 million sixty to seventy years from now.[2] All of this has occurred and will occur in an area of 371,000 square kilometers (slightly smaller than California), making Japan the fifth most populous country in the world, after China, India, the Soviet Union, and the United States, but with a population density higher than any country except the Netherlands and Belgium.[3]

Extremely limited natural resources furnished by the home islands contrast with the vast amounts of manpower which have been and will continue to be available for Japan's economic development. The terrain is mostly mountainous and rugged, leaving only one-fifth of the territory suitable for agriculture even with use of the most advanced technology and methods of land utilization. Chief compensations are a favorable climate, abundance of water and certain types of coal, and ready access to maritime food resources and to important shipping lanes. Aside from these factors, however, the country is poor in raw materials for industrial operations and,

---

[2] Ayanori Okazaki, "The Present and Future of Japan's Population," *Japanese Paper No. 4*, Twelfth Conference, Institute of Pacific Relations, Kyoto, Japan, September-October, 1954 (Tokyo: Japan Institute of Pacific Relations, 1954), p. 6, mimeographed. For another analysis of Japan's future population growth, with slightly higher projections, see Irene B. Taeuber, "Recent Population Developments in Japan: Some Facts and Reflections," *Pacific Affairs*, XXIX (March, 1956).

[3] Per square mile of cultivatable land, however, Japanese population density is now already double that of second-ranking Belgium.

even with full exploitation of tillable acreage, fails to be self-sufficient in meeting minimum food requirements. For example, at
present Japan must depend on foreign sources for all of her raw
cotton and bauxite, more than 90 per cent of her crude oil and
sugar, 75 per cent of her salt and iron ore, 20 per cent of her coal,
and about 20 per cent of her food staples. It is in the face of these
facts that the fast-growing Japanese population, geared to industrialization, assumes somewhat startling proportions.

The Japanese labor force now numbers well above 40 million
persons, or more than 45 per cent of the total population. In Japan,
nearly two-thirds of the population over fourteen years of age is in
the labor force, a high proportion when compared to the United
States where less than 55 per cent of the same age group belonged
to the labor force in 1950. A partial explanation may be found in
the large number of female workers in Japan—more than 41 per
cent of the total labor force. Moreover, the Japanese labor force
is growing, both absolutely and proportionately. Total increase
since 1947 has been 7 million, and the influx is expected to continue at the rate of about 750,000 per year for the next five years,
which will bring the total to about 45 million by 1960.[4] Since both
birth and death rates are declining, the number of persons in the
working population will increase in proportion to the total population. This will mean that employment opportunities must expand
rapidly if workers are to maintain their present income levels.

Precise measurement of unemployment in Japan is exceedingly
difficult. The impression left by official government statistics is that
the rate of unemployment is relatively low, averaging between 1
per cent and 2 per cent in recent postwar years. However, this
count is based only upon those who consider themselves to be in
the work force and who are completely out of work. Disguised,
hidden, or "latent" unemployment and underemployment, especially
in the form of unproductive self-employment, part-time jobs, and
work in small family enterprises, are widespread [5] and may include

---

[4] Okazaki, pp. 10-11. For labor force statistics covering recent years, see
Rōdō Hakusho (Labor White Paper), 1957 (Tokyo: Division of Labor Statistics and Research, Ministry of Labor, 1957). Each *Rōdō Hakusho* is cited hereafter as *Labor White Paper*.

[5] For an interesting discussion of this problem, see Tokutaro Yamanaka, "On
Latent Unemployment—An Interpretation as an Economic Problem," *The
Annals of the Hitotsubashi Academy*, VI (April, 1956), pp. 1-11; and Shigeto
Tsuru, "Employment in Japan: Problems and Prospects," *Far Eastern Survey*,
XXVI (July, 1957), pp. 97-103.

as much as 10–20 per cent of the labor force. On the other hand, low official unemployment figures indicate the resiliency of Japanese labor in adapting itself to various sectors of industrial activity.

Despite Japan's rise in fifty years to the position of sixth leading industrial nation in the world, agriculture still supports a major portion of her working population. As much as 40 per cent of the labor force is engaged in agricultural and forestry occupations, while 12.5 million farmers with their family members work some 6 million farms. Total agrarian population exceeds 38 million, and farms tend to be extremely small, varying from .75 to 12.5 acres.[6]

As shown in Table I, more than 25 million persons in Japan are found in nonagricultural employment. Of these, almost one-third are engaged in manufacturing, while a slightly smaller proportion is found in wholesale, retail, finance, insurance, and real estate fields. An additional 2 million are in transportation, communications, and public utilities; more than 4.5 million in services; more than one million in government; more than 1.8 million in construction; and about 500,000 each in mining and in fishing. Employment in services and commercial undertakings has been growing the most rapidly.

Japan's labor force distribution contrasts sharply with that of other advanced industrialized countries. Despite a downward trend, as late as 1953 more than 45 per cent of total employment was in "primary" industry (farming, forestry, and fishing), compared to 12.2 per cent in the United States, 5.0 per cent in Great Britain, and 23.2 per cent in West Germany. Moreover, Japan's "tertiary" employment (commerce, transportation, communication, public utilities, and services) of more than 31 per cent of the labor force

---

[6] In 1951, 35.6 per cent of all farms were smaller than 1.2 acres, even though 4.5 acres are considered a minimum for full-time farming in Japan. The small farm, made even smaller by the occupation land reform, is more prevalent today than prior to World War II. In 1941, only one-sixth of all farms had fewer than 1.2 acres. In addition, acreage under cultivation has also declined from about 14.4 million in 1941 to less than 12.6 million at present. On the other hand, the agricultural labor force has increased in this period from 13.5 million to about 17 million. See Robert S. Schwantes, *Japanese and Americans, A Century of Cultural Relations* (New York: Harper & Bros., 1955), pp. 59-60 and p. 60, fn. 36; Hiromi Arisawa, *Level of Living in Japan*, Economic Series No. 5 (Tokyo: The Science Council of Japan, Division of Economics and Commerce, March, 1955), pp. 9-10; Tetsugoro Noda, "Agriculture: Its Recovery and Development," *Contemporary Japan*, XXIV, Nos. 1-3 (1956), pp. 47-54; and Kazushi Ohkawa, "Economic Growth and Agriculture," *The Annals of the Hitotsubashi Academy*, VII (October, 1956), p. 47.

TABLE 1. DISTRIBUTION OF THE JAPANESE LABOR FORCE, 1951 AND 1956
   (in thousands)

	1951 (average)	1956 (average)	Change
Population	84,330	90,060	5,730
Total Labor Force	36,620	42,920	6,300
Employed	36,230	42,280	6,050
Unemployed	390	640	250
Employment by Industry:			
Agriculture and Forestry	16,170	16,820	650
Fisheries	520	580	60
Mining	510	460	−50
Construction	1,360	1,820	460
Manufacturing	6,300	7,660	1,360
Wholesale, Retail, Finance, Insurance, Real Estate,	5,150	7,040	1,890
Transportation, Communication, Public Utilities	1,840	2,070	230
Services	3,230	4,640	1,410
Government	1,140	1,170	30
Unclassified	10	20	10
Totals	36,230	42,280	6,050

Source: *Labor White Paper, 1957* (Tokyo: Division of Labor Statistics and Research, Ministry of Labor, 1957).

is relatively high compared to her "secondary" employment (mining, manufacturing, and construction) of less than 23 per cent. Only in the United States is tertiary employment substantially higher than secondary. In Great Britain they are about equal, and in West Germany the tertiary group is smaller.[7] Undoubtedly, the vast numbers of Japanese engaged in petty trades and services—partly out of lack of employment opportunities in industry and agriculture—account for this seeming imbalance of labor force utilization.

Wage- and salary-earners comprise a minority of the Japanese labor force, whereas in the United States three out of every four in the labor force are paid employees. Scarcely 40 per cent, or about 17.5 million persons (including only 620,000 in agriculture), receive wages and salaries in the employ of others, while 32 per

[7] *Wages in Japan* (Tokyo: The Daily Labour Press, Inc., 1954), p. 45. See, also, "The World's Working Population: Its Industrial Distribution," *International Labour Review*, LXXIII (May, 1956), pp. 501-21.

cent are family workers, productively employed but not receiving wage and salary payments on a regular basis. Almost one-fifth of these family workers are engaged in nonagricultural occupations. At least 25 per cent of the labor force are proprietors and self-employed, but probably no more than two-thirds of these employ paid workers. Within the employee group, nearly 60 per cent are manual laborers and apprentices and another 7 per cent are day workers. A sizable proportion, about 35 per cent, is composed of managerial, clerical, and technical personnel.[8]

INDUSTRIAL STRUCTURE

The relationships between managers and managed in the industrial process are basically patterned by the units of economic activity which bind the two groups together. The statistics of the preceding section indicate that only a minor portion of the Japanese labor force is directly involved in "modern" types of industrial relations. Since the beginning of her industrial expansion, a major feature of Japan's economic structure has been the proliferation of very small enterprises alongside relatively few giant establishments. No doubt the rapid rise of Japan as an industrialized nation could not have been achieved without the growth of both types of entrepreneurial organization. While the huge units became the keystone of modern industrialization, the small enterprises, too, have served as important means for economic development.

Japan's transition from an agrarian to an industrialized economy saw an exceedingly large proportion of her population remain attached to traditional occupations, both in agriculture and in small shops, handicrafts, petty trades, and personal services. Although these grew in the backwash of modern industrial enterprise, their growth and spread served to maintain traditional modes of economic behavior with pervading results for industrial relationships even in the large undertakings. What their growth reflected, of course, was sparseness of capital available for large-scale investments, depleted even further by war damage and postwar dismantling of plant and equipment. As Lockwood points out, the Japanese economic transformation was remarkable in that it did provide outlets for

---

[8] *Labor White Paper, 1957*, pp. 302-3, and *Industry and Labour*, IX (January 15, 1953), pp. 39-40. See, also, "The World's Working Population: Its Distribution by Status and Occupation," *International Labour Review*, LXXIV (August, 1956), pp. 174-92.

productive energy through a huge network of small undertakings.[9]

This admixture of entrepreneurial units flourishes today in Japan. The 6 million farming establishments, each employing only a small number of persons and contributing little to the national product, exist alongside some 3,750,000 nonagricultural establishments. In March, 1952, about 93 per cent of the latter were small individual enterprises; 95,000 were partnership, joint-stock, or limited companies; and 165,000, or 4.8 per cent of the total, were corporations. Only the corporations employed significant numbers of workers, but even among them merely 1,700 establishments had as many as 500 employees each.[10]

Both large and small nonagricultural establishments are critically important to the Japanese economy in terms of employment. About one-fourth of the nonagricultural labor force is found in the large companies, if the line between large and small is drawn at 100 employees—a relatively low number compared to "large" firms in other industrialized nations, but in Japan only 0.3 per cent of the establishments fall into this group. Companies with fewer than thirty employees furnish more than 60 per cent of nonagricultural employment.[11] Companies with fewer than twenty employees furnish almost 54 per cent of nonagricultural employment and comprise more than 96 per cent of the total number of establishments. Eighty-one per cent of all manufacturing plants have nine employees or less and provide 23 per cent of employment in manufacturing. At the other end of the scale, factories which employ more than 500 workers each comprise less than 0.2 per cent of the total number of factories and account for close to 23 per cent of manufacturing employment.[12] Union membership since the war period has been highly concentrated among the large units.

---

[9] Lockwood, p. 578.

[10] About 85 per cent of all nonagricultural enterprises were capitalized at the equivalent of $3,000 or less, while a bare 0.2 per cent had capital valued as high as $150,000. See Sakurabayashi Makoto, Rōshi Kankei No Nihonteki Seikaku, ("Characteristics of Japanese Labor Relations") Seni Keizai (Textile Economy), No. 21 (December, 1953), pp. 14-15; and Rōdō Kumiai Chōsa Hōkōku (Report on the Survey of Labor Relations), July, 1952 (Tokyo: Ministry of Labor, April, 1953), p. 6. Capitalization is computed on the basis of 360 yen to $1.00, the official exchange rate.

[11] Wages in Japan, pp. 48-49. For international comparisons, see "The Size of Industrial Establishments," International Labour Review, LXXIII (June, 1956), pp. 634-44.

[12] Wages in Japan, pp. 48-49. By way of comparison, in 1947, manufactur-

The past decade has seen rapid expansions and contractions in the small enterprise sector of Japanese industry. A heavy turnover continually occurs among these establishments. Small undertakings multiplied quickly during the postwar economic chaos, which virtually paralyzed operation of the big units; the majority of the new labor force participants tended to drift into the very small operations. For example, despite a sizable increase of more than 3 million (about 12 per cent) in the labor force between 1951 and 1953, employment of regular workers in enterprises with thirty or more employees remained almost stationary.[13] In contrast, during the two marked recessions of postwar Japanese economy, in 1951 and 1953, the small enterprises were driven into bankruptcy by the hundreds.

If we examine each component of Japan's industrial structure to determine its productive contribution relative to its proportion of the labor force, economic imbalances are readily noted. Primary industry employs nearly half of the labor force, but accounts for less than one-fourth of the value of national product. Secondary industry, with slightly more than one-fifth of the employment, contributes almost one-third of the product; while tertiary industry, embracing about one-third of the total work force, furnishes a little less than half the output value.[14] How these disparities appear in income levels and distribution is discussed in a later section of this chapter.

In the manufacturing sector, textiles, metals, machinery, foodstuffs, and chemicals are leading industries both in value of output and in amount of employment. Together, in 1950 they produced almost 78 per cent of the value output in manufacturing production, while employing about 72 per cent of the factory workers.[15] It is particularly among these that large-scale private businesses

---

ing firms with more than 500 employees in the United States accounted for 1.9 per cent of all manufacturing firms, but for more than 35 per cent of the total manufacturing employment; while American manufacturing firms with fewer than ten workers made up almost 50 per cent of all manufacturing enterprises, they provided only 3.5 per cent of manufacturing employment.

[13] *Year Book of Labor Statistics, 1952* (Tokyo: Division of Labor Statistics and Research, Ministry of Labor, 1952), pp. 17, 31; and *Year Book of Labor Statistics, 1953,* pp. 15, 25.

[14] *Wages in Japan,* pp. 45-46.

[15] *Japan in Industry, 1954* (Tokyo: The Oriental Economist, 1954), p. 13. See, also, George Rosen, "Japanese Industry Since the War," *Quarterly Journal of Economics,* LXVII (August, 1953), p. 449.

are found, often surrounded by thousands of small firms. Yet, even among these major manufacturing sectors, considerable disparities abound. In 1950, textiles accounted for about one-fifth of manufacturing employment and output, but machinery, although equal to textiles in employment, yielded only one-seventh of the total product. Metals, with 12 per cent of the employment, produced one-sixth of the output; chemicals with 9 per cent of the workers, and foodstuffs with nearly 10 per cent, each accounted for approximately one-eighth. All other manufacturing industries—which include ceramics, woodworking, printing, finishing and repairing, gas and electricity, and so forth—together provided more than 28 per cent of the factory jobs, but only slightly above 22 per cent of the production value.[16]

Since 1930 the Japanese industrial structure, especially manufacturing, has undergone significant transformations, principally as the result of militarization in the decade before the war and partly because of the postwar readjustments. As shown in Table II, the principal changes have been a decline by more than one-third of the proportion of value output contributed by textiles and a reduction of about three-fifths in the ratio of textile jobs to total manufacturing employment. In contrast, metals doubled its proportion of output and employment, while machinery doubled its employment ratio and increased its share in production by 40 per cent. The relative positions of other manufacturing industries have remained approximately the same.[17]

LEVEL AND DISTRIBUTION OF INCOME

Despite industrialization, Japan could barely bring her huge and growing population above the level of subsistence, even before the destruction wrought by the war. Her military aggression is commonly attributed to this fact. In 1952, when Japan finally regained her prewar level of income, national income per capita was still only $172 per year, merely one-tenth of the United States average, less than one-seventh of Canada's, one-sixth of Sweden's and Switzerland's, less than one-fifth of Britain's, one-fourth of France's, and hardly a third of West Germany's and Italy's.[18]

[16] Japan in Industry, 1954, p. 13.

[17] Ibid., pp. v, 13.

[18] Ryokichi Minobe, "A Statistical Survey of Japan's Poverty," Contemporary Japan, XXIII, Nos. 1-3 (1954), pp. 193-99. Per capita income, however, has

Table II. OUTPUT AND EMPLOYMENT BY MANUFACTURING INDUSTRIES IN JAPAN, 1930, 1935, AND 1950 (percentages)

	Production Value			Employment		
Industry	1930	1935	1950	1930	1935	1950
Total	100.0	100.0	100.0	100.0	100.0	100.0
Textiles						
Cotton Spinning	7.2	8.1	5.6	7.1	6.8	3.2
Cotton Weaving	7.0	5.9	4.3	6.6	5.6	4.1
Other	19.8	16.9	11.8	37.4	28.1	14.3
Metals	8.7	17.3	16.4	5.2	9.4	11.7
Machinery	10.3	13.5	14.1	10.9	16.1	21.0
Chemicals	15.5	16.7	13.2	7.6	10.1	8.5
Foodstuffs	15.9	10.8	12.5	8.7	7.0	9.0
Other	15.6	10.8	22.1	16.5	16.9	28.2

Source: Japanese Ministry of International Trade & Industry, as cited in *Japan in Industry, 1954* (Tokyo: The Oriental Economist, 1954), p. 13.

On the other hand, Japan's postwar recovery, while not as re-markable as West Germany's, has been admirable in face of more than a 25 per cent increase in population and loss of almost half her territorial empire. Real national income per capita in 1946 had fallen to 52 per cent of the 1934-36 level. Slowly recovering, this index reached 69 by 1949, and stimulated by the boom of the Korean War, it rose to more than 83 just a year later. In 1953 the index finally broke through the prewar level with national income attaining 106.2 per cent of the 1934-36 figure. An upward course has since continued.[19] 1956 and 1957, for example, were boom years with industrial production reaching a level more than twice that of the mid-1930's.

Throughout the postwar period, Japan's economy experienced severe price imbalances which in other economies might have been accompanied by serious declines in real national income. A ram-pant inflation persisted for four years after the surrender, with the

continued to improve, absolutely and relatively, reaching $184 in 1953 and more than $200 by 1956. See Yuzo Morita, "The National Income and the Standard of Living of Japan," *Japan Quarterly*, III (January-March, 1956), p. 108, and *The Oriental Economist*, XXV (July, 1957), pp. 343-45.

[19] "Ten Years of Japan's Postwar Economy," *The Oriental Economist*, XXIII, No. 540 (October, 1955), pp. 501-2. See, also, Jerome B. Cohen, *Japan's Economy in War and Reconstruction* (Minneapolis: University of Minnesota Press, 1949), pp. 447-68, and Morita, pp. 107-8.

official Consumer Price Index for Tokyo rising by 1949 to a point
200 to 300 times the 1934-36 level. The steepest jump occurred between 1947 and 1948 when this index advanced by close to 75
per cent. Actually, inflation struck even harder as prices on black
markets, where more daily necessities were bought and sold, rose
at three to four times this rate.[20] The inflation was halted by the
occupation-sponsored Dodge Plan, which eliminated government
deficit borrowing and inflationary note issues, ended government
subsidies to private business, stabilized the rate of exchange, and
placed controls on prices. By 1950 the Consumer Price Index actually had dropped. But the sudden emergence of Japan as a crucial
U.N. supply base in the Korean conflict brought on a resumption
of price rises. With the Korean stalemate in 1952, inflation again
tapered off; under the government's austerity program since the
Korean truce in 1953, price levels have held fairly constant.

Partly as the result of the inflation, income distribution in Japan
in the postwar years has tended toward greater equality. Put realis-
tically, poverty has been shared more widely.[21] Nevertheless, wide
disparities still exist. Although employing almost half of the population, primary industry furnishes only about one-sixth of the total
national income, while secondary and tertiary industry share the
remaining five-sixths about equally. Average per capita income
in each of the latter sectors is about three times that in agriculture.

On the other hand, the price inflation, particularly in food staples,
has benefited farmers. Proprietors in general have gained during
the postwar period, their share in the national income rising from
about one-third before the war to more than 40 per cent by 1952
(see Table III). Similarly, wage- and salary-earners achieved an
advance from less than 40 per cent to more than 45 per cent, a relatively high proportion for this group, which comprises only a little
more than one-third of the labor force. The chief losers in the postwar period have been the receivers of rent and interest, whose
share declined drastically from 18 per cent before the war to about
3 to 4 per cent at the present time. This reduction has been due in
large measure to the occupation-sponsored land reform program

---

[20] "Ten Years of Japan's Postwar Economy," p. 502.

[21]Arisawa (op. cit., p. 38), estimates that somewhere between 20 per cent
and 25 per cent of all Japanese households are "destitute," that is, they fail
to earn enough to provide for minimum living costs.

Table III. DISTRIBUTION OF NATIONAL INCOME IN JAPAN FOR SELECTED YEARS, 1934-52

	1934-36	1946	1947	1948	1949	1950	1951	1952
Wages and Salaries	38.9	30.8	32.6	42.2	41.8	42.4	43.3	47.2
Individual Proprietors								
Farmers, Foresters, Fishermen	13.7	33.9	31.3	27.9	23.8	23.0	21.9	20.5
Others	17.6	31.3	34.8	27.7	25.0	22.0	20.7	21.6
Rent and Interest	18.2	3.5	1.9	1.7	1.8	2.1	2.1	2.4
Corporate Profit	8.7	1.1	1.1	2.6	5.3	9.9	10.9	8.1
Other	2.0	0.6	1.7	2.1	2.3	0.1	1.1	0.1
Total	100.0	100.0	100.0	100.0	100.0	100.0	100.0	100.0

Source: Adapted from Hiromi Arisawa, *Level of Living in Japan*, Economics Series No. 5 (Tokyo: The Science Council of Japan, Division of Economics and Commerce, March, 1955), p. 7.

and the elimination of absentee ownership in the farm areas. Corporate profits, on the other hand, amounting to 8–10 per cent of the national income, have remained fairly stable.[22]

The increase in the proportion of the national income going to employees deserves special comment because the aggregate hides significant relationships within the group. Although the share of employees as a whole has increased, large disparities have continued among the subgroups. Using the average monthly wages of workers in firms with 500 or more employees as 100, in May, 1956, the index for the firms employing nine workers or less was 57; for firms employing 10 to 29 workers, less than 63; for firms employing 30 to 99 workers, less than 70; and for firms employing 100 to 499 workers, less than 80.[23] Between 1949 and 1952, the trend for all of the categories under the "500 workers or more" class was toward a smaller ratio even though money and real wages for all increased steadily during this period.[24] Since about 1953, however, employees in the small firms have gained slightly over those in large firms.[25]

---

[22] *Ibid.*, p. 7. For comparisons with other countries, see Morita, pp. 109-10.

[23] *Labor White Paper, 1957*, p. 174.

[24] Sakurabayashi, p. 20.

[25] *Labor White Paper, 1957*, p. 174. See, also, Shigeto Tsuru, "Internal Industrial and Business Trends," *The Annals of the American Academy of Political and Social Science*, CCCVIII (November, 1956), pp. 92-93.

In any event, wage differentials by size of firm appear to be much wider than those in most other industrialized countries.[26]

Glaring discrepancies in wage rates also exist from industry to industry and between male and female workers. Although industrial wage differentials on the average have tended toward greater equality over the past twenty years, Japan still has one of the largest ranges in wages by industry among the advanced industrial nations.[27] Similarly, despite a gradual closing of the sex differential, the wages of female workers have remained notoriously below those of male workers in comparison with other countries.

Nonetheless, membership in the wage-earning class generally offers distinct income advantages. Thus, the average paid employee received 12 per cent more in 1951 and over 21 per cent more in 1952 than the average member of the total labor force.[28] In most other industrialized nations the ratios are usually the reverse. Thus, a wage-earner in industry, at least in the large firms where "ability to pay" is relatively high and the workers are fully organized, receives higher income than workers in most other walks of Japanese economic life.

In the postwar period, real wages recovered more rapidly than real per capita national income, although they had fallen below the 1934-36 level somewhat more than the latter had. For example, with 1934-36 as 100, the real wage index for manufacturing stood at only 30 in 1947, but it climbed to more than 66 by 1949, and above 92 by 1951. In 1952 the index exceeded 102, and in 1953 it climbed to more than 107.[29] In light of the disparities between the small and large firms, the "pull" of the latter was most responsible for raising average real wages during these years. This did not mean, however, that wage-carners were appreciably better off than they had been before the war. Growth of average family size and alterations in the quality and availability of various goods and

---

[26] See, for example, Yamanaka, pp. 1-2.

[27] "Changing Wage Structures: An International Review," *International Labor Review*, LXXIII (March, 1956), p. 280.

[28] *Wages in Japan*, p. 5.

[29] *Ibid.*, p. 28. See, also, Boris S. Yane, "Wages in Japanese Mining and Manufacturing," *Monthly Labor Review*, LXXVIII (May, 1955), pp. 547-52. By 1956, real wages in manufacturing had increased an additional 25 per cent. See *Labor White Paper, 1957*, p. 157.

services probably still left most worker households at a lower standard of living in 1953 than in 1934-36 (see Table IV).

Table IV. INDEXES OF REAL NATIONAL PER CAPITA INCOME, CONSUMER PRICES,
AND REAL MONTHLY INCOME OF WAGE-EARNERS IN JAPAN FOR SE-
LECTED YEARS 1934-52

	Real National Income Per Capita	Consumer Prices	Real Monthly Income of Wage-Earners [a]
1934-36	100.0	100.0	100.0
1949	71.9	2369.0	57.8
1950	78.1	2199.0	69.1
1951	85.6	2555.0	72.0
1952	100.0	2661.0	84.0

[a] Tokyo only, adjusted for changes in family size.

Source: Hiromi Arisawa, *Level of Living in Japan*, Economic Series No. 5 (Tokyo: The
Science Council of Japan, Division of Economics and Commerce, March, 1955),
pp. 4, 15.

WORLD TRADE AND INDUSTRIAL PRODUCTIVITY

Pervading all aspects of Japanese economic life is the critical
importance of access to raw materials and to trade outlets in world
markets. International trade, accounting for more than a third of
Japan's national income, is vital to most of her modern industrial
operations. For example, the textile industry, employing over 2
million workers, depends almost entirely upon imports of raw cotton, wool, and other fibers and upon foreign purchases of a major
portion of its output. These examples may be multiplied, for few
of the major industries are self-sufficient either in terms of basic
national resources or domestic trade outlets. Accordingly, the Japanese economy is extremely sensitive to world market conditions
and heavily dependent upon trade policies of foreign governments.
To compete successfully in international trade, Japanese industry
must constantly seek legitimate means to increase productive efficiency and cut costs.

Although during the postwar period Japan has been able to recover its prewar production level and to make rapid advances in
productivity, recovery of foreign trade has lagged seriously. Within
a few years after the war ended, the foreign trade of most nations,
even those devastated by war, exceeded prewar levels. As late as
1953, however, Japan had recovered only 31 per cent of exports

and 54 per cent of imports compared to the 1937 volume.[30] Although the government's austerity program since 1953 has led to
marked improvements in overseas trade and foreign trade balances,[31] restrictions on the entry of Japanese goods into various
markets, new sources of foreign competition in traditionally Japanese selling areas, the cutting of trade connections with continental
Asia and the Soviet bloc, and the inability of Japanese industry to
keep costs from rising continue to be stubborn barriers to full recovery. Unfavorable trade balances have been barely compensated
by some 4 billion dollars of American aid, troop spending, and
special military procurements over the past ten years. In turn, the
expansion of production and employment opportunities has been
seriously hampered, although the extent to which postwar output
has grown is remarkable in face of the relatively low level of raw
material imports. Moreover, the hope for domestic market expansion, while offering a vast potential as a means for attaining Japan's
economic viability, rests in the last analysis upon stepping up the
flow of imports and exports.

It is not possible to discuss here all the political and economic
intricacies of Japan's foreign trade problem. For our purposes, it
suffices to point out that the stringent pressures generated by the
problem give rise to some of the most crucial issues in the relations
between workers and employers. Attempts to increase productivity
as a means of improving Japan's foreign trade position disturb industrial relationships at both local and national levels. Moreover,
the intricate interdependence of Japanese industrial operations,
geared as they are to the vicissitudes of world trade conditions,
has made industrial conflict difficult to contain. Repercussions are
apt to be immediate, severe, and widespread.

Today, Japan is seeking to solve the pressing problem of raising
productivity by economizing on the use of imported raw materials,
fully exploiting what natural resources she does possess, effectively
deploying the labor force, and taking other measures to reduce
costs for competitive pricing in world markets. Overseas markets,

---

[30] *Ibid.*, pp. 67-68.

[31] In 1956, exports had recovered to 86 per cent and imports to 111 per cent
of the 1934-36 level. Also, for the first time in the postwar period, Japan
achieved a favorable annual trade balance in 1955. The favorable balance
amounted to a half billion dollars. See *Japan Report*, II (November 15, 1956),
pp. 4-5, and III (July 10, 1957), p. 3, mimeographed.

of course, also must be open, and Japan's recent admission to the General Agreement on Tariffs and Trade (GATT) organization is an encouraging example of meeting this need. On the other hand, productive resources must be carefully combined, especially in view of the extremely rapid population increase. Exceptionally strong incentives for capital accumulation must be offered, and the flow of capital must be effectively co-ordinated and controlled. The degree of such controls and the control policies themselves raise political questions of intense concern for rival political groups within the country. In turn, fundamental ideological issues are likely to be evoked, especially as Japan is torn between the East and the West in their cold war conflict.

These problems have been rooted in Japan's industrialization process, in which the sudden transition from agrarianism to industrialism was aggravated and unbalanced by a reckless militarism that ended in disaster. For the foreseeable future, Japan has few prospects of an immediate solution to these problems. Economically, the situation could easily worsen for certain important sectors of the population, if not for the nation as a whole. The years ahead will be ones of transition, and the outcome will depend upon the efficacy of the institutions which determine the process of achieving Japan's place in the world economy.

INSTITUTIONS OF INDUSTRIALIZATION

Modernization of the Japanese economy in the short space of fifty years required intense and concentrated use of its productive resources, abundant in unskilled manpower but extremely deficient in skilled labor, technical know-how, basic raw materials, and capital. Successful management of these factors in catapulting Japan to a position among the leading powers was a feat of no small magnitude. It evolved principally through tight controls exercised by three organized institutional groups in Japanese society—the government bureaucracy, the military, and the industrialist clique known as the *Zaibatsu*.[32]

---

[32] It is appropriate to add still a fourth group to Japan's ruling elites in the prewar industrializing era—the landlords. This group is not discussed here because of its more remote role in the actual processes of industrialization. It should be noted on the other hand that at least in the early period of Japan's industrialization the landlords used their rental proceeds for industrial investment and in this way provided a chief source of capital for new industries. By and large, however, they remained identified with the control of social and

This triumvirate early worked out their mutual relationships and guided Japan through its era of industrialization. Utilizing the concept of a unifying Emperor System and indoctrinating the population with a sense of national destiny, the combination avoided what other Asian nations failed to avoid—economic and political colonization of Japan by the West. In fact, the very industrialization of Japan was predicated upon meeting the threat of Western invasion. Except in the earliest stages of the transformation, Japan relied little upon borrowed foreign capital. Instead she managed to meet her own requirements through internal savings, favorable trade balances, and foreign invasion. For this objective, the three major institutions worked in reasonable harmony until Japan reached the limits of peaceful economic expansion. After the Manchurian Incident in 1931, the system broke down. The military group virtually subdued the bureaucracy and *Zaibatsu* and eventually led Japan into the China and Pacific Wars.

In this schema, there was little room for the development of other effective organized interest groups. Farm, labor, and small merchant groups offered no serious challenge.

Although the huge mass of peasants continued to grow along with economic expansion and industrialization, they remained wedded to traditional forms of social organization and, except in sporadic instances, offered relatively little resistance to the ruling cliques.[33] Despite improvements in agricultural methods and techniques, the agrarian system remained intact. Even today, except for the notable shift in formal land ownership brought about by the postwar reform,[34] social organization in agriculture has undergone

political life in the rural areas and tended to refrain from direct participation in industrial management except as members of their group entered the military or government bureaucracy. The postwar reforms, of course, significantly shook the hold of the landlords in the agrarian areas.

[33] Tenant farmer grievances against landlords, however, mounted steadily after World War I. In 1935, for example, landlord-tenant disputes reported by the Japanese government numbered close to 7,000. See David E. Lindstrom, "Outlook for the Land Reform in Japan," *Contemporary Japan*, XXIV, Nos. 1-3 (1956), p. 88; Andrew J. Grad, *Land and Peasant in Japan, An Introductory Survey* (New York: Institute of Pacific Relations, 1953), pp. 133-34; and L. I. Hewes, Jr., *Japan—Land and Men: An Account of the Japanese Land Reform Program, 1945-51* (Ames: Iowa State College Press, 1955), pp. 33-35.

[34] The postwar land reform virtually eliminated the traditional system of farm tenancy. Before the reform was achieved, almost half the arable land was tenanted. Today, less than one-tenth is farmed by tenants. See Ohkawa, p. 47.

little change. Intensive land use, principally achieved by improved fertilization and crop control, permitted an increase in food and other farm produce to sustain rapid population growth even though acreage expansion was small in proportion. While the population rise furnished recruits for the new industrial and military operations, a large part of the increment was absorbed by farm units already in existence. Peasant living standards remained at traditional, near-poverty levels, and only scant protests were raised against the farmer's plight from time to time.

Likewise, the growing industrial labor force did not assume a position of importance in the complex of group interests that led Japan through its industrializing era. Efforts to organize a labor movement failed to catch fire to any significant degree. Culturally, the notion of a labor movement had two strikes against it from the beginning. The concept of a mass movement, even one based upon conservative ideology, was foreign to basic institutional relationships long characteristic of Japanese society. A horizontal amalgamation of workers ran counter to traditions of vertical loyalties stemming from the age-old consanguinal family system and feudal relationships. Ingrained superior-subordinate relations were fortified by religious and ethical precepts of Buddhism, Confucianism, and Shintoism, which stressed self-discipline, nonmaterialism, fatalism, and fixed social stratification, and, after the Meiji Restoration, by an Emperor System, which affirmed the monarch's "divinity" and required conformity and subservience of all groups to the aims of "The Imperial Polity" (*Kokutai*). The ruling cliques, whose functions were central in achievement of these aims, were conceived as "assisting" the Emperor in his "divine" mission. This left little room for an actively protesting labor movement.

Industrialization in Japan not only caused little social upheaval in traditional agricultural organization, but also deterred an overflow of discontent from the old rural to the new urban sectors. A distinct urbanized proletariat developed much more slowly in Japan than in the nations that experienced the Industrial Revolution of the eighteenth and nineteenth centuries. The earliest recruits for Japan's new industry were largely females, the "surplus" daughters of the struggling farmers. In fact, until fairly recently, many in Japan considered industrial work as befitting only women; the manly occupations were considered those attached to agriculture.

The industrial labor force was hardly committed to industrialization in any conventional sense. Workers perceived industrial work as supplementary to agrarian pursuits. Even though they might find their temporary attachment to industry extending over long periods, they constantly hoped to return to the family farm. Second, third, fourth (and usually more) sons of farm families, who had no rights of primogeniture, drifted into factories, but they aspired to resume agrarian life within the security of the family system, even though they actually had no real prospect of returning to the already overcrowded villages and farms. Especially after the Manchurian Incident of 1931, when Japanese industry turned increasingly to munitions and other heavy production, workers were drawn mainly from distressed and overpopulated farming areas, rather than from open labor markets in cities. In some cases, plants were located among the paddies to take advantage of the plentiful rural labor supplies.

In any event, the worker was likely to be only a half-proletarian, dividing his time between factory and field. The working class was unstable and, in effect, largely migratory. Only a relatively small hard core of workers sheltered by systems of paternalism were permanently in industry, for example, in the machinery manufacturing plants; the rest, notably in the huge textile mills, were temporary, or at least considered themselves temporary. These labor market characteristics help to explain why industrial plants experienced frequent shortages of labor despite the huge growth of population. Shortages derived to a large extent both from rapid labor turnover and from lack of industrial labor skills. Workers floated between farm and factory with in-between stops in the growing myriad of small shops and industries. In view of these conditions, establishment of effective trade-unionism was extremely difficult.

A powerful merchant group also had little chance to emerge. The central government deliberately initiated modern industrialization. In contrast to Western European industrialization, the Japanese industrial development was not the product of forces growing out of a disintegration of feudalism following an outburst of private entrepreneurship. Industrialism was imposed upon an ongoing social organization. Only after the government had firmly established certain basic units of modern industrial production—especially for armament and textile production—were they turned over to select private managements, who in many cases continued to receive state subsidies. It was this entrepreneurial group that came to be known as the *Zaibatsu,* relatively advanced in management expertise and completely trustworthy for the promotion of nationalistic aims. This elite was drawn principally from a small number of well-disciplined family groupings traditionally identified with the ruling feudal clans of the past either as family members (lower samurai) of these clans or as merchants who had long served the commercial and financial needs of feudal lords. Each of the *Zaibatsu* —recognized by such familiar names as Mitsui, Mitsubishi, Sumitomo, Yasuda, and others—eventually came to control well-articulated economic empires within Japan, embracing virtually all types of modern manufacturing, trading, and financial operations.

The small enterprises that grew in large numbers alongside these modern combines were left to themselves unless they threatened to compete directly with the *Zaibatsu,* in which case they were absorbed. Yet, they did not come to constitute a sturdy middle class which could threaten the position of the ruling groups. By nature and interests they were highly heterogeneous and served primarily local and traditional needs. Some, however, such as those producing silk, ceramics, lacquerware, and other indigenous products, did find ready overseas markets and in the aggregate assumed an important position in Japanese foreign trade. Their function complemented the *Zaibatsu* operations, and they were often sustained by *Zaibatsu* marketing, financing, and subcontracting arrangements. In addition, they served as shock absorbers for economic fluctuations in the industrializing process, thereby assuming many risks which the *Zaibatsu* preferred not to undertake. On the other hand, despite the wide latitude afforded petty enterprise, economic development was not left to mere chance. Investment capital was procured by taxing the peasants and by controlling proceeds from foreign trade. Each operation of any magnitude had a specific role to play in terms of the national polity and found its appropriate place within the well-articulated *Zaibatsu* structures. All three ruling groups had some say in these allocations.

Labor recruiting practices in the development of modern industrial enterprise deserve brief comment here. To meet labor requirements, management relied upon recruits drawn from the large mass of unskilled available in the growing agricultural population. And the early development of a universal public education system was designed in part to overcome the most glaring deficiencies in needed work skills. By and large, the industrial labor force was made up of marginal workers whose productivity was low, perhaps even negative, in the agrarian sectors. As a result, labor market flows came under the firm direction of industrial managers who utilized traditional organizational concepts for the task. In their view, any other approach was likely to thwart desired relationships and give rise to the formation of interest groups, such as trade-unions and left-wing political parties, which would threaten the sought-after objectives.

Accordingly, the structure of the labor markets became a set of vertical or "manorial" channels, whereby workers in search of employment could not expect to float freely from one labor market to another but were confined to specific routes, usually between a given farm area and a given factory or enterprise, in some instances geographically separated by hundreds of miles. Company recruiters, with specific territorial assignments, and so-called "labor bosses," who commanded the allegiance of close followers, were commonly depended upon to meet the particular needs of each specialized unit of the *Zaibatsu* operations.

Arrangements such as these served to fortify the position of the *Zaibatsu*. In a brief space of two or three generations, this system of industrialism became firmly rooted. It grew imperceptibly in the blur between agriculture and industry, nurtured by traditional cultural norms inherent in the family and feudal systems. It was accepted as a major means of fulfilling the nationalistic goals widely shared among the Japanese population. Thus, a tenacious industrial institutionalism confronted the occupation in its attempts at reform after the surrender.

OCCUPATION REFORMS [35]

Major occupation reforms extended into civil, religious, political, and economic life. A new Japanese constitution was written. The educational system was revised. The military, of course, was eliminated. The basis for farm ownership was drastically altered. Control of industry was formally restructured, the civil service system revamped, and a trade-union movement reborn.

---

[35] For fuller discussion of occupation reforms and policies, see Robert A. Fearey, *Occupation of Japan; Second Phase, 1948-1950* (New York: Macmillan, 1950); Edwin M. Martin, *The Allied Occupation of Japan* (Stanford: Stanford University Press, 1948); Robert B. Textor, *Failure in Japan* (New York: John Day, 1951); Harry E. Wildes, *Typhoon in Tokyo* (New York:

Aside from demolishing the military, the occupation gave initial and primary emphasis to revising Japan's political system. Freedom of speech, assembly, and press was immediately proclaimed. Thousands of political prisoners were released from jails, and the banished returned from overseas. Ground was laid for a new political configuration, and encouragement was given to the formation of popular political parties supporting virtually any ideology other than ultranationalism.

The new Japanese constitution, written largely by occupation authorities, was promulgated within fifteen months after the surrender and took effect on May 3, 1947. Its chief features provided that the Emperor be stripped of "divine" status and become a constitutional monarch. Theoretically, the people obtained complete sovereignty, restricted for the duration of the occupation by rules and regulations laid down by the Supreme Commander for the Allied Powers (SCAP), who was General Douglas MacArthur. Ultimate government power was placed in the hands of a popularly elected bicameral Diet. In turn the lower house members selected a prime minister whose cabinet would be responsible to the Diet, not to the Emperor. Powers of the central government were considerably reduced, and local government autonomy concomitantly increased. Prefectural assemblies and governors were made independent of central government control and were popularly elected. A check-and-balance system within government was partially structured. While the government bureaucracy remained virtually intact, except for the abolition of the nefarious Home Ministry and the shifting about of various administrative agencies (including the creation of a Ministry of Labor in 1947), the civil service was reformed and made responsible to the Cabinet and Diet, ending its existence as an independent entity.

Education was a special target of the occupation. Because the schools had been highly instrumental in promoting traditional cultural concepts believed to be at the basis of Japanese militarism, the teaching of Shintoism and Japanese ethics was banned from the curriculum. Instead, individualism was to be stressed in instruction. Teachers were screened for their ideological leanings and the ultranationalists were purged. Educational opportunities were

Macmillan, 1954); and *Political Reorientation of Japan: September 1945 to September 1948: Report of Government Section, Supreme Commander for the Allied Powers* (Washington: Government Printing Office, 1949).

widened. Compulsory schooling was increased from six to nine years, and discrimination between sexes abolished. Special stress was placed upon social studies and "unbiased" instruction in political affairs. Finally, control over the educational system was divorced from the central government's Ministry of Education and placed in the hands of autonomous local bodies. These measures, however, were only slowly implemented, as they required drastic shifts in the philosophical and social orientation of educators, training and retraining of suitable teaching and administrative staffs, and preparation of needed facilities and instruction materials.

Agriculture and the large industrial combines were the principal focus of economic reform. The end of farm tenancy and the breakup of large land holdings virtually by expropriation took place in 1947 and 1948. A new land-owning class was created almost overnight, enhancing the political, economic, and social independence of the peasant masses.

In industry, the reforms were not as thoroughgoing. Only the very top business leaders were purged, barred from returning to their posts for life or from engaging in political party activity, and plans for dissolving the *Zaibatsu* were but partially carried out.[36] However, the formal legal connections among the separate enterprises of each combine were broken, and open holding-company control ceased to exist. Some measures to prevent monopoly and restraint of trade were also enacted, although they did not proceed to the point of actually breaking up the major operating units into smaller ones. Stock dispersal was encouraged in hopes of achieving widespread popular ownership of corporations.

In spite of the enormous damage to plant and equipment, the changed position of Japan in world markets, and the immediate postwar prohibition of armaments production, the Japanese industrial structure remained essentially intact both in terms of product-mix and general patterns of ownership and control. Occupation authorities rejected Socialist and other left-wing arguments for nationalization, preferring to foster private enterprise on the American model.[37] At first, there was some strong advocacy of reducing Japanese industry almost entirely to small shops and factories, but eventually the pressure of the cold war, the dire need for economic

---

[36] See T. A. Bisson, *Zaibatsu Dissolution in Japan* (Berkeley: University of California Press, 1954).

[37] *Ibid.*, pp. 4-5.

rehabilitation without increasing American aid burdens, and the ideology of private enterprise led SCAP to abandon any serious tampering with the long-existing industrial structure.

Because the central interest of this study lies in Japan's postwar industrial relations, at this point it is helpful to outline occupation reforms dealing specifically in this area.[38] The first direct treatment of the problem came in the United States Policy Directive of September 22, 1945, issued from the White House, which ordered that "encouragement shall be given and favor shown to the development of organizations in labor, industry, and agriculture, organized on a democratic basis." SCAP immediately moved to implement these instructions by commanding the Japanese government to draw up legislation to protect the rights of wage-earners. Later, the new Japanese constitution, as the highest law of the land, also embodied these fundamental concepts.

Provisions of the Trade Union Law (TUL), passed by the Diet in December, 1945, complied with MacArthur's instructions. This act, which went into effect April 1, 1946, established a type of public labor policy which already had achieved firm hold in the free West. To some extent, the Wagner Act served as its model, although it was also drawn from proposals seriously considered by the Japanese Diet during the "liberal" era of the 1920's. The law's basic philosophy was to encourage trade-unionism as a means for protecting the economic interests of the wage-earner vis-à-vis the employer. Accordingly, it guaranteed workers the right to organize, to bargain collectively, and to strike. In addition, the measure afforded protections against employer discrimination for union activity by workers. All who worked for others for remuneration—except certain categories of public workers such as firemen and police—were permitted to organize and join unions of their own choosing. To administer the act, special tripartite agencies known as the labor relations commissions were established at the national level and in each of the forty-six prefectures.

The second major step in the labor reform followed in September, 1946, with the adoption of the Labor Relations Adjustment Law (LRAL). This act was designed to facilitate peaceful settlement of labor disputes and, within the framework of the Trade Union Law, spelled out the functions of the labor relations com-

---

[38] These are taken up more fully in Chapter VI.

missions in promoting mediation, conciliation, and voluntary arbitration. Except in certain vital public utility industries, the stress in dispute adjustment was upon voluntarism, but at the same time the commissions were instructed to encourage the formation of independent labor organizations.

A third major reform came in April, 1947, with the passage of the Labor Standards Law (LSL). Here, the objective was to place the power of government on the side which would assure wage-earners certain minimum standards of work whether or not they formed trade-unions. Essentially, the act incorporated the principal conventions of the International Labor Organization and also included provisions bearing on conditions peculiar to the Japanese industrial scene, such as the regulation of worker dormitories. To mention only some of the major items, the law provided minimum protection for women and minors, regulated hours of work, stipulated procedures for discharge, and enabled the government to place wage minima in effect. An additional enactment outlawed feudalistic labor recruiting practices and widened the public employment service, while still other protective legislation, passed soon after the Labor Standards Law, regulated employment of seamen and adopted new systems of industrial health insurance, workmen's accident compensation, and unemployment benefits. There is little doubt that the Japanese labor code, as written, took long steps to come abreast of, and in some respects surpass, minimum standards prevailing in most advanced industrial nations. A Ministry of Labor, in part replacing the previous Home Ministry, was established in August, 1947, to administer the bulk of these new laws.

THE COURSE OF SCAP LABOR POLICY

How did the labor reforms fare during the seven years of occupation? Chronologically, three phases may be distinguished. The first, from 1945 to 1948, was a period of open encouragement and enormous expansion of organized labor. The second, 1949-51, saw restrictive revisions in the occupation's attitude and policy toward organized labor. In this period the trade-union movement ceased to grow and underwent reorganization. The third was a period of stabilization, or rather, watchful waiting, in preparation for Japan's attainment of independence through the peace treaty of April, 1952.

Spectacular results immediately seemed to follow SCAP's initial encouragement for unionism. By 1949 the labor movement was able to claim as many as 7 million members, or more than 50 per cent of the nonagricultural work force, organized into some 35,000 constituent unions. Nowhere in the world had union growth of this magnitude occurred so quickly.

However, despite SCAP's guidance and appeal for "business" unionism of the American type, almost from the beginning the top leadership of the Japanese labor movement devoted its major energy to political activity. Two principal national centers, separated chiefly by ideological differences, were established within a year after the surrender. On the right, the revived prewar *Sōdōmei* (*Zen Nihon Rōdō Kumiai Sōdōmei*), or Japan General Federation of Trade Unions, tied itself closely to and officially supported the new postwar Socialist party. On the left, the militant *Sanbetsu* (*Zenkoku Sangyōbetsu Kumiai Kaigi*), or All-Japan Congress of Industrial Labor Organizations, was openly dominated by Communist elements. More often in competition than in co-operation, these centers, by making incessant demands for wage increases and all types of enlarged welfare benefits, added to the chaos of Japan's postwar economy and openly agitated to unseat the conservative party government and to effect a thoroughgoing revolution in Japan's political, economic, and social structure. The upsurge of the labor movement soon threatened occupation objectives themselves and led to General MacArthur's dramatic ban upon a general strike call early in 1947.

Although the general strike ban marked the beginning of the second phase in occupation labor policy, later in 1948 and 1949 the Diet, upon occupation suggestion, took legislative steps to restrict organized labor. Until then, as in most phases of Japanese economic reform, the occupation had maintained a "hands-off" approach with the exception of the general strike ban. The Japanese were left to work out of their own chaotic situation. Soon after the East-West cold war became a reality, however, Allied aims shifted toward strengthening the Japanese economy through more direct aid and controls. The emphasis of the occupation changed from reform to rehabilitation.

As a result, SCAP moved to contain the Japanese labor movement within the confines of the new situation. An occupation order following the general strike in 1947 prohibited government work-

ers from engaging in any dispute actions. Now after a rash of localized walkouts by public employees in the spring of 1948, SCAP
took specific action to define the permissible role for this sector of
organized labor. This step was of vital importance to the entire
movement, since government worker unions, with more than 2
million members, accounted for over one-third of total union membership and were leading centers of political agitation.

The first revision of the Trade Union Law came in July, 1948,
when General MacArthur "suggested" that the Diet enact legislation to limit the union rights of government workers. SCAP proposed to distinguish between civil servants and workers in government-owned enterprises by granting the former only the right to
organize and the latter the right both to organize and bargain.
Neither group was permitted to strike. Two new laws adopted soon
afterwards applied these principles to central government workers.
Civil servants were removed entirely from coverage of the Trade
Union Law, while compulsory dispute adjustment procedures were
established for government enterprise workers. A short time later
the Diet passed similar enactments covering local government workers.

Japan's economic rehabilitation began in earnest during 1948
and culminated with the adoption of the so-called Dodge Plan in
1949. Inasmuch as Communists and other left-wing elements, rather
than Japanese Fascists and ultranationalists, now constituted the
chief threat to the occupation's objectives, steps to minimize radical
influence accompanied the rehabilitation measures. These eventuated in the so-called "red purge," intensified with the outbreak of
the Korean War. Each of these programs had immediate repercussions upon the Japanese labor movement and severely affected
the course of postwar industrial relations.

The Dodge Plan came after four years of rampant inflation and
rather slow production recovery. In the wake of the Plan's disinflationary measures, both government and business operations
retrenched during 1949 and 1950 by cutting work forces and tight-
ening managerial methods. In addition, because the Dodge Plan
specified that wage increases could be justified only by rises in productivity, there was stiff resistance to union economic demands.
As a consequence of the program, the price spiral came to a sudden
halt. The conditions under which union growth had previously
flourished changed completely Many smaller enterprises folded up

altogether and with them their new union organizations. In some of the larger companies, personnel cuts were used to eliminate union leadership and to lessen the attractiveness of union membership. Only after the Korean conflict began in mid-1950 did this trend begin to reverse, as once again the demand for Japanese goods brought a rise in prices and expansion of production.

Removal of left-wingers from positions of influence actually began as early as 1947 when certain unions eliminated their Communist leadership through so-called "democratization leagues," popularly known as the *Mindō*. The split of the Japanese labor movement between *Sōdōmei* and *Sanbetsu* facilitated the "red purge." In 1948 *Sōdōmei* abandoned any further attempts to work with *Sanbetsu* after their joint co-ordinating organization known as *Zenrōren* (*Zenkoku Rōdō Kumiai Renraku Kyōgikai*) or the National Liaison Council of Japanese Trade Unions, had clearly fallen under Communist domination. The Dodge Plan retrenchment then offered further opportunity to evict extreme radical elements from industry.

Actually, the occupation did not give forthright sanction to the anti-Communist drive until after the Korean War began. Early in the summer of 1950, SCAP ordered a purge of Communist officials from government posts and suspended publication of *Akahata*, the Communist newspaper. By the end of August, the Japanese Attorney General, with SCAP approval, ordered the dissolution of *Zenrōren*. Taking their cue from these actions, both governmental administrators and private business managements quickly moved to rid themselves of left-wing elements. The purge lasted only a few months, but by the end of 1950 almost 12,000 persons had been removed from government, union, or industry positions.

In the course of these developments, *Sanbetsu* rapidly disintegrated. By 1949 it had suffered numerous defections, and the way was now prepared for the formation of a new unified trade-union center to be led by *Sōdōmei* and dissident groups of *Sanbetsu*. This was achieved in July, 1950, with establishment of *Sōhyō* (*Nihon Rōdō Kumiai Sōhyōgikai*), or the General Council of Trade Unions of Japan, which soon embraced over half the organized workers and today is the principal Japanese labor center.

The shift in occupation policy also called for rewriting the Trade Union and Labor Relations Adjustment laws. Like the earlier legislation restricting government workers, revisions adopted in mid-1949 aimed at curtailing the political orientation of trade-unions.

They also attempted to strengthen unions as economic institutions in dealings with employers. While the amendments increased the government's power to take action against threats of general strikes and other critical work stoppages, they provided clearer and more precise legal protections for workers and unions than had been originally enacted against unfair employer practices. Also, while unions were made subject to more exacting stipulations to gain legal protection and status as bona fide organizations, they were no longer required to register with state authorities.

In terms of industrial relations, the Dodge Plan, the "red purge," and the revision of the basic labor laws brought a virtual halt to trade-union growth. In less than two years, union membership declined from a high of 7 million to slightly more than 5 million. Concurrently, management regained status and power. Employers, private and public, now began to ignore union demands for improvements and in general took the initiative in economic activity. The heyday of organized labor's challenge appeared to be over; the desultory third phase of the occupation began. The labor movement was occupied largely in reorganizing itself, while a calm settled on the industrial relations scene during the wait for the transition from occupation to independence.

The peace treaty, placed in effect in the spring of 1952, opened a new era in Japanese industrial relations which has continued to the present. End of the occupation created a vacuum in the power structure of Japanese society. New political alignments began to regroup around issues of rearmament, continuance of occupation reforms, direction of national economic policy, and nature of the peace treaty itself. The Socialist party, which from the beginning had been precariously united, split and resplit. In the fall of 1951 two separate parties—the Left Wing and the Right Wing—were established and remained apart for four years. Even among the conservatives, considerable splintering took place over issues and positions of power. As for the trade-unions, Sōhyō, which originally announced its dedication to economic movement and political neutralism, began to be involved openly in political questions within two years after its formation. Communist influence reappeared in the trade-unions, especially as Sōhyō began increasingly to oppose American foreign policy and to advocate Japanese "neutrality" in the cold war struggle. Sōhyō's major efforts were now concentrated on government elections, three of which took place between 1952 and 1955, while its major strike activities aimed as much toward unseating the conservative government as toward achieving economic gains for the workers. All these moves, which met only small success, precipitated a new split in the labor movement. In the spring of 1954, dissident groups created *Zenrō Kaigi* (*Zen Nihon Rōdō Kumiai Kaigi*), or the Japanese Trade Union Congress, as an organization to counter the political emphasis and policies of *Sōhyō*.

These events, then, provide the background against which a cross-cut analysis of Japanese industrial relations during the postwar period is undertaken in the chapters that follow.

II

THE JAPANESE

MANAGERIAL SYSTEM

The system of management which evolves in the process of a nation's industrialization is believed to be a basic determinant of the type of industrial relations that emerges. In deciding to initiate, expand, reduce, or maintain entrepreneurial operations, management inevitably adopts attitudes and policies likely to shape the response of the work force which commits itself to industrial supervision, discipline, and co-ordination.

This chapter examines some of the major characteristics of the management system, as evidenced in Japan's industrial expansion, which today persist as influential factors in Japanese industrial relations. The full importance of these characteristics will be seen later in their relationship to the types of trade-unionism and collective bargaining which have grown up in postwar Japan. Here, we shall be concerned principally with traditional concepts of Japanese industrial management and the extent to which they have carried over into the postwar period. In particular, we shall give attention to management's organizational form, access to its ranks, the place of the industrial relations executive, and the impact upon industrial relations of recent changes that now seem to be occurring in managerial approaches. Although the treatment here is general, impressionistic, and unsupported by specific details, it does grasp the essential elements useful for the discussion in the remainder of the study. Actually, the subject demands much additional research, but, unfortunately, at the present time only very limited data are available.

The occupation took few direct steps to reshape management methods in the operating units of business enterprise. Rather, it envisioned that changes at this level would come about through

31

basic institutional reforms such as purge of top business leaders, breakup of the *Zaibatsu* cartels, formation of labor unions, prohibitions of various labor market practices, democratization of educational and political opportunities, abolition of the military, land reform, and so forth. The occupation anticipated that the effects of these reforms would seep gradually into day-by-day activities and eventually manifest themselves in changed managerial attitudes and practices. However, except for the requirements relating to management behavior set forth by the Trade Union, Labor Relations Adjustment, Labor Standards, and similar laws, there was little direct assault upon operating management per se.

THE TRADITIONAL CONCEPT OF JAPANESE MANAGEMENT

Probably the outstanding management practice in Japan's developing industrialism was the incorporation of traditional family behavior patterns within enterprises technologically similar to their Western counterparts. Japanese traditions of personal loyalty, subservience of subordinate to superior, and close interdependence of individuals within tightly knit social units were transposed readily from the long-established family system of the earlier feudalistic agrarian society. The Japanese avoided most of the social and cultural upheavals which usually accompanied industrialization in other countries.[1] Basic pre-existing patterns somehow remained and in some instances took on even bolder forms.

In the relatively smooth transition to modern industrialization, the agricultural community suffered no traumatic breakdowns, but, by and large underwent orderly expansion utilizing long-established modes of social organization. For most Japanese, it is likely that the shift from almost pure agrarianism to advanced industrialization, even though it occurred in a mere half century, came almost

---

[1] For a detailed analysis of Japan's prewar industrialization, see William W. Lockwood, *The Economic Development of Japan, Growth and Structural Change, 1868-1938* (Princeton: Princeton University Press, 1954). Additional standard works on this subject in English are E. Herbert Norman, *Japan's Emergence as a Modern State* (New York: Institute of Pacific Relations, 1940); G. C. Allen, *Japanese Industry: Its Recent Development and Present Condition* (New York: Institute of Pacific Relations, 1940); and *A Short Economic History of Japan, 1867-1937* (London: Allen and Unwin, 1946); E. B. Schumpeter (ed.), *The Industrialization of Japan and Manchukuo, 1930-1940: Population, Raw Materials and Industry* (New York: Macmillan, 1940); and John E. Orchard, *Japan's Economic Position, The Progress of Industrialization* (New York: McGraw-Hill, 1930).

imperceptibly. There was ready accommodation to the material trappings of Western civilization. Despite the movement from farm to factory, most workers remained oriented toward their family or farm units. Entering a shop or factory did not in most cases represent a sharp break with a cultural pattern which workers generally accepted. Management's structuring of the work situation to mirror traditional social relations further facilitated the transformation.

Another reason for this relatively smooth transition lay in early allocation of control over industrial development in the hands of the few tight-knit *Zaibatsu* family groupings. The interesting point of this policy—fostered by a government itself based on the familial concept of the Emperor System—was that these families had long possessed expertise in commercial enterprise as money-changers and bankers for the clan lords of the pre-Restoration era. They were rigidly disciplined in family in-groupism and tradition and, as family entities, were slavishly devoted to their functional role as entrepreneurs in Japanese society.[2] Accordingly, they could be intrusted to carry forward with full energy and efficiency the degree of industrialization needed to thwart attempts by foreign powers at reducing Japan to colonial status and to bring Japan abreast of such nations economically and militarily. State sponsorship and subsidy early converted this notion into concrete fact.

The early outburst of economic individualism and attempts at self-determination in Japan were insignificant compared to those that marked the industrial awakening of the West. A strong bourgeois middle class failed to emerge. There was little of the widespread ferment and withering competition out of which sprang the entrepreneurial types identified with the West's Industrial Revolution. In terms of the nature of management, the Japanese approach to industrialization meant that the family system was an integral part of the process and that, through the *Zaibatsu* arrangement, underlying concepts of family relationships could be utilized fully in developing and controlling industrial operations, of even the largest magnitude.

Despite the fact that this pattern of managing Japan's modern industrial development left in its wake consequences undesirable by Western material standards, the system received a wide popular

---

[2] Marion J. Levy, Jr., "Contrasting Factors in the Modernization of China and Japan," *Economic Development and Cultural Change*, II (October, 1953), p. 187.

toleration and considerable forthright support. Although income disparities were large and distribution of authority prevented emergence of political and social democracy, the very smoothness of the transition, whatever the material and power results, lay in preserving a cultural pattern that afforded most Japanese a degree of the psychological, social, and economic security which long had prevailed. For some, this security even increased; for only a few did it actually lessen.

Japanese management paternalism was based on still other factors; geographical, technological, and economic conditions also spurred the development. The proximity of agricultural and industrial areas for a long time blurred any sharp distinction between urban and rural populations. Agrarian patterns of family organization were carried over readily into the urban sectors.

Sparseness of essential raw materials and lack of investment capital gave further impetus to preserving the family pattern. There was little alternative but to resort to the extensive use of unskilled labor. In the feverish attempt to catch up with other industrialized nations, the government and *Zaibatsu* had to rely mainly upon this method, although at the same time they did use techniques such as heavy taxation of peasants, establishment of a national system of education, sending many Japanese abroad to learn industrial techniques, and so forth.

The reliance upon manpower as a substitute for capital meant that labor markets had to be created almost overnight which would provide a steady flow of large numbers of willing workers. This was best assured by maintaining family identifications intact. Otherwise, a disgruntled, rootless proletariat might have arisen not only to challenge managerial controls, but also to upset an orderly flow of manpower to the expanding enterprises.

In sum, the paternalism of Japanese management was a logical outgrowth of the combination of feudal traditions and intense nationalistic motivation that spurred the burst of modern economic enterprise. Since the goal of nationalism was widely and consciously shared throughout Japanese society, industrial enterprise was conceived as the means of building a stronger and stronger national entity, which would preserve long-established modes of social relations, rather than merely as a means of reaping economic gain for the individual. Here, of course, was a sharp contrast with the early Western system of laissez faire, which first and foremost gave sanction to individual self-aggrandizement and self-dependence without regard to the consequences for the social structure.[3] In organizing modern Japanese enterprise, the traditional family hierarchy, with management as the paternal head, was a ready instrument for quick and orderly industrial development. If this approach to industrialization seemingly left management free from outside interference in its operations, it was not because private enterprise per se was conceived as the means to achieve the "greatest good for the greatest number," but because select managing families could be relied upon better than any other group to direct energies in behalf of national growth and strength. With nationalistic aspirations almost unanimous among the Japanese (except for those few who altogether deplored nationalism), Japanese management differed from other segments of the society mainly in terms of function rather than objectives. Social harmony was to serve the purpose of industrialization, and industrialization was to preserve social harmony. Nationalism and familial patterns of organization went hand in hand.

"PATRIARCHALISM" AND "DESPOTISM" IN JAPANESE MANAGEMENT

Two fairly distinct types of management may be discerned as evolving in Japan's industrializing process. Both were tradition-oriented.[4] One, which may be termed "patriarchal," emphasized cooperative aspects inherent in the traditional family system of Japan. The other, termed "despotic," stressed the authoritarianism in this system. Actually, in most cases an admixture of both elements was present, although it is likely that one or the other tendency emerged more strongly in any given enterprise.

---

[3] This is not to say that nationalism was the only motivation for the industrialization of Japan. Undoubtedly, individual strivings were also important. But, in contrast to the West where the ethos of individualism was predominant, the controlling cliques in Japan relegated the ideology of atomism to the background. Although ownership of industry was technically private (with the exception of the earliest establishments which the government operated), actually there was only a small semblance of free competition in the market place for the vital sectors of the Japanese economy.

[4] As used here, the terms "patriarchalism" and "despotism" are intended as objective conceptualizations, not value judgments. Similar terminology may be found in Weberian sociology dealing with "traditional authority." See *Max Weber: The Theory of Social and Economic Organization*, trans. A. M. Henderson and Talcott Parsons (New York: Oxford University Press, 1947), especially pp. 341-58.

"Patriarchalism" appeared most naturally in the huge mass of small enterprises which were organized typically on a consanguinal family basis. It was in the large Westernized enterprise that "despotism" received stronger emphasis. The present analysis is focused on the latter because it has been among these for the most part that a distinct wage-earning class emerged. However, because the coexistence of the numerous small enterprises alongside the very large had a pervasive influence upon the managerial approach in the latter, it is useful to discuss the essence of patriarchalism first.

Patriarchal management in Japan retained the socially responsible characteristics of the traditional kinship system. Although it gave little encouragement to individualists, and indeed individualism was frowned upon if not actually punished, each member of the organization was recognized as an integral and important cog in the functioning of the whole enterprise. Conformity to the purposes of the unit rested upon fostering and structuring the situation to achieve complete identification between superior and subordinate. The reward was life-long security within the group and full acceptance of one's functional role.

In obtaining this complete identification, subordinates looked to the employer for every means of personal security, morale was likely to be high, and mobility into and out of the enterprise was apt to be virtually nonexistent. Once these elements took firm hold, the system grew upon itself. Often with a family as its core, the organization would develop its own special traditions—in patterns of authority, processes of communications, specialization of functions and skills, technological adaptations, division of income, and even in customs, religious practices, and symbols. A homogeneity of interests evolved regardless of position held or function performed. Each enterprise was a self-contained social organization and had only weak bonds with others. Workers were not likely to be conscious of their status as wage-earners because they felt that they shared little in common with workers in other enterprises. They were inwardly oriented toward their own enterprise group and their whole lives, from birth to death, were intimately bound to their enterprise community. While they were keenly conscious of their subordinate status in the organizational hierarchy, they placed full trust in their employers. The workers recognized that the patriarchal manager, like the traditional Japanese family or clan chief, placed the interests of the whole enterprise ahead of his own individual wants. The employer, typically, required few material goods to distinguish himself from his workers; what extra physical comforts he enjoyed were deemed appropriate for his function, not a display of his wealth.

In this set of circumstances, workers possessed little drive for self-determination and did not participate in decision-making except when the patriarchal employer might consult them before making a final judgment. Outside ideology and appeal could rarely assault or dent these self-contained organizations.

Patriarchal managers also felt wholly responsible for the welfare of their workers [5] both on and off the job and provided a variety of benefits. These usually included housing, medical care, financial aid for important ceremonies, clothing and food, and so forth. The patriarch often bestowed special gifts in the form of holidays and travel funds, undertook to send workers' children to school, led in religious ceremonies, provided for the aged and retired, and even arranged marriages and adoptions. In addition, wages were not conceived of simply as remuneration for work performed, but were more in the nature of allowances paid out of the general funds of the enterprise in accordance with one's need and status in the enterprise community.

Status in this type of enterprise came principally with age, although factors such as family size, technical skills, and degree of education were also given some weight. Similarly, regular payment of wages, customarily on a monthly basis, served more as confirmation of the status hierarchy and less as a matter of economic equity in producing income. In many cases, in fact, employers held wages for the workers in the form of savings to be drawn upon when needed. Wage rates typically were low, since many workers' expenses were paid on a group basis through the enterprise itself. However, it was, and still is, common practice for management to grant special cash bonuses on certain occasions, notably at the New Year and summer Buddhist festivals, in order to provide workers with extra funds to purchase gifts. Often these amounted to a sizable portion of the worker's annual cash income.

---

[5] The Japanese express the relationships between superior and subordinate through the various concepts of *on, gimu, giri,* and *ninjō.* Roughly speaking, *on* is the incurring of obligations; *gimu,* the performance of duties; *giri,* a type of reciprocity in the performance; and *ninjō,* human feelings which are suppressed when in conflict with *gimu.* See Robert S. Schwantes, *Japanese and Americans, A Century of Cultural Relations* (New York: Harper & Bros., 1955), pp. 17-19.

On the other hand, these practices made for fairly loose accounting procedures, and it was difficult for management to compute costs with any accuracy. Cost consciousness was not apt to be a strong characteristic among members of the patriarchal enterprise, although the efficiency gained through centralized direction and close co-operation probably served to counteract some of the non-accountable losses.

Closest possible contact between manager and managed was necessary to carry out the patriarchal approach effectively. In small shops, face-to-face, day-to-day interaction readily occurred. If the enterprise grew larger, management then began to utilize dependable assistants as channels of communication and donors of welfare benefits, and often subdivided the work force into small units, each with its own *oyabun,* thus creating a pyramid of father-child (*oyabun-kobun*) relationships within the larger enterprise organization.[6] In some instances, management suggested that the workers form their own mutual benefit societies in order to facilitate communications and co-ordinate the welfare activities. These organizations might have become means for worker protest, but what little protest they summoned, rather than expressing dissatisfaction with the patriarchal system per se, usually was directed at the employer's failure to carry out his responsibilities in serving the welfare needs of the workers. Although a group of this sort sometimes brought individual grievances to the attention of management, such an organization resembled a trade-union only slightly. As a rule, it made no attempt to challenge management's decision-making authority or to bargain for terms of employment with management.

Subordinates felt a deep sense of obligation and duty to the patriarchal employer, and their common loyalty, fortified by family, religious, and other traditional values, heightened their conformity. Workers readily placed the needs of the enterprise well ahead of their own. At times, they were willing to become self-sacrificing, in some cases even to an extreme degree. So, in all likelihood, was the employer.

From the outside, despotic systems closely resembled the patri-

---

[6] *Oyabun* may be translated as "boss" but connotes a parental relationship. For an interesting description of this system of relationships in various settings, see Iwao Ishino, "The *Oyabun-Kobun* Institution: An Introductory Analysis of a Ritual Kinship System in Japan," (unpublished Ph.D. thesis, Harvard University, 1954).

archal, but the inner spirit fundamentally differed. As firms grew in size, and especially as welfare programs expanded and became more complex,[7] the cost of administering a patriarchal approach overburdened management's time, energy, and resources. Although paternalism was not abandoned, a heavy strain was placed on the sense of mutual obligation between superior and subordinate. Management and workers were likely to be suspicious of one another, simply because it was difficult to reproduce the family structure faithfully in a large plant as levels of authority were added. Welfare programs became the means of controlling or minimizing unrest among the workers. Although managements typically strove to be benevolent in exerting their despotic control, essentially this was a negative approach, in contrast to the positiveness of patriarchalism. No longer did as strong a feeling of a self-contained enterprise community exist.

As a result, authoritarianism grew—an experience hardly foreign to most Japanese, who recognized it as part of the traditional family system. The despotic employer also required a considerable staff of assistants, now to serve as a police corps rather than as a means of increasing his sensitivity to subordinates' needs. No risk was taken which might upset the tranquillity of the regime. Special pains were taken to recruit docile workers; any worker displaying aggressive tendencies was quickly and surely rooted out even if he did manage to pass through the recruiting sieve. *Oyabun,* or "labor bosses," were relied upon to provide the enterprise with small groups of well-disciplined employees, who usually continued to work together as a unit. In addition, decisions were made at the top, or, if at lower levels, within the meaning of well-defined orders from above.

In the despotic case, the wage system reflected the employer's evaluation of an individual's or group's loyalty to the enterprise, which might or might not coincide with conventional attributes of status. Management seldom tolerated attempts by workers to have a voice in deciding terms of employment, or, for that matter, in communicating dissatisfaction for the superior's consideration.

---

[7] Welfare programs, in fact, typically were broader in scope and provided greater benefits as the large firms grew more and more profitable. Such a development was particularly noticeable by the beginning of the twentieth century, especially after a rash of strikes and labor unrest in the late 1890's and early 1900's.

Any move by the workers to act in an independent or organized fashion was perceived as a threat to the authority structure. Unions were quickly crushed, in some cases by inflicting physical punishment on their instigators. When they did manage to form and persist, the management usually moved in and took control of the organization.

Although the foregoing presents the despotic type of Japanese management in its extreme, actually it was not necessary for despotism to become very overt, since workers rarely resisted the system. Lack of open protest was due in part to fear, but also in part to wide social approval of paternalism as a legitimate approach both in daily family life and as a means for achieving the long-run nationalistic aims of the State. Even those groups of workers who did perceive their separate interests as a laboring class were diverted from protest by contradictory tendencies within themselves to accept traditional relationships.[8] Had it been clear that despotism served only the personal wants of managers and entrepreneurs, the attitude might have been radically different. But individual selfishness was not an important element even in despotism, for a strong sense of self-denial in behalf of the national entity existed even at the top.

In both patriarchal and despotic systems of management, basic relationships between workers and management were essentially the same. Each was a vertical structure, which taken altogether matched the fabric of Japanese society in general. Horizontalism, or bargaining among competing interest groups where the parties are on equal terms, at least legally, and act collectively, was virtually nonexistent in prewar Japan. It could evolve possibly where patriarchal elements were strong, where the employer closely consulted and communicated with his workers, and where the latter in organizing might develop a bona fide union. But these were highly

---

[8] On the other hand, as shown by the history of the Japanese labor movement (see Chapter III), workers were not completely docile at all times. While worker docility, explained largely by its agrarian roots, thwarted independent labor activity, at the same time the threat to return to the farm served in some instances to strengthen the position of the industrial wage-earner vis-à-vis the industrial employer. On the whole, however, especially after World War I, there was a growing realization among the workers that it was becoming increasingly difficult to return to the overpopulated rural areas. This perception gave rise to contradictory attitudes—among the great bulk of the workers, a resignation to and acceptance of industrial work; among a small segment, frustration with and protest against their lot.

exceptional instances, since subordinates, out of their sense of duty to the employer and security in the group, usually preferred to rely upon management's beneficence rather than to seek any lasting self-determination. Even when horizontal relations did arise, they mainly served *ad hoc* purposes and then reverted to the traditional vertical pattern.

INTERNAL MANAGEMENT ORGANIZATION

Analysis of the way in which management organizes itself internally helps to delineate the nature of major practices and policies which give shape to industrial relations. Of major relevance for this purpose are size of the managerial staff, its levels of authority and responsibility, and access to managerial positions.[9] These factors, however, are clearly discernible only in large-scale enterprise, and for this reason attention here is focused on management organization typically found in units which were originally parts of the *Zaibatsu* combines.

In the early development of these organizations, it may be noted, considerable study was made of Western industrial counterparts. As a result, the organizational forms instituted for them often closely corresponded to those of large foreign operations. Despite these outward appearances, however, Japanese managerial organization principally reflected the traditional vertical patterns of Japanese society.

A notable characteristic of the managerial hierarchy of modern Japanese enterprise long has been its relatively large complement of personnel in comparison with both its American and Western European counterparts. Several factors explain this. One reason was the complexity of the *Zaibatsu* empires,[10] which were not confined to a single industry or group of related industries as were American trusts and European cartels. The operations of one *Zaibatsu* combine usually ranged over areas of marketing, finance, and manu-

---

[9] These factors are similar to those employed by Harbison and Burgess in comparing Western European and American management. See Frederick H. Harbison and Eugene Burgess, "Modern Management in Western Europe," *The American Journal of Sociology*, XL (July, 1954), pp. 15-19. See, also, Clark Kerr, Frederick H. Harbison, John T. Dunlop, and Charles A. Myers, "The Labour Problem in Economic Development: A Framework for Reappraisal," *International Labour Review*, LXXI (March, 1955).

[10] For descriptions of these organizations, see T. A. Bisson, *Zaibatsu Dissolution in Japan* (Berkeley: University of California Press, 1954).

facturing and were integrated both vertically and horizontally. Each
constituent unit, therefore, was likely to possess management functionaries to provide links with every other constituent unit. In effect,
such an organizational interlacing contributed to the multiplica-
tion of management personnel. In addition, because of the extreme
shortage of capital, Japanese enterprise utilized vast quantities of
inexperienced and unskilled labor as a substitute, necessitating a
proportionately large supervisory and co-ordinating staff.

Finally, there was a tendency stemming from family and feudal
traditions for Japanese entrepreneurs to organize their operations
by delegating a narrow range of functions to each management
member. As the *Zaibatsu* combines grew in complexity, the reign-
ing families typically loosened their direct control by inaugurating
systems of "*banto* administration," whereby trusted managers, or
banto, were given responsibility for specific subsidiary operations.[11]
The *banto* became the top managerial elite of prewar Japan.[12] In
turn, each *banto* developed his own band of faithful underlings.

In this system, the management functionary was expected to devote himself utterly to his job and to attain high proficiency. Thus,
officials would become thoroughly versed in those relatively few
special tasks which were their own exclusive concern and responsibility. This method of assigning functions gave rise to widespread
"empire-building," as higher executives added to their status and
prestige by increasing their entourages. Thus, not only were there
the usual tiers of an organizational hierarchy, but also each major
official was surrounded by a special set of staff assistants who were
his personal followers and apprentices. Each unit comprised a small
society in and of itself, and the management organization was made
up of a congerie of such units.

Five or six distinct management levels were found in the typical
enterprise. At the top, a board of directors (*jūyakkai*) was composed of the owners or their representatives (usually officials from
the parent holding company), the enterprise manager (*shachō*),
and several of the executives in charge of key functional divisions

---

[11] The origin of the *banto* system may be traced to the 1890's. See Robert
A. Scalapino, *Democracy and the Party Movement in Prewar Japan* (Berkeley:
University of California Press, 1953), p. 260, fn. 28.

[12] In view of these sub-layers of *banto,* SCAP reforms, which "purged" only
the *Zaibatsu* family members and stripped them of their wealth, penetrated
but little into the managerial system itself.

(*buchō*). These key division executives, along with the other division chiefs (finance, sales, production, research, general affairs, etc.),[13] made up the second level of management. Section heads (*kachō*) within each division were in the third tier. Members of the fourth group (*kakarichō*), who were in charge of subsections, were responsible for supervising the actual operations of the enterprise. They resembled foremen in American industry in terms of job responsibility, but unlike American foremen, they were apt to be office personnel who did not directly command the workers under them, nor did they appear frequently in the shops.[14] At the fifth level were the "shop bosses" or "work chiefs" (*shokuchō*). Although they were first-line supervisors, they possessed little management-delegated authority and actually were not considered a part of the management organization.[15] Finally, at the lowest level were the group leaders or leadmen (*kumichō*) who assisted the shop bosses in overseeing the work.

Foremanship in the Japanese enterprise was not the distinct identifiable entity it is in American industry. No sharply drawn line could be made between the management and nonmanagement groups. Immediate supervision essentially spread over the tiers of subsection chiefs, shop bosses and leadmen. As will be indicated later, access to each of these positions differed markedly. The subsection chief post was the first step in the climb up the managerial ladder, and the shop boss title was the highest a member of the working group could reach, as a rule.

The major point in this intricate organizational pattern is that it was designed not to delegate authority down through the hierarchy, thereby decentralizing decision-making, but to concentrate decision-making at the very top. In this respect, traditional Japanese management, despite its large size, contrasts with the American managerial system and resembles the traditional Western European.

---

[13] In relatively few cases were there separate personnel divisions. The personnel or industrial relations functions were usually handled by sections within each division or were a part of the activities of a general affairs division for the whole enterprise.

[14] Also, as assistants to the subsection chiefs, there usually were staff members (*kakariin*) who carried out specialized supervisory functions and technical work.

[15] Japanese vocabulary makes a sharp distinction between those considered in the management cadre (*shokuin*) and those not (*kōin*). "Shop bosses" (*shokuchō*) were usually among the latter.

Each member functioned to facilitate top management's role in deciding policy on virtually all matters. Every plan had to be drawn up in detail and scrutinized by the top officials. Then it was to be executed without deviation or discretion. Subordinate officials acted under strict orders from above. Imaginative innovation or experimentation not explicitly authorized by superiors brought few rewards. Little leeway was permitted for this type of executive growth and development.

ACCESS TO MANAGEMENT

For management to operate in this fashion produced distinctive features in its methods of staffing. Once a candidate was selected, he spent his career with the enterprise. Movement between enterprises was not condoned, and tacit agreement existed among managements not to bid away officials from one another. Indeed, there was little room for this to occur, since talents and training, in the context of the above-described management organization, were utilizable as a rule only by the enterprise to which the executive initially became attached. What shifting around occurred usually was within units of the particular *Zaibatsu* empire, and this would happen only upon assignment, not out of individual choice.

Even horizontal movement from division to division within an enterprise was exceptional. The management novice could expect to move upward only within the division for which he was recruited. If he was transferred to another division, it was likely to be a temporary shift, and he soon would return to his original post. His status and advancement depended upon the superior of whose entourage he was considered a member. As a result, an executive was not apt to be well-rounded in his knowledge of the enterprise as a whole, although he became expert in his permanently assigned function. These conditions created problems of co-ordination in the management organization and further propelled decision-making to the very top. Also, at times sharp rivalries would generate among the divisions and sections as distinct interests arose within the management structure. It is likely that only traditional Japanese self-discipline and common recognition that the enterprise served the purpose of nationalism prevented open splits within management ranks.

One result of this system was to place special demands for conformity upon younger executives. To obtain recognition—which for all practical purposes took the form of ascending the management ladder according to age, length of service, or year of university graduation—the junior official first had to display mastery of a technical subject of immediate usefulness in the operation of his division. In addition, his loyalty to superiors had to be unquestionable, and he was wise to avoid self-assertiveness or personal claim for individual achievement. He submerged his contribution in the work of his unit, permitted credit to redound to his superior executive, and bided his time in waiting to rise in the hierarchy.

Access to management followed a long preparatory process. In Japan, members of the working class rarely rose to managerial ranks. Workers remained workers (when not farmers or petty tradesmen), although it was possible for their children to aspire to entry into management, provided the channels leading to this status were opened for them by family or patrimonial connections. Selection of management candidates rested upon traditional concepts in the family system. The requirements were rigorous, for once hired, the novice virtually was taken in as a member of a family-like group, and in some cases, he was legally adopted. An excellent school record was necessary not only to demonstrate the applicant's capacity to master useful techniques, but also to show his unswerving loyalty to superiors, acceptance of authority, self-discipline and self-denial, and his ability to co-operate within tight-knit groups. A degree from a university or technical school was a prerequisite in most instances, and the schools the applicant attended, from kindergarten through college, were of utmost importance. Some companies followed a policy of hiring new management personnel with the same educational background or geographic origin. Thus, an enterprise might become identified with a particular university or with a particular prefecture.

Accordingly, commitment to a career in management and, for that matter, in the bureaucracy and military, began at a very early age. Since family connections and sponsorship were important, nepotism and self-perpetuation tended to mark the managerial class. At times, however, management did reach out to incorporate promising young men, whatever their backgrounds, into its ranks because of the need for managerial talent during the rapid industrialization. The establishment of nationwide compulsory education aided in the early discovery of students with managerial abilities. At times, also, the traditional patronage and adoption system brought forth bright youngsters from working class or peasant families. However recruited, the candidate was selected while young and quickly was forced into a mold of strict conformity with management purposes and practices.

This process created a fierce class consciousness in the Japanese management group. Neither property ownership nor the rise of a vocal working class, both critical causes of the class consciousness of European entrepreneurs, became crucial factors in evoking the class awareness of Japanese management. The required channels of access, the severe competition to gain admission, the exacting criteria for acceptance, and the patterns of vertical relationships within management itself all gave a special stamp to the Japanese management elite which arose from its key functional role in industrializing Japan within the framework of an intense nationalism.

INDUSTRIAL RELATIONS FUNCTION IN POSTWAR MANAGEMENT

Prior to the postwar period, management placed little emphasis upon the industrial relations function. The need for specialists in this area was confined largely to technical assistance in recruiting labor and in administering welfare benefits. Typically, labor control sections were located within the major operating divisions and were not staff groups servicing the enterprise as a whole. A specialized central division dealing with industrial relations, even in an advisory staff capacity, would have constituted a threat to vested interests within management. In view of the way in which management typically had been structured, with its intervening congeries of managerial personnel between the owning families and the rank-and-file workers, there was little recognition of a need for a coordinating, centralized policy and function for industrial relations. It is here that significant developments occurred within management in the postwar period.

The impact of the defeat threw Japanese management into confusion, uncertainty, and near-paralysis. *Zaibatsu* leaders were among those held responsible for wreaking a disastrous war and therefore were purged or threatened with purge.[16] Initial occupation plans

[16]Actually, the penetration of the purge was not very deep. In all, only 380 business leaders were removed from their positions, while an additional 1,967 were declared ineligible to hold public office. For the extent of the purge and efforts at business deconcentration, see Allan B. Cole, *Japanese Society and Politics: The Impact of Social Stratification and Mobility on Politics*, Boston University Studies in Political Science, No. 1 (Boston: The Graduate School of Boston University, June, 1956), pp. 78-89.

called for the dissolution of the combines, a breakup of their operations into small units, and even the abolishment of some. Under these conditions, traditional management could take no initiative in planning or co-ordinating production.

Moreover, the basic driving force of Japanese industrialization had been momentarily swept away—ultranationalism had failed and was condemned. The foreigner now occupied the Empire. To continue to operate many of the enterprises seemed rather purposeless; it was not even known what type of economy would be permitted. The situation worsened as inflation mounted, black markets flourished, and raw materials became unavailable. Much of the plant and equipment had been destroyed or damaged by bombing and fire; what remained was run-down from over-use or obsolete as the result of Japan's failure to keep technologically abreast during the war years.

SCAP at first gave little guidance for the direction in which Japanese industry might be rebuilt; its policy was to leave Japan to recover by its own efforts, and to intervene only to prevent mass starvation, disease, or unrest inimical to occupation objectives. In the postwar interim, management was uncertain what function it should perform, and its efforts were devoted largely to preserving what capital it still possessed and to maintaining the work force which was permanently attached to the enterprise. Almost four years passed before management was to reassume full entrepreneurial functions.

Organized labor's sudden growth immediately after the surrender further confounded management. With unions receiving encouragement and legal status, management was little inclined to resist their inroads; in fact, some managements accepted them openly as a means of currying the authorities' favor. Management yielded traditional prerogatives, gave in to most union demands, and in some instances permitted union leaders to take over plant operations. Numerous joint union-management production committees were established, and unions frequently took charge of personnel functions such as hiring, transfer, promotion, discharge, and discipline. Recalcitrant managers were subjected to kangaroo courts, barred access to plants, and, in some cases, physically abused.

By 1949, with the shift in occupation policies, management had regained power. Now there was emphasis upon management's crucial role in rehabilitating the Japanese economy. The authorities contained the challenge of unions as industrial efficiency became the most pressing problem. Managerial talents were urgently needed to bring about expanded production, as a means both of relieving economic stress and of assuring the West of a dependable source of strength in the struggle with the Soviet bloc.

Nonetheless, the first four years of occupation produced what appears to be a significant transformation in the Japanese managerial system, with important implications for industrial relations. Despite certain weaknesses, unions had become a new force to be reckoned with in the management function. The new postwar constitution and reform laws, despite their embryonic development, were forcing management to take account of a much wider range of interests among the public (which also found expression in newly established popular political parties) than existed before the surrender. Moreover, with the widening of educational opportunities, men who did not necessarily share the ethical values and philosophies of prewar management were beginning to enter managerial positions. Essentially, traditional concepts of management organization were undergoing a change. This took shape in the rise of industrial relations specialists within the management hierarchy.

Emphasis on industrial relations in management received inspiration from several sources. In part, it was an attempt to emulate the model provided by developments in American management organization; however, if it had been purely so, the effect would have been primarily "window-dressing." Concrete experience also advanced these specialists within management ranks.

In the early flush of unionization, many management personnel, including in some instances the top manager himself, joined the unions, especially since the unions typically were organized on an enterprise basis. Union membership frequently extended well up into management ranks, and management officials not uncommonly initiated the new worker organizations and served as officers. Everyone had become a member of the working class! Actually management people found much in common with the workers as inflation mounted and critical shortages developed; the strong political orientation of the new unions, in close alliance with the new postwar left-wing parties, placed a premium upon intellectual leadership at all levels. The university or technical school graduate and the trained clerk and lower management official, as well as the intellectuals of the prewar labor movement, were some of the most likely candidates for union leadership, especially in view of their knowledge of management operations and access to management information.

This phenomenon did not necessarily represent a conscious attempt by management to capture or dominate the unions, although such a result actually may have followed, but it met the need for providing leadership for the work force in a situation where customary industrial relationships had suddenly broken down. Later, when management regained status, these functionaries, although no longer permitted under the revised Trade Union Law to remain in unions, frequently found themselves torn between management and union interests.

Developments such as these had their effect upon the outlook of management and in turn gave impetus to the emergence of industrial relations specialists in the enterprise. These specialists began to perform a function which traditional management organization could not—the integration of the union into the enterprise community. But at the same time, a new interest group within management had arisen and gained status, aided by the establishment of management associations which dealt exclusively with industrial relations and by the reorganization of internal management structures, which placed industrial relations specialists in key policy-making positions.

Management associations which specialize in industrial relations are essentially a postwar development in Japan. However, there were antecedents. For example, during the 1920's the so-called Harmonization Society, or *Kyōchōkai,* was formed, financed by private and government subsidies, with the major purpose of promoting labor-management co-operation.[17] Resembling somewhat the American National Civic Association, the *Kyōchōkai* was principally an organization of "progressive" employers of the patriarchal type. While it sought trade-union participation, the small labor movement, shot through at that time by ideological conflict, hastened to condemn the Society. Although instrumental at first in framing proposals for liberalizing Japan's labor legislation, the *Kyōchōkai* principally functioned as a research and study organization.

Later, in 1931, the major enterprises established the National

---

[17] *Industrial Labour in Japan,* Studies and Reports, Series A (Industrial Relations), No. 37 (Geneva: International Labour Office, 1933), pp. 131-33.

Federation of Industrial Organizations, or *Zenkoku Sangyō Dantai Rengō Kai*, whose chief objective was to bring pressure upon the Diet and other government authorities to defeat proposals for a trade-union law. Such a bill, previously offered on several occasions during the 1920's, almost secured passage in that year. Also, during the war period, when the government formed all-embracing industrial patriotic associations not unlike the Nazi German or Fascist Italian labor fronts, management groups had to co-ordinate their planning through them as a means of controlling the labor market for military and production purposes. These were among the first organizations dissolved by the occupation.[18] Otherwise, few specialist associations were organized in the prewar period although general employer federations, often active in public policy formulation on labor matters, may be traced back to the turn of the century.[19]

After the war, formation of management associations began in order to erect common defenses against bargaining demands of the new trade-unions. Leadership came primarily from ex-*Zaibatsu* enterprises, and organizations were formed on both regional and industrial bases. Among the very first was the *Kantō* Employers Association, which was organized in June, 1946, and comprised firms in the Tokyo area. The occupation permitted these to operate so long as they did not attempt to monopolize or cartelize product markets.

In 1948, after a year or more of preparation, the separate associations established a national organization exclusively concerned with industrial relations, *Nikkeiren* (*Nihon Keieisha Dantai Remmei*) or the Japanese Federation of Employers' Associations. A federation of federations, *Nikkeiren* includes thirty-two industrial and nine regional associations, with the latter, in turn, subdivided into prefectural and local groupings. Membership in *Nikkeiren* is by enterprise, and affiliation is obtained only through participation in one of the constituent associations. There is no direct affiliation with the national organization.[20] By the early 1950's, *Nikkeiren*

---

[18] The Patriotic Industrial Association, or *Sampō* (*Sangyō Hōkokukai*) and the Patriotic Labor Association, or *Rōmu Hōkokukai*, were both dissolved on September 30, 1945. See Miriam S. Farley, *Aspects of Japan's Labor Problems* (New York: John Day, 1950), pp. 31-33.

[19] *Industrial Labour in Japan*, pp. 70-85.

[20] Secretariat, Japan Federation of Employers' Associations, *Constitution, Officers, Items of Work, Outline of the Development of Employers' Associations in Japan, the Structure of Japan Federation of Employers' Associations* (Tokyo: The Federation, 1951), pamphlet.

claimed over 18,000 enterprises as affiliates, two-thirds of which came via the industrial association route. Among the company members are almost all of the major enterprises. Accounting for about 70 per cent of the total industrial employment, these large firms dominate the organization.[21] Many members, moreover, have joined at both industrial and regional levels, thereby increasing their influence in *Nikkeiren's* activities.

In general, however, *Nikkeiren* and its affiliates have not been strong centralized organizations directly involved in collective bargaining. For the most part, they have been research, educational, and lobbying centers for management. Although in some instances *Nikkeiren* has given support to industry-wide bargaining with trade-unions, notably in coal mining, cotton spinning, and shipping, its major role in collective bargaining has been to assist individual enterprises through research and educational activity. Most of its work in this connection has been in economic analysis of collective bargaining issues, study of personnel administration, and promotion of so-called scientific techniques for executive selection and training, supervisory development, productivity improvement, and so forth. Special emphasis, for example, is given to collection and dissemination of information about industrial relations systems of other countries, particularly the United States, Great Britain, Scandinavia, and West Germany.

A major function of *Nikkeiren* is to provide a voice for employers in the formulation and administration of public labor policy. Here, *Nikkeiren* stands alongside still other management organizations which also have been established or re-established since the end of the war. The most notable of these, all of which are general rather than specialized associations, are *Keidanren* (*Keiei Dantai Rengōkai*) or the Federation of Economic Organizations, the Japanese Chamber of Commerce and Industry, and the Medium and Small Business Enterprises Association. Only *Nikkeiren*, however, has gone into the detail of labor policy, while the others have confined themselves to fairly general pronouncements. On the other hand, the other employer associations have not always wholeheartedly accepted *Nikkeiren* viewpoints. Conflicts have been sharp, particularly over proposals for revising the Labor Standards Law, for

[21] E. Daya, "Freedom of Association and Industrial Relations in Asian Countries: I," *International Labour Review*, LXXI, No. 4 (April, 1955), p. 373.

whose emasculation the export and small enterprise groups especially have pressed.

Divergencies among managements stem in part from differing economic interests among enterprises, but also in part from conflicting attitudes of management executives within enterprises. For example, although *Keidanren* comprises virtually the same company membership as *Nikkeiren*, at least in terms of embracing most of the ex-*Zaibatsu* enterprises,[22] it is generally recognized that on labor matters *Keidanren* is the more conservative. It has been in *Nikkeiren* that the new industrial relations specialists have been able to exert their greatest influence, while more traditional types of management executives have concentrated their strength in *Keidanren*. Yet, because membership in *Nikkeiren* is on a company basis through affiliated industrial and regional associations, the influence of the industrial relations specialists is not necessarily predominant.[23] Nonetheless, the *Nikkeiren* structure has helped to institutionalize the new functional division within management. Its most active members are industrial relations specialists, and the work of the association staffs primarily services this group. Even though the specialized associations were formed to deal with the labor problems thrust upon management by occupation reforms, at the same time it is likely that they assure and enhance status for the industrial relations specialists who arose within management during the postwar period. This in turn has given opportunity for new concepts to arise to challenge the traditional managerial system.

Within individual managements, the ascent of industrial relations specialists has injected new ingredients. One has been the mere addition in many situations of another tight-knit suborganization as part of the management structure. In such cases, industrial relations has added nothing much new to management except to increase its sectionalism and the possibility of subgroup rivalries within the enterprise. Another ingredient, however, lies in the nature of industrial relations divisions because of their inherent interest in organizational relationships within the entire enterprise. By becoming involved in over-all policy planning of wage sys-

---

[22] At the industry level, only in a few cases—notably in coal mining—are there both general and specialized management associations. Usually, only one industrial association exists, but affiliates with both *Nikkeiren* and *Keidanren.*

[23] Specialized industrial relations associations with membership on an individual basis have also been created, but are of little significance beyond educational and research activities.

tems, conditions of work, welfare administration, communications, allocation of responsibility and authority, application of labor laws, recruitment and training of workers and supervisors, and so forth, the industrial relations specialists have exerted a horizontal influence throughout the whole management structure. Moreover, during the period when management was in a state of collapse because of postwar uncertainties, these new specialists took what little initiative there was and began to assume leadership in the management organization. One evidence of this was the trend to concentrate all personnel decisions in the hands of the industrial relations executive and make him a member of the board of directors. Another was his role as management spokesman in dealing with the unions. Still another was the not infrequent duplication of supervisors at the shop level—the phenomenon of two line organizations within one management. Often one supervisor reported to his traditional line superior and another to the industrial relations division.

Thus, the importance of industrial relations specialists in postwar management grew as the result of at least two factors. The first was that they began to acquire expertise in meeting the requirements set forth by the occupation reforms. The second, and probably of greater importance, was that they were in positions to gain the confidence of the rank-and-file workers by assuming major responsibility for the latter's welfare. Direct experience with, and often in, the new union organizations usually enhanced their status.

POSTWAR EMPLOYER PATERNALISM

It is probably correct to say that the role of the industrial relations specialist in postwar Japanese management has helped to dispel despotic tendencies inherent in the traditional approaches.[24]

---

[24] Not all of these have been stamped out by any means, however. One of the most significant postwar labor disputes, which aroused widespread reaction throughout Japan and had international repercussions, was the strike of the Omi Silk Company workers during 1954. This enterprise, engaged mainly in cotton spinning, employed over 10,000 workers, mostly young females under 20. The stoppage, lasting over three months, was one of the longest labor disputes in Japanese history. The issues, involving wages, hours, and working conditions only to a minor extent, were principally concerned with the utter control by the employer over the personal lives of the workers. In seeking recognition as the bargaining agent, the textile workers union received nationwide support, but only after an embittered struggle did management finally give in to this demand. Commonplace among large firms only a little more than ten years ago, this type of management is now considered archaic in Japan.

Management has now turned in other directions, and its principal choice seems to be either a resurrection of patriarchalism or fostering of horizontal relationships between employers and wage-earners. In general, it may be said that the trend has been toward the former.

The emphasis upon industrial relations as a specialized over-all management function has had the effect of increasing the attention given to worker interests within the enterprise. This has occurred both at the top policy-making level and in day-to-day operation of the shop. Industrial relations staffs typically have assumed some supervisory functions and often have acted as intermediaries between workers and other management executives. Moreover, since the new postwar laws provide numerous protections for wage-earners, old-line managements no longer are likely to feel so personally responsible for their employees as they once did. As a result, the industrial relations group has frequently assumed these responsibilities.

Developments such as these have served to strengthen managerial paternalism of the patriarchal type. Even though Japanese management has given considerable lip service to democratization of industry and has undertaken serious study of foreign techniques of personnel administration [25] and in some cases put them into practice, the chief result so far has been that the industrial relations divisions, which for the most part carry out these activities, have tended to strengthen the traditional patriarchal approach. This has evolved directly from face-to-face dealings by the industrial specialists with the rank and file and union leaders, and indirectly from the influence they have exerted upon other management executives.

If Japanese workers no longer possess as strong a sense of loyalty and mutual obligation toward traditional management as they once did, they appear to have transferred these attitudes to the industrial relations specialists because of the latter's immediate and almost exclusive concern with their interests. Given the tenaciousness of the family system in Japanese culture, which was not likely to be swept away in the few short years of occupation and reform, workers have readily sought protection from new patriarchs. This

---

[25] One example has been a widespread interest in the training-within-industry programs developed in the United States during the war. Dissemination of information about these techniques came largely from SCAP and *Nikkeiren*, and in 1951 a first group of Japanese visited America to study training-within-industry. In general, the study of "human relations in industry" is receiving growing attention within Japanese management circles.

need has been met in part by the industrial relations experts in management, in part by trade-unionism. The widespread phenomenon of enterprise-wide unionism, to be discussed subsequently, attests to the latter tendency.

In concentrating principally upon the welfare of the enterprise's members, industrial relations specialists and union leaders find themselves in fairly high accord with one another. Strong and stable enterprise-wide unions provide support needed by the industrial relations group to enhance its status within management and, in turn, are supported by this new element in management. Had Japanese unionism been founded on some other organizational basis, it probably would have constituted a larger threat to the industrial relations specialists, and their attitude toward unions might have been very different. What the present situation often amounts to, then, is a mutual obligation—the workers pay loyalty to the industrial relations group in exchange for recognition of their permanent membership in the enterprise as symbolized by the union organization. In view of the traditional verticalism in Japanese society, the industrial relations executive is likely to be at the top of the resulting pinnacle. In turn, despite temptations to yield to outside political and ideological appeals, enterprise union leaders also tend to work closely with the industrial relations officials within management as a means of solidifying their own positions in the union structures.

Even though the industrial relations executives may sincerely believe in developing horizontal relationships in Japanese industry, existing conditions permit only slow progress in this direction. Despite attempts to introduce advanced personnel practices from abroad such as job classification and evaluation, incentive systems tied to production, training-within-industry, etc.,[26] an emphasis upon increased welfare benefits and employment security measures, especially those not likely to disrupt the ongoing status structure among the workers, appears to predominate. Working out such welfare provisions with the unions, rather than introducing sudden innovations in managing the work force, takes on a character more in the traditional patriarchal vein. Moreover, since labor contract administration has yet to become a central concern in Japanese

---

[26] See, for example, Japan Federation of Employers' Associations, *Analysis of Personnel Practices in the Principal Industries in Japan* (Tokyo: The Federation, 1953), and Noda Nobuo and Mori Goro, *Rōmu Kanri Kindaika no Jitsurei* (*Examples of the Modernization of Labor Administration*) (Tokyo: Daiamondo-sha, 1954).

industrial relations,[27] the supervisory structure, typically controlled by an industrial relations division, retains still other attributes of the old patriarchal system. In this context, then, a chief function of the enterprise unions appears to lie in providing management with a constant reminder to carry out its responsibilities toward workers who are permanent members of the enterprise. Management's failure in this respect is likely to bring loud protests from the union and threats of succumbing to outside political and ideological influences. A function of the industrial relations specialists is to guard management against such failures.

This situation places the industrial relations specialists in somewhat of a dilemma. On the one hand, the need to increase Japanese industrial productivity leads to their attempts to introduce new personnel practices and approaches, particularly those identified with managerial efficiency in American industry. On the other hand, however, any sudden adoption of these techniques is likely to disrupt established relationships with consequences that would increase the difficulty of meeting this need. The safer course has been to rely on traditional methods of patriarchalism, which, despite their limitations, did, in fact, initially succeed in launching the phenomenal industrial expansion of modern Japan.

One management problem, for example, has been whether to attempt development of a foremanship such as that found in American industry. Earlier it was mentioned that by tradition first-line supervisors in Japanese enterprise usually have not been part of the management cadre and that authority of immediate supervision has been extremely limited.[28] As the highest post to which rank-and-file workers may ascend, the rank of shop boss has been considered less a management representative, but more a symbol of the reward for wage-earners who devote their lives to the enterprise.[29] Thus,

---

[27] See Chapter V.

[28] As in other industrialized countries, the position of the first-line supervisor deteriorated during the period of economic expansion. The earliest Japanese "foremen" usually possessed full authority in recruiting, hiring, training, and disciplining their workers not only in the work situation, but also in life outside the plant. These functions, however, tended to be taken over by the foreman's superiors, especially the subsection chiefs, with the growing tendency toward despotism and the elevation of the early foremen, once trained, to subsection chief posts.

[29] In a labor market such as Japan's, which sharply distinguishes between those who are permanently and temporarily attached to enterprises, this symbol takes on even greater economic and social significance.

especially in his role of an *oyabun* ministering to the personal needs of employees under him, the Japanese "foreman" typically has served as a link which strengthens the identification of the workers with the management and the enterprise. Despite his exclusion from the process of managerial decision-making, his function has been to reinforce his group's self-discipline, already inherently strong as a result of commonly held cultural values, customs, and language. In this way, although he has identified himself almost completely with the working class, at the same time his presence has lessened the need for that type of supervision found in industrial societies characterized by individualism and social mobility. In turn, this arrangement has permitted management to concentrate upon internal technical specialization, without being overly concerned with industrial relations. It is likely that organizational factors such as this may have contributed heavily to Japan's success in rapid industrialization. To convert the Japanese "foreman" into a true member of management, in the image of his American counterpart, so to speak, runs the risk of undermining group discipline and morale, impeding productivity, and further upsetting the managerial system.[30] In most cases, industrial relations specialists seem to prefer to leave the situation as it is or at best to change it most gradually. In the meantime, they would continue to assume the major responsibility themselves for managing relations with the work force. As a result, vertical relationships of the patriarchal type have tended to perpetuate.

Although management's patriarchal approach has increased the consideration given to worker interests, in any large organization the system is necessarily difficult and clumsy to administer, especially when it is urgent to increase productive efficiency. This means that a search for an alternative is probably inevitable. Earlier discussion pointed out that patriarchalism contains seeds of both democracy and despotism in industrial relations, so that either could logically result from the existing situation. Management specialization in industrial relations and widespread unionism, even in its enterprise-based form, are new factors on the Japanese scene which afford a strong basis for the development of horizontalism. These did not exist prior to the occupation.

---

[30] It may be added that the size of the task of retraining "foremen" to assume managerial functions beyond their present "watchdog" role appears highly formidable.

On the other hand, should hostile political, economic, or cultural forces threaten to submerge either of these new institutions, despotism would likely return to Japanese industry. Here, the time factor is especially important. Despotism could *quickly* re-emerge, but development of horizontalism is apt to be very *slow*—only as experience in joint consultation, collective bargaining, and contract administration gradually accumulates, and as changes in the access to management strengthen the new interest in industrial relations.

The solution to Japan's productivity problem, which will become increasingly serious as long as population growth continues, may rest in part upon the spread of horizontal relations throughout her society. Although the vertical patterns effectively helped Japan vault from backward agrarianism to advanced industrialization and provided orderly processes for rapid economic development, they are now likely to impose serious limitations even when they assume the patriarchal form. It is for this reason that the postwar changes in Japanese management are of critical significance, for on them in part depends whether Japan's economic viability and freedom in human relationships may coexist. In part also, the outcome depends upon the nature of trade-unionism.

III

THE TRADE - UNION
MOVEMENT: ORIGINS,
GROWTH, DEVELOPMENT

The emergence of labor unionism represents one of the most re-
markable changes in the institutional structure of postwar Japan.
Union growth has been phenomenal. Like those of all other countries, however, the Japanese labor movement exhibits its own dis-
tinguishing characteristics in terms of organizational form, economic
and political function, and major guiding philosophies. In part, the
explanation lies in environmental factors already noted, in part,
in internal elements to be explored. But before undertaking discussion of these points, first it is necessary to describe the movement's historical roots in the prewar era and to outline its growth
and major developments during the postwar period.

PREWAR UNIONISM [1]

Even though independent trade-unions did not exist in Japan at
the time of the surrender in August, 1945, a prewar labor movement
had originated in the late nineteenth century soon after Japan first
undertook modern industrialization. Despite numerous fits and
starts, trade-unionism managed to endure until it was virtually
obliterated in the 1930's by Japan's military dictatorship; nonetheless, it left a heritage of some significance for the present-day
movement.

The early Japanese labor movement was of necessity confined

---

[1] Unless otherwise noted, materials in this section are drawn largely from
Okochi Kazuo, "Rōdō" ("Labor"), in Yanaihara Tadao (ed.), *Gendai Nihon
Shoshi* (*A Short History of Modern Japan*), II (Tokyo: Misuzu Shobo, 1953),
pp. 111-214. See, also, Suehiro Izutaro, *Nihon Rōdō Kumiai Undō Shi* (*History
of the Japanese Labor Union Movement*) (Tokyo: Kyodo, 1950), pp. 9-105;
and Eitaro Kishimoto, "A Short History of the Labour Movements in Japan,"
Kyoto University Economic Review, XXI (April, 1951), pp. 39-56.

to a very limited sector of the industrial labor force. While the beginnings of Japanese industrialization go back to the 1860's and 1870's, when large-scale factories were first built with foreign technical assistance to produce munitions for defense and textiles for foreign exchange, manning of these establishments did not immediately create a large permanent wage-earner group. To a considerable extent industrial jobs were filled by recruiting for temporary hire females and younger sons of peasants who regarded factory work as a means of supplementing the meager incomes of their families. At that time probably a majority of wage-earners were women. Moreover, low wage competition of the females and the loss of status perceived to be involved in industrial work often discouraged males from entering the new factories. Men drifted into heavy work only, and even then on a temporary basis. Thus, except for a relatively small hard core of workers who were brought in as full-fledged members of the new family-like enterprises, the early wage labor force was for the most part transient—surplus sons and daughters of farm families, prison laborers, unemployed artisans, dispossessed lower *samurai*, and the like. This type of labor force, moreover, predominated at least until the First World War and even to the present has remained a salient characteristic of Japanese industrialism.

By Western standards, the treatment which the temporary workers received was deplorable. Employers gave little consideration to conditions of employment. Hours were long, rest periods were unheard of, the speed-up and stretch-out were everyday practices. For all this, wages were a pittance, and often the workers saw little of their incomes, since it was a common arrangement to make payments in advance directly to the parents and to withhold the balance of earnings until the employment period terminated.

During the 1870's, 1880's, and 1890's, industrial workers registered scattered protests against such conditions. Strikes are known to have occurred in some coal and metal mines, in textile mills, and among handicraft workers. Most of them, however, were spontaneous and unorganized and did not become the basis of a lasting union movement. Protest against the industrial conditions also was registered by various new political groups, taking names such as the Oriental Socialist Party (*Tōyō Shakaitō*) in 1882, the Rickshaw Party (*Shakaitō*) in 1883, and the Oriental Liberal Party (*Tōyō Jiyūtō*). However, they were able to attract only small followings among the wage-earners and enlisted mainly tax-oppressed farmers, bankrupt ex-noblemen, intellectuals, and reactionary traditionalists.

The earliest bona fide unions came into being during the interim between the Sino-Japanese War of 1895-96 and the Russo-Japanese War of 1905-6. It was in these years that development of Japan's heavy industry leaped forward. Numerous labor disputes, although usually small and limited in scale, occurred at this time. In 1897, the Labor Union Promotion Society, or *Rōdō Kumiai Kiseikai,* was established in part to bring pressure upon the government for enactment of factory legislation. In the same year, the Workers' Volunteer Society (*Shokkō Giyūkai*)[2] and the Association for the Study of Socialism (*Shakai Shugi Kenkyūkai*) were founded to disseminate the idea of trade-unionism.

Under the guidance of the *Rōdō Kumiai Kiseikai,* unions were organized in the steel industry, the railways, shipbuilding yards, printing establishments, and among cooks. These had some measure of success in organizing. For example, in 1899 the steel workers union claimed a membership of more than 5,000 organized in about forty local branches.

On the other hand, few of the prominent leaders came out of the wage-earner class. Those who did were skilled craftsmen rather than unskilled workers. For the most part, in fact, the leaders were theologians and intellectuals, many of whom had been in the United States as students or workers and had been involved with American Federation of Labor activities in the San Francisco area. Accordingly, the guiding ideology was not revolutionary but an admixture of Christian socialism and Gompersism. Its aim was to educate the working class, and it emphasized a pragmatic, business-type unionism. Such men as Jo Tsunetaro, Sawada Hannosuke, Abe Isoo, Katayama Sen, Takano Fusataro, and Murai Tomoyoshi, some of whom had been divinity students in the United States, are identified with this early organized movement.

Even the nonrevolutionary unionism of this period was too much for the ruling Japanese cliques to swallow. Although already seriously weakened by divided leadership, by employer opposition, and by an economic depression that set in at the turn of the century,

---

[2] Interestingly, the *Shokkō Giyūkai* was originated in San Francisco by a small group of Japanese who worked in California and had become members of AFL unions.

the labor unions were dealt a death blow with the promulgation of the Public Peace Police Act in 1900, which suppressed them altogether. When the union leaders turned to political action out of desperation, they met similar suppression. In 1901 the government outlawed the Social Democratic party on the very day it was established. Three years later, even the "educational" Socialist Association was obliterated. Although the formation of a Socialist party was tolerated in 1906 following the unrest produced by the Russo-Japanese War, the police kept it under strict surveillance and in 1910 ordered its dissolution when an alleged plot to assassinate the Emperor was discovered.[3]

Government suppression of the embryonic labor movement drove the leadership into hiding and toward left-wing ideologies. Katayama Sen, for example, at first an adherent of Gompersism, later embraced communism and eventually fled to the United States and then to Soviet Russia. Others who had visited America in the early 1900's, such as Kotoku Shusui (who at first was a parliamentary Socialist), now were far more taken by the anarchistic approach of the Industrial Workers of the World than by AFL business unionism. The Socialist party itself, while it lasted, was rent with factionalism, reflecting the scramble for a guiding ideology.

A few years later, about the time of the First World War, the Japanese government began to relax its attitude toward labor organization. In 1912, what may be described as the beginnings of a durable movement came in the establishment of the so-called *Yūaikai*, or Friendly Love Society, under the leadership of Suzuki Bunji, who was associated with the Unitarian church and had come to know the Webbs during their visit to Japan about that time.[4] Like the earlier *Rōdō Kumiai Kiseikai*, *Yūaikai* avoided revolutionary ideology and was principally a mutual benefit and education society, advocating employer-employee co-operation. Again orientation toward AFL philosophy predominated, especially after Suzuki visited the United States during the war period, attended AFL conventions, and came to know Gompers personally.[5] In the

---

[3] For a discussion of the beginnings of Japanese socialism, see Hyman Kublin, "The Origins of Japanese Socialist Tradition," *The Journal of Politics,* XIV (May, 1952), pp. 252-80.

[4] Robert S. Schwantes, *Japanese and Americans, A Century of Cultural Relations* (New York: Harper & Bros., 1955), p. 78.

[5] *Ibid.,* p. 79.

meantime, *Yūaikai* grew from an original membership of 10,000 to 30,000 in 120 unions by 1920.

The environment now began to favor trade-union growth in Japan. Although on the side of the Allies in the war, Japan was virtually a nonbelligerent and took advantage of this opportunity to undertake rapid economic expansion and to enter world markets which the warring countries could no longer supply. Heavy industry grew as a result, and more and more workers found themselves in a permanent wage-earner status. Moreover, as Japan suffered from a severe inflation and shortages began to develop, worker resentment mounted, culminating in the rice riots of 1918. It was at this point that the Japanese government adopted a liberalized attitude toward the labor movement, declaring that it would not oppose the "wholesome development" of trade-unions.

Yūaikai now engaged openly in organizing activities. In 1919 it changed its name to the Great Japan Labor Union Federation (*Dai Nihon Rōdō Kumiai Sōdōmei Yūaikai*). In 1920 the name was changed again to the League of Labor Unions (*Rōdō Kumiai Dōmeikai*) and finally in 1921 to the Japan Labor Federation (*Nihon Rōdō Sōdōmei*), in short, *Sōdōmei*. Two years later, *Sōdōmei* claimed a membership of 100,000 in some 300 unions.

The Japanese union movement achieved additional status after the formation of the ILO in 1919. The ILO especially criticized the Japanese government for selecting labor delegates to this body without consulting the trade-unions. Although the government never went so far as to give the unions legal status, it was sensitive to the criticism and eventually nominated labor delegates to the ILO from among union leaders in accordance with their membership following.

In the decade of the 1920's, there were encouraging signs of growth. Almost every year showed an expansion of union membership. By 1925, 250,000 workers were organized in 450 unions, and by 1930, the figures had reached 350,000 and 700 respectively. In 1931, the highest proportion of organization for the prewar period was attained. Nevertheless, although there were 370,000 members in 818 unions, this did not exceed 8 per cent of the industrial work force. In fact, the Japanese Seamen's Union accounted for at least a third of the membership. Unions actually achieved their maximum membership in 1936 with more than 420,000 workers organized in slightly less than 1,000 bodies. But, because of rapid expansion of the munitions industry in the early 1930's, this figure represented only a little more than 5 per cent of the industrial wage-earners.

Yet, despite these favoring circumstances, the Japanese labor movement began to suffer from internal defections and splits which had been evident earlier and were to continue to plague it for the remainder of the prewar era. The impact of the Russian Revolution, the re-emergence of earlier leaders who had now turned to radical ideology, and the failure of Gompersism to catch the imagination of the Japanese worker (especially in face of the severe postwar depression and AFL support of the American Oriental exclusion policy) contributed to internecine warfare that soon developed. In this "liberal" period of Japanese history, the 1920's, the labor movement was principally a battleground for competing ideologies imported from abroad. It was caught between the victory for democracy and the sudden outburst of bolshevism. As a result, no indigenous philosophy grew as the main theme of Japanese trade-unionism.

Ideological contests within the trade-union movement of this era served to reduce the small effectiveness it had. In 1922, the Socialists, Syndicalists, and Communists failed to come to agreement over the issue of establishing a single unifying labor center. By this time, splits developed within *Sōdōmei* as it swung to the left, largely under syndicalist influence, abandoned the Suzuki philosophy, and supported Marxist class-struggle theory. At first the anarcho-syndicalists seemed to be at the top of the three-way struggle, but following the great Tokyo earthquake in 1923, the syndicalist influence rapidly declined and the bolshevists grew in strength. The major contest was now between the Socialists and Communists. In 1925, *Sōdōmei* split in two when the right wing attempted to oust the Communists. Shortly thereafter a centrist group also pulled out. By 1927, three competing centers were in existence: the Japanese Council of Labor Unions (*Nihon Rōdō Kumiai Hyōgikai*) on the left, the League of Japanese Labor Unions (*Nihon Rōdō Kumiai Dōmei*) in the center, and *Sōdōmei* on the right. Each, moreover, supported a different political party, heightening the ideological differences.[6] In 1929, further confusion was

---

[6] The Communist party, formed in 1921, was ordered dissolved in 1923 and its leaders were jailed. A new Socialist party was organized in 1926.

added when one faction within *Sōdōmei* withdrew and joined the centrist group to form the National League of Labor Unions (*Zenkoku Rōdō Kumiai Dōmei*).

The Manchurian Incident, the rise of the militarists to power, and the Great Depression failed to unify the labor movement. Instead, the splits deepened as leftists moved further left and rightists further right. By the mid-1930's, moreover, the government's policy of toleration ceased. In 1936, the May Day celebration, which had been initiated in 1920, was banned, and a year later the leftward-drifting Japanese Council of Labor Unions was declared illegal. Right-wing groups in the meantime began to endorse Japan's militaristic course, with *Sōdōmei* as early as 1934 re-embracing union-management co-operation and in 1937, after the Shanghai Incident, renouncing resort to strikes. In 1938, the right-wing government workers union dissolved of its own accord, while *Sōdōmei* as a whole followed suit in July, 1940, after the government had outlawed all unions. Concurrently, the government established its own "labor front," the *Sangyō Hōkokukai*, popularly known as the *Sampō*, initiated in 1938 and reorganized two years later. With this, any semblance of independent trade-unionism lapsed into history.

Failure of the prewar movement to achieve any modicum of solidarity meant that it constituted only the weakest of challenges to the ruling cliques. With the Japanese nation virtually committed to defend itself against foreign invasion, military or ideological, this is perhaps not surprising, since unionism was virtually imported from abroad and never could escape from its own internal conflicts over what "stranger" philosophy to follow. Organizing energy was spent in rival attempts to take away from one another those limited sectors of industry amenable to organization—notably among the maritime trades, land transportation, and the mines. Except for these few groups, the only other sizable concentrations of permanent wage-earners were in the *Zaibatsu* manufacturing and commercial operations, which were virtually unassailable by unionism. The organization of trade-unions followed scattered industrial or craft lines and the unions functioned largely as demonstration and political bodies. Collective bargaining was rare and labor agreements few.[7] Except for a few moderates, such as Matsuoka Komakichi, who arose from the working class, top leaders were mostly left-wing

---

[7] See Chapter V.

intellectuals, whom the rank and file readily abandoned in favor of Japanese militarists and nationalists. A heritage of contradictory features thus was left to the postwar labor movement.

POSTWAR GROWTH

The growth of the Japanese trade-union movement immediately after the war was phenomenal. More than 500 unions, claiming at least 380,000 members, formed within five months after Japan's capitulation to the Allied Powers in 1945. In this brief period, the movement reattained its prewar size. The great bulk of the growth occurred during 1946, when nearly 5 million workers entered the unions and more than 17,000 union bodies were established. By July, 1947, membership reached close to 5.7 million and the number of unions exceeded 23,000. Still another million members and 10,000 unions were added during the following year. Thus, between the time of the surrender and early 1949, the number of Japanese unionists grew from zero to about 7 million. More than 50 per cent of the industrial labor force was organized, and, with the turnover of unions and union membership during the period, a considerably larger percentage of workers had had some experience with trade-unions.

In 1949 the postwar expansion came to a halt under the pressures of the reversals in occupation labor policy, recovery of management's status and power, disinflation and retrenchment of the Dodge Plan, and "red purge" of trade-union leadership. But also, the union movement had reached a saturation point. Nearly all major enterprise units had been organized. All that remained was the vast sea of unorganized workers in the myriad of medium and small industry.

Between July, 1949, and July, 1950, union membership declined by almost one-seventh to about 5.8 million. More than 5,000 unions disappeared. Although during the ensuing twelve months total membership managed to remain constant, there was an additional net loss of about 1,500 union bodies. Only after mid-1951 did the growth resume, but at a slow pace, increasing by approximately 150,000 new members each year. The present level is again slightly above 6.6 million, while the number of union bodies has regrown to about 36,000, mainly owing to reorganizations rather than to the creation of wholly new unions.

On the other hand, the union movement has failed to keep pace with the growth in the industrial labor force since 1950. The proportion of organized among the industrial workers has declined slowly from year to year and is less than 37 per cent at the present time. Although this figure still compares favorably to the 35 per cent organized in the United States and the 45 per cent in Great Britain, the comparison should not be over-emphasized because of significant differences between Japan and these countries in the ratio of industrial workers to the total labor force.

As would be expected, 60 per cent or more of the union members are from the major urban areas such as Tokyo, Osaka, Fukuoka, and Kobe. Nevertheless, unionism is a nationwide phenomenon with even the most remote rural prefectures having some union organization.[8]

Table V. PREWAR AND POSTWAR GROWTH OF JAPANESE TRADE-UNIONISM

Year[a]	No. of Unions	Membership	Year	No. of Unions	Membership
1918	107		1938	731	375,191
1919	187		1939	517	365,804
1920	273		1940	49	6,455
1921	300	103,412	1941	11	895
1922	389	137,381	1942	3	111
1923	432	125,551	1943	3	155
1924	469	228,278	1944	—	—
1925	457	254,262	1945	509	380,677
1926	488	284,739	1946	17,266	4,925,598
1927	505	309,493	1947	23,323	5,692,179
1928	501	308,900	1948	33,926	6,677,427
1929	630	330,985	1949	34,688	6,655,483
1930	712	354,312	1950	29,144	5,773,908
1931	818	368,975	1951	27,644	5,686,774
1932	932	377,625	1952	27,851	5,719,560
1933	942	384,613	1953	30,129	5,842,678
1934	965	387,964	1954	31,456	5,986,168
1935	993	408,662	1955	32,012	6,166,348
1936	973	420,589	1956	34,073	6,350,357
1937	837	395,290	1957	36,084	6,606,275

[a] 1918-46, as of the end of the year; 1947-57, as of June 30.
Source: Except for 1957, *Year Book of Labor Statistics, 1956* (Tokyo: Division of Labor Statistics and Research, Ministry of Labor, 1957). For 1957, Division of Labor Statistics and Research, Ministry of Labor, news release, December 4, 1957.

[8] *Yearbook of Labor Statistics, 1956* (Tokyo: Division of Labor Statistics and Research, Ministry of Labor, 1957), p. 372.

Union coverage in Japan, when measured on an industry-by-industry basis, reflects the coexistence of large and small enterprises.[9] Transportation, communications, and public utilities, which are composed almost entirely of large operating units, have been particularly vulnerable to trade-unionism. More than 70 per cent of their nearly 2 million employees are organized in more than 8,000 union bodies. Similarly, the mining industry, where most of the 500,000 employees work in large operations, is two-thirds organized in about 1,000 unions. In contrast, industrial enterprises in agriculture and forestry, with close to 650,000 workers, have a mere 7.5 per cent rate of organization in less than 600 unions, and only 28 per cent of some 200,000 fishery workers are members of fewer than 150 unions. In other sectors where small enterprises abound—wholesaling, retailing, finance, insurance, and real estate, which employ about 3 million persons—fewer than 17 per cent of the workers are organized, principally in the large banks and investment institutions. Altogether these fields have about 4,600 unions.

Services, which embrace a work force of close to 2.9 million in fields such as automobile repair, education, amusements, and recreation, have an organization rate of about 33 per cent. This relatively high figure, however, is explained by almost complete unionization of Japan's 600,000 public school teachers. In these service industries, approximately 5,000 unions have been established. Of the more than one million civil servants in local and national government, about 55 per cent are members of trade-unions, although organization is more widespread in the central government ministries than among the prefectural, municipal, town, and village government organs.

Despite its typically small units, the construction industry usually abounds with unions that make up the backbone of the labor movement in many industrial countries. In Japan, however, less than one-third of its 1.3 million construction workers belong to unions.

Similarly, while manufacturing, with its concentrations of manpower, is normally expected to constitute the bulk of trade-union

---

[9] See *ibid.*, p. 303, for a breakdown by industrial sectors in 1951, 1952, 1953; *Labor White Paper, 1956* (Tokyo: Division of Labor Statistics and Research, Ministry of Labor, 1956), p. 399, for 1954 and 1955; and Division of Labor Statistics and Research, Ministry of Labor, news release, December 4, 1957, for 1956 and 1957.

membership, this industrial sector in Japan has no more than 35 per cent of its 5.8 million workers organized. Within manufacturing, organization rates vary from a high of almost 75 per cent in the chemical industry to less than 10 per cent in furniture, apparel, and wood. Other high penetrations in manufacturing include about two-thirds in primary metals, rubber, and transportation equipment and over one-half in oil and coal products. Altogether, however, both in numbers of members and of union bodies, manufacturing makes up less than one-third of the present Japanese trade-union movement. Transportation, communications, public utilities, education, and the civil service account for a larger proportion. These are areas which are mainly composed of large operating units or where the government exercises a significant control through direct ownership or regulation.

In terms of union organization, statistics for manufacturing amply demonstrate the contrast between large and small industry. In 1953, unions existed in only 4.5 per cent of the manufacturing enterprises employing fewer than thirty. Enterprises with thirty to ninety-nine employees were less than one-fourth unionized. On the other hand, firms in the 100–499 employee category and those with 500 or more were organized 70 and 90 per cent, respectively.[10] It has been the large-scale enterprises, private and governmental—those largely identified with the old *Zaibatsu* cartels and military establishment—which have furnished the bulk of unionism in postwar Japan. These, of course, are the very sectors of the Japanese economy which are synonymous with the modern industrialization of Japan—coal mining, shipping, cotton textile spinning, chemicals, transportation, communications, electricity and gas, steel and iron, government bureaus, and so forth. All are key operations and figure heavily in Japan's dependence upon world trade. In contrast, sectors which are rooted in the traditional culture have not been especially amenable to union organization.

THE FIRST POSTWAR TRADE-UNION CENTERS: SANBETSU AND SŌDŌMEI

Before turning to the structural and functional characteristics of Japan's postwar unions, it is well to review the major developments

[10] *The Labor Union Movement in Postwar Japan* (Tokyo: The Daily Labor Press, Inc., 1954), pp. 16-17. See, also, *Rōdō Kumiai Chōsa Hōkoku* (Report on the Survey of Labor Unions), July, 1952 (Tokyo: Ministry of Labor, April, 1953), p. 6.

in the labor movement during the past decade.[11] The main events concerned attempts to establish nationwide trade-union centers.

Once the occupation gave the go-ahead signal for union organization, almost immediately there were efforts to establish a unified labor center. Mindful of the splits that had plagued the prewar movement, the initial postwar leaders, principally those who had been at the helm of the defunct *Sōdōmei*, set forth to avoid the earlier ideological conflicts. They envisaged a single national federation modeled after elements in both the CIO and AFL. While it would emphasize industrial organization, voluntarism, and economic activity, the federation was prepared to embrace any variety of organizational form which facilitated fuller unionization, especially if industrial unionism did not appear feasible for the time being.

This plan was somewhat of a vain hope, for the thousands of Communists, Syndicalists, and other left-wingers who had been released from jail or repatriated from overseas strongly advocated a politically inclined, highly centralized movement based on strict industrial unionism. As the rivalry grew, SCAP stood by without evidencing any official preference for either proposition, although it is alleged that some of its labor affairs officers favored the latter.

Actually, for many months after the occupation began, the leaders of both groups did attempt to lay a basis for a single unified center which would reconcile each notion of trade-union organization and philosophy. The effort proved futile. By August, 1946, two competing national centers made their appearance within a few weeks of one another. On the right and supporting the newly established Social Democrat party was the revived *Sōdōmei* (*Nihon Rōdō Kumiai Sōdōmei*) or the Japanese Federation of Labor. On the left stood *Sanbetsu* (*Zen Nihon Sangyōbetsu Rōdō Kumiai Kaigi*) or the National Congress of Industrial Unions, predominantly under Communist party control, but with some elements favoring the

---

[11] For more detailed surveys in English of the Japanese labor movement during the occupation period see Miriam S. Farley, *Aspects of Japan's Labor Problems* (New York: John Day, 1950); Iwao Ayusawa, *Post-War Developments in Organized Labor* (Tokyo: Foreign Affairs Association of Japan, 1953); and Evelyn S. Colbert, *The Left Wing in Japanese Politics* (New York: Institute of Pacific Relations, 1952). The more recent developments as well as the earlier period are dealt with in *The Labor Union Movement in Postwar Japan* (Tokyo: The Daily Labor Press, Inc., 1954), and Solomon B. Levine, "Prospects of Japanese Labor," *Far Eastern Survey*, XXIII (May and July, 1954). This section is based largely on these sources.

Socialists and other left-wing groups. Shortly afterward, a centrist group established the Japanese Congress of Labor Unions (*Nihon Rōdō Kumiai Kaigi*), but it proved to be of no great consequence. The prewar sectionalism had quickly re-emerged. The main difference, of course, was that now the movement no longer had to struggle merely to exist. Instead it received every encouragement. Given this freedom, however, the rivalry was even sharper than it had been in the prewar era.

During this period, *Sanbetsu* claimed almost twice the membership strength of *Sōdōmei*. Organized almost entirely on a national industrial union basis, *Sanbetsu* comprised twenty-one components with 1.6 million members. Its major constituents were government workers, miners, electric power, transportation, and other heavy industry groups. *Sōdōmei,* a confederation of twenty-four prefectural federations and four industrial unions with a membership of over 850,000, drew its support mainly from light industry and the smaller enterprises. It was well represented in textiles and shipping.

Together, at their height, the two centers could muster only about 50 per cent of the labor movement membership. At least half the organized workers did not affiliate with any of the centers, but remained in a variety of "neutral" or "independent" bodies—industrial, regional, enterprise, and in a few cases, craft unions. Although *Sanbetsu* and *Sōdōmei* competed to win over the independents, they made relatively little headway in this direction after the initial organizing period.

Despite their conflicting positions in ideology and organization, the two centers did manage to work together in certain instances. Most notable of these were the formation of a joint struggle committee to seek wage increases, especially for the government workers in the fall of 1946, and the founding of *Zenrōren* (*Zenkoku Rōdō Kumiai Renraku Kyōgikai*) or the National Liaison Council of Japanese Trade Unions in the spring of 1947. The instances of collaboration were related to one another; in effect they were attempts by one federation to gain control over the other.

The 1946 struggle committee fell into the hands of Communist leaders among the government workers and took the lead in threatening the general strike of early 1947. When the occupation moved to outlaw this action, the *Sōdōmei* elements withdrew rather than incur the ire of SCAP, thus bringing the joint committee to an end. On the other hand, formation of *Zenrōren* in March, 1947, promised somewhat greater success. With the Communists rebuffed by the February 1 general strike ban, *Sōdōmei* and the non-Communist elements of *Sanbetsu* seized the opportunity to assume leadership during the chaotic inflationary situation. As a result, *Zenrōren* attracted many of the neutral unions, and its affiliates soon embraced as many as 4.5 million union members. However, the Communists quickly began to reassert themselves, and a year later *Zenrōren,* like the earlier joint committee, had come under their domination. *Sōdōmei,* realizing its failure to "capture" the *Sanbetsu* unions through this method, withdrew from *Zenrōren* in 1948, and many of the neutrals followed suit. By the end of 1949, *Zenrōren* had fewer than 800,000 members.

Attacks upon *Sanbetsu's* Communist domination switched course after *Sōdōmei's* failure to control *Zenrōren.* These took the form of internal "democratization" movements, or the *Mindō,* which now received occupation blessings in view of the opening of the cold war. *Mindō* had its beginnings during the fall of 1947 within the independent but Communist-dominated National Railway Union, an organization of 400,000 members. Here, during the bitter contest between left and right, the *Mindō* group made considerable headway. At about the same time, various right-wing union leaders established an anti-Communist league, which gained official *Sōdōmei* support by January, 1948. A month later, after defections occurred within the Communist leader group, the *Mindō* spread into *Sanbetsu* itself.[12]

Under these internal pressures, SCAP and Diet restrictions upon government worker unions, and the 1949 revisions of the Trade Union and Labor Relations Adjustment laws, *Sanbetsu* began to crumble. Disaffiliations occurred steadily during 1948 and 1949. By the end of 1949, *Sanbetsu* had been reduced to half the membership it had two years earlier. Some of the unions which withdrew still embraced the ideal of pure industrial unionism and established *Shinsanbetsu* (*Zenkoku Sangyōbetsu Rōdō Kumiai Rengō*) or the National Federation of Industrial Organization with 200,000 members in late 1949. Most of the unions that had pulled out remained completely unaffiliated. Only a few entered *Sōdōmei.*

The demise of *Sanbetsu* gave rise to a new attempt at establish-

---

[12] The *Mindō* movement also spread into *Sōdōmei* as a protest against alleged dictatorial control by federation leaders. This, however, did not assume the significant proportions achieved in *Sanbetsu.*

ing a unified national labor center for the Japanese trade-union movement under right-wing control. With the Communists on the run, SCAP gave every encouragement for such a development. The implementation of the Dodge Plan was designed to produce the economic stability and expansion which would undercut the Communist appeal. The retrenchment of government and business operations in 1949 offered an opportunity to get rid of left-wing elements among the workers.[13] The revision of the labor laws in 1949 and the "red purge" of 1950 further relegated the Communists and their sympathizers to the background.

With occupation approval, the Japanese Attorney-General decreed the dissolution of *Zenrōren* as inimical to occupation objectives in late August, 1950. By this time, also, SCAP had suspended publication of the Communist daily paper, the *Akahata*, ordered the dismissal of Communists from newspaper staffs, and required the government to remove twenty-four members of the Communist central committee from public offices they held. Then, late in August the Labor Ministry announced its interpretation of the labor laws as permitting discharge of Communists from employment under the guise of retrenchment,[14] and in October it directed the prefectural governments to allow employers to dismiss Communists as "destructive" elements within their enterprises. Beginning in September, the government began to remove all known Communists from public service. Private employers quickly emulated this action. By December, 1950, nearly 11,000 had been discharged from private industry and more than 1,000 from government agencies. Among them were 2,546 union officials, mainly from *Sanbetsu* unions.[15] The Communists had gone underground.[16] The way was now open for an untrammelled right-wing labor movement.

---

[13] It is estimated that 700,000 workers were dismissed as the direct result of retrenchment measures.

[14] Somewhat earlier the Central Labor Relations Commission had reached a similar conclusion in an unfair labor practice case.

[15] The "red purge" came to an end by late 1950. Early the following year, however, *Nikkeiren* approached occupation officials to support another purge. The proposal was rejected as a "union busting" proposition.

[16] The Communist party, however, was not declared illegal. Whereas in the general election of January 23, 1949, the Japan Communist party gained 35 of 466 seats in the lower house of the Diet with almost 10 per cent of the popular vote cast—the high point of Communist popularity, in the following election of October 1, 1952, the Communists failed to gain a single seat winning only 2.5 per cent of the vote. The party won one lower house seat

THE FORMATION OF SŌHYŌ

Sōhyō (*Nihon Rōdō Kumiai Sōhyōgikai*) or the General Council
of Trade Unions of Japan was inaugurated on July 12, 1950, as the
new unified labor center. As such, it was a convergence of the
Mindō movement, *Sōdōmei, Shinsanbetsu,* and various unaffiliated
national unions, all of which were anti- or non-Communist. Actually,
however, the formation of *Sōhyō* came after more than eighteen
months of effort, preparation, and compromise.

In the fall of 1948, as a means of countering Communist domination of *Sanbetsu* and *Zenrōren, Sōdōmei* and the *Mindō* groups
in the independent National Railway Union and in *Sanbetsu* established a joint council to promote "democratization" of all labor
unions. This council, taking the name of the National Congress of
Japanese Trade Unions (*Zenkoku Rōdō Kumiai Kaigi*), formally
began in February, 1949, with a claimed membership of over 1.5
million. In the following July, it resolved to place principal emphasis on promoting affiliation with the new free world labor organization, the International Confederation of Free Trade Unions, then
in the process of formation. This move served to attract additional
adherents from among unions that had broken away from *Sanbetsu*
or had been independent. In the meantime, SCAP, through its Economic and Scientific Section, also began to encourage the establishment of a pro-ICFTU national labor center.

It was *Shinsanbetsu*, advocating the reconciliation of pure industrial unionism with political neutrality, which first took the initiative
to create the new unified organization. However, the support of
Shinsanbetsu wavered. Internal divisions, mainly of an intellectual
nature, arose in part from an aversion to joining up with distrusted
Sōdōmei elements and former *Sanbetsu* groups and in part from the
alleged political nature of the ICFTU itself. Accordingly, despite
its initial role in launching the new federation, *Shinsanbetsu* actually voted to withdraw in February, 1950, six months before *Sōhyō*
was inaugurated. But then in November, after *Sōhyō* was already
established, it elected to join the new center. However, it was an
unenthusiastic affiliate and, in July, 1951, withdrew from *Sōhyō*

in the April, 1953, election and two in the election of February 27, 1955, but
was unable to register more than 2 per cent of the vote cast. In July, 1955, the
party, after four years of semi-underground activity, again came out into
the open.

with half of its original membership. Although it often aligns with *Sōhyō* on economic and political issues, it has not since reaffiliated.

Sōhyō's establishment involved other uncertain compromises as well. Even though the unions which participated in its preparatory meetings embraced more than two-thirds of the labor movement membership, only about half of them were represented when *Sōhyō* finally was inaugurated. The majority of the affiliates were unions of government employees, and the leadership came from former *Sanbetsu* unions such as the postal workers and from independents such as the national railway workers. Many unions preferred to adopt a "wait and see" attitude. Others, like the *Shinsanbetsu*, felt that *Sōhyō* required too great a deviation from their basic tenets. The most serious problems centered around developments within *Sōdōmei*, which with its one million members would have been a principal component of the new *Sōhyō*. Difficulties related to *Sōdōmei* were both political and organizational.

At that time, unity among the Socialists was at best precarious. The Socialist-led coalition government, which had been in office during most of 1947 and early 1948, had failed to stem inflation and the party had become involved in a series of embarrassing bribery scandals. These developments gave rise to internal dissension, which intensified with the Dodge stabilization program, revisions of the labor laws, and anticipation of the impending peace treaty. *Sōdōmei* readily reflected the schisms of the Socialists, since its leadership for the most part tended to advocate support of the more conservative pro-Western right-wing.[17] It is quite likely that this group feared that it would be swallowed up in the new federation by its opponents within the Social Democratic party. While the rival factions within *Sōdōmei* on the whole were willing to submerge their political differences in a new labor center which would rout out the Communists and give support to American foreign policy and the ICFTU, their jockeying for position made for fragile unity.

In addition, *Sōdōmei* had been built upon a gerrymandering and pragmatic basis, related to the personal influence of its leaders, rather than along any predetermined organizational principle such

---

[17] Matsuoka Komakichi, for example, the prewar labor leader and former chairman of *Sōdōmei*, was a right-wing Socialist and served as speaker of the lower house in 1947 and 1948 during the term of the Socialist-led coalition government.

as industrial or craft unionism. At the same time, however, a strong sentiment for industrial unionism did exist within *Sōdōmei*. The challenge to *Sōdōmei's* leadership came over the issue of organization. The immediate question was whether *Sōdōmei* would retain its separate identity within *Sōhyō* or would be broken into components of *Sōhyō* on the basis of industrial unionism. The matter did not come to a head within the new national center but within *Sōdōmei* itself at its national convention in November, 1950. During the debate, the pro-dissolution forces made charges, some attributed to SCAP officials, that right-wing leaders of *Sōdōmei*, especially in the textile workers union, were collaborating with management groups. When a motion to dissolve *Sōdōmei* was introduced, the right-wing delegates withdrew from the meeting and left the issue undecided. Four months later, however, the left-wing faction recommended and voted formally for *Sōdōmei's* dissolution. About the same time, the right wing, which now controlled only about a third of the original membership, reconstituted *Sōdōmei* as a separate federation. The latter, of course, did not affiliate with *Sōhyō*, especially since left-wing *Sōdōmei* elements by that time had become the major officers of the new national center.[18]

The two major unions considered to be in the *Sōdōmei's* right wing—the textile workers and the seamen—along with some smaller right-wing units, nevertheless decided to cast their lot with the new *Sōhyō*. These, it should be pointed out, were industrial-type unions, and, while inclined politically to support the right-wing Socialists, they felt that at this time abandonment of *Sōhyō*, which was supposed to dedicate itself to political neutrality and support of ICFTU, would only reopen the deep divisions that had always plagued the Japanese labor movement. Their affiliation, however, was to prove tenuous and they withdrew three years later.

Sōhyō's earliest pronouncements gave every indication that it would provide a national trade-union leadership along the lines of the American model. They stressed democracy within unions, unalterable opposition to communism, intention to concentrate upon economic activity, and desire to join the ICFTU *en bloc*. When the Korean War broke out within a few days after *Sōhyō*

---

[18] *Sōhyō's* first secretary-general, the most powerful post in the organization, was Shimagami Zengoro, a former *Sōdōmei* official. He was succeeded by Takano Minoru, also formerly of *Sōdōmei*, in 1951. Takano remained in this post until July, 1955.

was inaugurated, a special convention condemned the North Koreans and upheld the action of the U.N., although it did oppose Japan's entry into the conflict as prohibited by her "peace" constitution.

This proved to be a short-lived position. Within a year, *Sōhyō* began to alter its emphasis, and by its third convention in July, 1952, it was no longer recognizable as originally chartered. Its turnabout began with the need to face up to the nature of the impending peace treaty and the question of Japanese rearmament. By 1950 the Social Democratic party itself was in the throes of debate over these problems, which eventually led to its formal split into Right and Left groups in the fall of 1951. The Left opposed a separate peace with the West alone, declared that under no conditions should Japan rearm, and supported Japanese neutrality of the type espoused by Nehru for India. While also in favor of "third force" neutrality and against rearmament, the Right was willing to accept a separate peace as the only practical alternative for regaining Japanese sovereignty. At its second convention in March, 1951, *Sōhyō* plunged into the problem and endorsed, in face of heated right-wing opposition, the so-called "four principles of peace"—neutrality, no rearmament, no military bases for foreign powers, and an over-all peace treaty. In July, *Sōhyō* capped its position with a condemnation of the proposed pact as "hardly satisfactory."

Dissension within *Sōhyō* emerged openly during 1952 and ended with defections in the following year. It was abetted by the seeming growth of Communist influence among *Sōhyō* unions, especially as the leadership undertook to strengthen industrial union organization and to concentrate power at the upper union councils. But the turn of *Sōhyō* toward unrestrained political action as its major preoccupation was the precipitating agent. This led not only to accusations that *Sōhyō* was abandoning its role as a trade-union center independent of political parties, but also to heated arguments over what political positions it should support.

SŌHYŌ SINCE THE PEACE TREATY

Restive under the restrictions imposed by the Dodge Plan and by the revised labor legislation, *Sōhyō* leadership, and particularly its principal officer, Secretary-General Takano Minoru, saw an opportunity for reasserting the labor movement's political influence as soon as the occupation ended and there could be an open contest to wrest governmental control from the conservative parties. Even before the San Francisco Peace Treaty went into effect, *Sōhyō* took concrete action to force the issue by organizing a nationwide protest against proposals made by the conservative Yoshida cabinet to revise the labor laws further and to enact antisubversive legislation on the grounds that it was necessary for the government to prepare to take over powers possessed by SCAP. In particular, the conservative parties contended that the central government would need authority to ban general strikes and to deal with "emergency" stoppages. Also, they proposed to modify the Labor Standards Law to bring it in line with "actual realities" of Japanese industry and alleged that legislation against subversives merely would continue occupation policy. General Ridgway, who had earlier succeeded MacArthur as SCAP, in fact had expressed support for proposals such as these in order to achieve an orderly transition from occupation to independence.

Sōhyō's protest movement took shape in a series of work stoppages. Five waves of twenty-four-hour nationwide walkouts were carried out under *Sōhyō* leadership during the spring and early summer of 1952 to bring pressure upon the Diet. These stoppages approached the proportions of general strikes, since most national unions, including thirty which were not affiliated with *Sōhyō*, joined in at various points. It is estimated that the largest walkout involved 3 million workers.

As a political movement, however, the drive was unable to muster enough strength to prevent passage of the new legislation, although in the end the conservatives offered no amendments to the Labor Standards Law and did agree to some compromises in the other enactments. On the whole, it was rather apparent that the unions themselves were poorly co-ordinated and divided in purpose during the campaign. Right-wing unions were concerned with the labor laws per se; left-wing unions focused on stopping the antisubversive measures and protesting against the peace settlement. Some unions, the coal miners for example, failed to join the walkouts when government authorities gave assurances that the revisions, particularly the antisubversive proposal, would not be used to restrict "legitimate" union activity. Moreover, the response was sporadic at the local and enterprise level, especially when *Nikkeiren,* with support of the Labor Ministry, advised employers to discharge or discipline workers for engaging in "unprotected" strikes and not to fear unfair labor practice charges. Still other unions concentrated on pure wage issues and once these were settled pulled out of the political protest. Finally, after the legislation was adopted at the end of July, 1952,[19] Premier Yoshida dissolved the Diet and called for new elections to be held in October as a means of reconfirming conservative party strength. Although the Socialists made gains in this election, the conservatives remained solidly in power.[20]

Sōhyō leaders did not give up easily. During the fall of 1952 they launched an even more vigorous political drive, partly in the hopes of unseating the Yoshida government and partly to recompense for the loss of prestige resulting from the failure of the spring campaign. This time the attack made use of direct economic weapons. It began with Sōhyō's demand for establishing a new principle for determining wages—the so-called "market-basket" formula, which called both for guaranteeing a minimum wage for all workers [21] and relating wage rates to a "theoretical" standard of living. This principle

---

[19] The major changes were (1) an addition of an "emergency adjustment" clause to the Labor Relations Adjustment Law, (2) removal of requirements for unions to be eligible to participate in the dispute procedures of the labor relations commissions, (3) extension of the list of government employees subject to the Public Corporation and National Enterprise Labor Relations Law, (4) enactment of a Local Public Enterprise Labor Relations Law, and (5) loosening of restrictions on overtime and night work for women and on underground work for male miners under the Labor Standards Law. See Chapter VI. In addition, the Diet created two public security agencies to investigate "subversive" activities.

[20] The October 1, 1952, election results were as follows in comparison with the previous alignment of seats in the lower house of the Diet:

	Prior to Election	Following Election
Conservative Parties:		
Liberal	285	240
Progressive	67	85
Socialist Parties:		
Left-Wing	16	54
Right-Wing	30	57
Communist Party	22	0
Others	17	30
Vacancies	29	0
	---	---
Total	466	466

See Paul S. Dull, "The Japanese General Election of 1952," *American Political Science Review*, XLVII (March, 1953), pp. 199-204.

[21] The minimum wage demand was set at 8,000 yen, estimated as the average monthly wage in Japanese industry at that time.

was to replace the prevalent practice in wage bargaining of keeping wages abreast of changes in living costs and of sharing the gains of increased productivity. The first of *Sōhyō's* targets were the coal mining and electric power industries, where two of the largest private industrial unions were affiliated with *Sōhyō* and where, of course, stoppages could quickly produce "emergency" situations which would test the government's willingness to utilize its new powers under the revised labor legislation. The wage demands under the formula were increases of 93 per cent and 52 per cent, respectively. To the employers these figures were preposterous, and in reply management offered wage reductions.

The biggest strikes in Japanese history then followed. Mediation by the Central Labor Relations Commission, whose award provided for small increases, proved of no avail, and the strikes continued for over two months, lasting late into December. In the meantime, with the Yoshida government returned to office, the cabinet considered enjoining the strikes under the new "emergency" powers unless a settlement was quickly achieved. As winter set in, public clamor for intervention reached an increasingly higher pitch.

Under these pressures, splits began to appear within the coal miners and electric workers unions, revealing the political nature of the entire affair. Several of the constituent enterprise unions broke ranks and returned to work. Then, in early December, the Prime Minister announced that he would seek an injunction. The coal miners executive committee divided in half over continuing the strike with a slim majority voting to end the walkout. In the end the terms of the commission's award were accepted, and the prolonged stoppages were over.

In the aftermath of these strike failures, dissension within *Sōhyō* crystallized. The defections in the coal and electric unions led to the establishment of rival national organizations which leaned toward *Sōdōmei*. In addition, the textile and seamen's unions now became increasingly impatient with the leftward-drifting *Sōhyō* leadership and began to protest against the almost exclusive concern of the national labor center with political activity. The conflict increased in intensity as the line between Right and Left Socialists was drawn tighter over the issues of the peace treaty, the United States Security and Administrative Agreements, Japanese neutrality in the cold war, and the question of rearmament. When Prime Minister Yoshida called again for new elections to be held in April,

1953, merely a half year after the earlier first post-occupation election, the factionalism further intensified.

Within *Sōhyō*, in February, 1953, the textile and seamen's unions, along with other right-wing groups, formally established *Minrōren* (*Minshu Shugi Rōdō Undō Renraku Kyōgikai*) or the National Liaison Council for Trade Union Democratization. *Sōdōmei*, in turn, affiliated with this group. Initially, *Minrōren* aimed to return *Sōhyō* to its original platform of principles but soon abandoned this hope.

By this time, *Sōhyō* had disavowed any intention to join the ICFTU *en bloc*, even though several of its important constituents, including the coal miners, seamen, textile workers, teachers, and private and national railway unions, had affiliated. In fact, at its July, 1952, convention, *Sōhyō* leadership criticized the ICFTU for allegedly attaching too much importance to Western Europe and for supporting the San Francisco Treaty, Japanese rearmament, and the U.N. action in Korea. In spite of the growing opposition within its ranks, *Sōhyō* leaders did not modify their positions.

The April, 1953, elections saw the Yoshida government returned to office but no longer commanding an absolute majority of seats.[22] *Sōhyō* leaders were now aroused by new government proposals to enact further labor restrictions, notably prohibition of labor stoppages in vital industries such as electric power and coal. As a result, during the spring and early summer of 1953, *Sōhyō* again launched a wave of political protest strikes. But lack of co-ordination was evident again; only 750,000 strikers could be mustered at any one time in three one-day walkouts. The right-wing unions were lukewarm to the maneuvers and ignored the protest, while the Diet

---

[22] The election of April 19, 1953, showed the following results in the lower house:

Conservative Parties:	
Liberal	202
Progressive	77
"Splinter" Liberals	35
Socialist Parties:	
Left-Wing	72
Right-Wing	66
Communist Party	1
Others	13
Total	466

See *Japan As It Is Today* (Tokyo: Ministry of Foreign Affairs, August, 1953), pp. 12-13.

proceeded to enact legislation prohibiting for a period of three years any stoppages which would cut off the nation's coal and electric fuel supplies.

The conflict within Sōhyō came to a head at its fourth convention in July, 1953, with the rejection of motions put forward by the seamen and textile workers to reaffirm Sōhyō's intention to join the ICFTU and to declare itself in open opposition to communism. The majority now chose to uphold the leaders' pronouncement that Sōhyō would seek to establish friendly relations with other trade-union bodies as well as the ICFTU, particularly the Red China Federation and other Communist-inclined groups in Asia.[23] Furthermore, the Sōhyō leadership embraced, although without the endorsement or rejection of the convention, a new "peace force" position, which condemned the United States for thwarting achievement of world peace and looked to Communist China and the Soviet Union as the promoters of global harmony. While they did not, however, go so far as to declare themselves communistic, their stand was enough to propel the seamen's union with its 100,000 members and two smaller right-wing unions out of Sōhyō immediately. By the fall, the textile union also voted to withdraw and numerous splinter groups—notably among the miners, electric power workers, teachers, auto workers, and railway workers—followed suit.

Although unwilling to abandon Sōhyō, still other unions, especially the synthetic chemical workers, now began to voice criticism of the extreme position taken by the Takano leadership. By continuing to favor a strict "third force" platform they held positions closer to the "mainstream" of the Left Socialist party than the Takano group. They therefore saw the "peace force" pronouncement of the Sōhyō leadership as a direct challenge to the party itself. The issue was drawn at the Left Socialist party convention held early in 1954 and ended in rejection of Takano's attempt to gain control over party machinery.

IMPACT OF RIVAL UNIONISM

Soon after the textile workers' withdrawal from Sōhyō, the right-wing unions, including Sōdōmei, took steps to form a separate rival

[23] The national railway workers union and the private railway workers union, two of Sōhyō's major constituents which had affiliated with the ICFTU, withdrew at this time from the free world labor federation.

labor center, and in April, 1954, established the new federation which took the name of *Zenrō Kaigi* (*Zen Nihon Rōdō Kumiai Kaigi*) or the Japanese Trade Union Congress. With its nucleus drawn essentially from *Minrōren*, total membership claimed exceeded 800,000. Significantly, in the new center *Sōdōmei* was permitted to retain its separate identity. Although supporting the Right-Wing Socialists, with whom *Sōdōmei* was directly affiliated, *Zenrō Kaigi* disclaimed any emphasis upon political action not strictly of a pure trade-union nature, declared that it immediately would seek membership as a federation in the ICFTU, and structured itself to give greater voice in its top leadership to the smaller unions. Furthermore, in opposition to *Sōhyō's* "market-basket" formula, which *Zenrō Kaigi* considered a mere political stratagem, the new federation supported wage increases based upon productivity and the financial conditions of individual enterprises and sought to promote union participation in management.

In the meantime, the conflict within *Sōhyō* sharpened. At its July, 1954, convention the "third force" unions led by Ota Kaoru, head of the synthetic chemical workers, directly challenged the leadership of Secretary-General Takano. The outcome was exceedingly close. Takano was re-elected secretary-general by a slim margin, and his "peace force" group retained possession of only eight of the fifteen seats on the *Sōhyō* executive council.

This result tempered *Sōhyō's* political position, for now the rival factions agreed to allow both "third force" and "peace force" views to coexist within the organization. Also, it was agreed to support any political party of the left except the Communists. In effect, this policy stalemated *Sōhyō* attempts at political action, although it probably helped to unify rank-and-file support for the Socialists. However, the outcome was only a temporary truce, not a reconciliation.

Sōhyō's political indecisiveness came at a critical juncture. By this time, the government's deflationary austerity program launched at the conclusion of the Korean War was in full swing. Threats of wage cuts, rationalization programs, and work force retrenchments were increasingly placing the unions on the defensive. What politicalism there was on the part of the unions was fanned by the "reverse course" policies of the Yoshida cabinet, which sought to increase the powers of the central government and to tie Japan closer to the United States. Acceptance of American military aid, expansion in the Japanese defense forces, centralization of control over the police, weakening of local government autonomy, and curtailment of political activities among public school teachers,[24] to name the major measures, brought forth constant protests from the *Sōhyō* unions. But *Sōhyō* made no serious attempt to repeat the widespread strikes of the previous two years, even though *Zenrō Kaigi* and the smaller *Shinsanbetsu* joined it in opposition to most of the government's proposals.

The situation within *Sōhyō* has remained uneasy. Probably the most significant trend has been a gradual submerging of the "peace force" group in favor of the "third force" position. In the fall of 1954, the Yoshida cabinet fell, more for reasons of internal ineptitudes than because of the growing left-wing strength. However, the general elections in February, 1955, returned the conservatives to power under the leadership of the Democratic party's Hatoyama Ichiro. Benefiting by this turnover, both the Right and Left Socialists, especially the latter, made notable election gains. Together they now commanded the bare one-third vote in the Diet necessary to block any attempt at revising Japan's "peace" constitution.[25]

The July, 1955, *Sōhyō* convention witnessed the ousting of Takano as the center's secretary-general. The Ota faction placed the name of Iwai Akira of the National Railway Workers Union in opposition to Takano. In the voting, Iwai received a slight plurality, but because of abstentions, he failed to gain the absolute majority needed for election. At this point Takano withdrew from the race and Iwai was acclaimed the winner. The "third force" Left Socialists also gained control of the executive council, but the "peace force"

---

[24] This measure was a severe blow to the Japan Teachers Union, *Sōhyō's* largest affiliate with more than 500,000 members.

[25] The results of the February 27, 1955, election for the lower house were as follows:

Conservative Parties:	
Democrat	185
Liberal	112
Socialist Parties:	
Left-Wing	89
Right-Wing	67
Communist Party	2
Others	12
Total	467

See *Japan Information*, II, No. 4 (Washington: Embassy of Japan, March 2, 1955), pp. 7-8, mimeographed.

group did retain substantial minority representation. Accordingly, no clear-cut triumph was evident.

Between the 1955 and 1956 conventions, the two factions quietly continued their struggle. Reunification of the Social Democratic party in October, 1955, tended to pull *Sōhyō* further away from the "peace force" line inasmuch as the "third force" position with the support of the Right clearly gained strength. Also, with the Ota-Iwai group in control of major organs of the center for the first time, *Sōhyō's* pro-Soviet emphasis softened. On the other hand, the "peace force" faction remained a power to be reckoned with, so that the Takano policies were not completely abandoned. For example, *Sōhyō* attitude toward the ICFTU underwent little perceptible change as the center continued its efforts to establish an international organization among Asian and African trade-union bodies in and out of the Communist camp.

The grip of the "third force" group strengthened in the 1956 convention. In addition to returning Iwai as the secretary-general, the Ota faction succeeded in gaining an absolute majority for its candidate for general chairman, Haraguchi Yukitaka, who previously had been serving as the chief ICFTU representative in Japan. Its representation on the executive council also increased. The only major concession toward the "peace force" position was to amend *Sōhyō's* constitution to make open collaboration with the Communists possible, but the Ota-Iwai-Haraguchi faction discounted this eventuality as very unlikely because of its control.

A major test of strength between the two groups also has taken shape in collective bargaining strategy. Rejecting the Takano emphasis upon "popular-front" campaigns and general protest stoppages such as those of 1952 and 1953, the Ota-Iwai leadership has stressed co-ordination of pure union struggles for wage increases. While not as openly political as the Takano approach, this tactic aims indirectly at undermining the economic policies, particularly wage-pegging, of the conservative government. Success on this score is believed to be the key to the general political success of the Socialists. Concretely, this development came to a head in *Sōhyō's* "spring offensive" of 1956, when both public and private industry workers sought wage advances simultaneously. In general, aided by Japan's economic upturn, this plan proved relatively effective— at least in the sense that the obvious failures of the Takano-led campaigns of mass protest were not repeated. Although the participating unions did not obtain all they were seeking, enough gains were registered to legitimize their claim to be effective guardians of the workers' interests.

Yet despite the change in leadership and in strategy, *Sōhyō* continues to give priority to political objectives. As if to recognize this, the Communist party emerged from hiding at the time of *Sōhyō's* 1955 convention and again began to advocate formation of a popular front with only a "modest" role to be played by the Communists. On the other hand, even though the long-sought rapprochement between the Left and Right Socialists has been achieved, the unified party still suffers from deep fissures within its ranks over principles of policy and positions of power. Apparently, the coalition has been aimed primarily at co-ordinating the hitherto disparate efforts to unseat the conservative government [26] rather than at mapping out a common program. That this situation remains difficult for the unions is seen in the continuing gulf between *Sōhyō* and *Zenrō Kaigi*, which show few signs of immediate merger. Because of the very failure to reconcile these different groups, politicalism is likely to remain a major theme in the Japanese labor movement.

The division among the union centers and their constituents takes its most dramatic form in the issue of international affiliation, particularly with the ICFTU. Only the fragmental *Sanbetsu* group openly joined the Communist-controlled World Federation of Trade Unions, and even then, upon voting affiliation in 1950, its adherents were closely divided. While some *Sōhyō* constituents have made occasional gestures toward the WFTU, the major controversy has centered about the free trade-union confederation. At the founding of *Sōhyō*, nineteen of its original major constituents immediately sought to enter the new ICFTU. These included *Sōdōmei*, *Shinsanbetsu*, and such large national unions as the coal miners, tex-

---

[26] The two principal conservative parties—the Democrats and Liberals—also effected unification in November, 1955. Following this merger, the lineup of seats in the lower house of the Diet was as follows:

Conservatives (Liberal Democrat Party)	300
Socialists (Japan Social Democratic Party)	154
Communists (Japan Communist Party)	2
Others (Farmer-Labor Party, independents, etc.)	8
Vacancies	3
Total	467

See *Japan Report,* I, No. 8 (Washington: Embassy of Japan, November 30, 1955), pp. 2-4, mimeographed.

tile workers, seamen, private railway workers, and the teachers. But with the ideological and political splits appearing in *Sōhyō* so soon after its formation, this did not come to pass. Because the left- and right-wing unions openly competed with one another for control of entry into the confederation, the ICFTU directly admitted national unions of both factions. These affiliates then compromised by forming a joint council, whose unanimous approval was required for any additional affiliations to the ICFTU. The arrangement, however, quickly proved embarrassing to the ICFTU as the joint council became the scene of conflict among the member unions. Disagreement produced stalemates, thereby detracting from the spread of ICFTU influence. *Sōdōmei* unions, for example, were unable to gain admission.

In turn, the ICFTU was reluctant to bypass the council and admit unions individually, lest such a policy would lead to withdrawals and to greater losses than gains in adherents. Furthermore, with the confused ideological position of most Japanese unions, it was necessary to rely heavily upon the Japanese themselves for passing upon eligibility of union organizations seeking to affiliate. In 1953 and 1954, the ICFTU headquarters dispatched several investigating missions to the scene in hopes of achieving a rapprochement among the Japanese ICFTU affiliates. The situation had become alarming not only because of the stalemate in the joint council, but also because of the criticism of the ICFTU by *Sōhyō* leadership and actual withdrawal from the ICFTU in 1953 of two major constituents, the national railway workers and the private railway workers.

No resolution to the problem began to appear until after the challenge to the "peace force" group's control in *Sōhyō's* 1954 convention. The ICFTU member unions voluntarily agreed to dissolve their joint council and to set up new machinery. Under the plan, the existing members, which included six *Sōhyō* unions—coal miners, metal and machine workers, broadcasting employees, teachers, communication workers, and municipal transport workers, together claiming a membership of over one million—and the four from the new *Zenrō Kaigi*—the seamen, textile workers, movie and theater workers, and garrison force workers, totalling over 410,000 members—comprised a co-ordinating committee and affiliated individually with the ICFTU. Shortly afterwards, *Sōdōmei*, which now had become a part of the *Zenrō Kaigi*, was admitted *en bloc* to the

ICFTU as a single affiliate. At the same time, a new co-ordinating council comprised of existing member unions was established to examine applications and to advise ICFTU headquarters on individual admissions. At this writing, however, only a few small additional unions [27] have been admitted under the new procedure. Thus, while ICFTU coverage in Japan is considerable, it falls far short of the original *Sōhyō* intention. Only a third of the total Japanese trade-union membership is affiliated, and only a third of the *Sōhyō* group has joined. The "neutral" unions and the bulk of *Sōhyō* unions have remained outside. *Sōhyō* itself remains isolated from the free world trade-union movement through its nonalignment policy.

---

[27] These include three regional organizations of electrical workers and a union of automobile workers. Both had previously broken away from *Sōhyō* national unions and affiliated with *Zenrō Kaigi.*

IV

THE TRADE-UNION MOVEMENT: STRUCTURE, FUNCTIONS, PHILOSOPHY

One must look behind the struggles over establishing national labor centers to discover the nature of the trade-union movement in postwar Japan. The political and ideological differences at this level furnish an explanation only in part. More fundamental clues lie in structural and functional relationships among the vast number of union organizations which constitute organized labor in Japan. Here its central theme is shown more clearly.

UNION STRUCTURE

One of the chief problems in structuring the Japanese trade-union movement has been how to weld together the numerous units at the level of rank-and-file organization into centralized co-ordinating federations. At present there are some 36,000 of these basic units. Most of them are small in size. Probably over 40 per cent of all these local organizations have less than fifty members, and 90 per cent have under 500 members. Somewhat less than half the organized belong to local units with fewer than 500 members, and more than one-third of the local units are found in small firms with fewer than 50 employees.[1]

The problem of unity and stability is complicated by a considerable turnover rate among the local unions. In a year in which total union membership showed only a small decline, July, 1950, to July,

---

[1] The large local unions, however, comprise the bulk of the membership. Local unions with less than 200 members account for somewhat more than 30 per cent of the organized workers, and those with fewer than fifty members have less than 6 per cent of the total membership. The average size local unit is only about 200 members. This is about half the prewar average and considerably smaller than the average size in the period immediately following the war. See Okochi Kazuo, *Nihon Rōdō Kumiai Ron* (*On Japanese Trade Unions*) (Tokyo: Yuhikaku, 1953), p. 114.

1951, 5,000 local units disappeared, while 3,000 new bodies were established. In each succeeding twelve-month period, 2,500 to 3,500 locals ceased to exist and 3,000 to 5,000 locals were created.[2] An annual turnover of 10 to 25 per cent, however, should not be surprising, given the newness of the institution, the precarious financial position of the smaller enterprises, and the instability of the national organizations themselves.

The structural feature most characteristic of Japanese trade-unionism has been its "enterprise" basis of organization. Probably more than 85 per cent of all basic union units, embracing almost 80 per cent of total union membership, are organized along enterprise lines; that is, their members are confined to a single shop, establishment, or enterprise. The remainder are divided about equally between industrial unions and craft organizations in which the local units are not based simply on enterprise membership. The "enterprise," or enterprise-wide, union typically includes all branches and plants of a firm whether engaged in the production of single or multiple lines, whether in one or several industries. In other words, it usually follows the structure of the enterprise entity. It may take either of two forms—a centralized enterprise-wide federation with local branches or an enterprise-wide confederation of local unions. The former is more prevalent. Where the enterprise has only one factory or shop, of course this distinction cannot be made. If the enterprise-wide federations and confederations are treated as single rank-and-file unions, the number of basic union units is about 19,000, rather than 36,000. The enterprise structural feature accounts for the major proportion of this reduction.[3]

In appearance, the enterprise union resembles the local of an industrial union, or an "intermediate" organization like the Ford or General Motors departments of the United Automobile Workers in the United States. However, the similarity ends about there. The essential distinction between the enterprise union and the local industrial union is that the former is a unit in and of itself; it is not merely an administrative component of a national union, nor is it simply an "inside" independent company-wide union. Although it is essentially autonomous, in most important cases it formally

[2] *Labor White Paper, 1957* (Tokyo: Division of Labor Statistics and Research, Ministry of Labor, 1957), pp. 270-72.
[3] *Ibid.,* p. 274.

joins with other enterprise unions into national, regional, or industrial federations.

A major characteristic of the enterprise union is its all-inclusiveness. More than 60 per cent of all the unions are "combined" organizations in that they include both white-collar and production workers.[4] Only 15 per cent solely embrace production workers, while the remaining 25 per cent are exclusively white-collar.[5] The large proportion of the latter, of course, reflects widespread organization in service and other tertiary industry, where there are few manual workers of the factory type.

Combined unions often suffer from diversity of interests among their members, and in recent years there has been a growing tendency for white-collar groups to break away and form their separate enterprise-wide organizations. Similarly, craftsmen and senior workers have sometimes agitated for separate union representation. The combined unions have responded to these moves by creating special divisions within themselves to represent these groups in union affairs. Frequently it is also the practice to divide the union officers equally between white-collar and production workers, who then alternate in the top posts.

The basic union units display a variety of affiliations to upper federations, as it is to be expected where there are several competing national labor centers. As shown in Table VI, in June, 1956, almost 42 per cent of the unions were affiliated with *Sōhyō*, most of them through national industrial unions and federations. These included about one-half of the total membership. *Sōdōmei* claimed a few more than 1,100 unions, or about 3 per cent of the total, with slightly above 7 per cent of the members. Affiliation to *Sōdōmei* came mainly through national industrial unions or federations and prefectural federations, with at least one-fourth of the groups participating in *Sōdōmei* via both routes. The remaining 700 unions in *Zenrō Kaigi* were for the most part affiliates of national unions and federations and embraced over 400,000 members. *Shinsanbetsu*, whose membership by that time had declined to a mere 36,000 or about 1 per cent of the total, embraced only 136 unions, most of which affiliated through national industrial unions and federations and the remainder through prefectural federations. *Sanbetsu*, which

---

[4] Okochi, p. 117.

[5] Production worker unions account for about 15 per cent of total union membership and white-collar unions for about 20 per cent.

TABLE VI. ORGANIZATIONAL STRUCTURE OF THE JAPANESE TRADE-UNION MOVEMENT BY AFFILIATION AND MEMBERSHIP, 1956 [a]

Organizations	Number of National Unions and Federations	No. of Local Unions				Number of Union Members
		Total	Affiliated through National Unions and Federations	Affiliated through Prefectural Federations	Affiliated through Enterprise Unions	
National Trade-Union Centers:						
Sōhyō	40	13,518	11,446		2,011	3,137,551
Zenrō Kaigi	13	1,828	1,495		70	661,965
(Sōdōmei)	(8)	(1,116)	(829)	(981)	(7)	(242,317)
Shinsanbetsu	4	136	88	47		36,135
Sanbetsu	2	120	120			12,078
Unaffiliated National Unions and Federations	35	4,671				1,083,314
Unaffiliated Local, Regional, and Enterprise Unions		13,925				1,451,818
Totals	94	34,073 [b]				6,350,357 [c]

[a] As of June 30.
[b] Total is smaller than sum of column because of multiple local union affiliations.
[c] Total is smaller than sum of column because of multiple memberships.
Source: *Year Book of Labor Statistics, 1956* (Tokyo: Division of Labor Statistics and Research, Ministry of Labor, 1957).

recently announced its dissolution, included about 120 unions with fewer than 13,000 members, affiliated through national industrial unions.

Yet, more than half of all the basic union units belonged to no national labor center. Over 17,000 unions, with an aggregate membership exceeding 2,500,000, remained unaffiliated. Some 4,700 unions with about one million members belonged to thirty-five national industrial unions and industrial federations which were independent or "neutral." More than 13,000 unions with 1.5 million members were affiliated with federations which were neither national nor industrial in scope or had no outside affiliation whatsoever.[6]

Dual affiliations also have not been uncommon. Some locals have affiliated with national unions belonging to one labor center, although they themselves have joined another either directly or through a constituent organization such as a prefectural federation. Some have refused to join a national center even though they belong to national unions which did. Still others have affiliated with a national center although they also belong to industrial, regional, or enterprise federations which have not. It is estimated that double affiliations involve about 300 unions with a membership between 150,000 and 200,000.[7]

The structures of the four major national labor centers are fairly similar. Each has espoused strict national industrial unionism, but all have departed from the principle.

Although almost all of *Sōhyō's* 3 million members are divided among about forty constituent national unions and federations, how purely "industrial" these constituents are is somewhat dubious. In the first place, close to two-thirds of *Sōhyō's* members are public workers, employed directly by the government or in government-owned corporations. Twenty-seven of the *Sōhyō* affiliates are unions of government employees. Most of these are restricted organization-

---

[6] The most recent membership figures (as of June, 1957) by status of affiliation are as follows:

Sōhyō	3,410,228	Sanbetsu	12,540
Zenrō Kaigi	782,459	Unaffiliated	
Sōdōmei	256,297	national unions	1,029,011
Shinsanbetsu	37,933	Other unions	1,534,275

See Division of Labor Statistics and Research, Ministry of Labor, news release, December 4, 1957.

[7] *Year Book of Labor Statistics, 1956* (Tokyo: Division of Labor Statistics and Research, Ministry of Labor, 1957), p. 370.

ally to a single government agency, ministry, or enterprise. Among the largest are the National Railway Workers (membership 370,000),[8] All-Communications Employees (membership 218,000), and National Telecommunications Workers (membership 152,000). In addition, at least fifteen other *Sōhyō* public workers unions, with a combined membership of more than 250,000, have the same organizational pattern.[9] The orientation of government unions toward traditional "departmentalism" in the Japanese government bureaucracy[10] and away from industrial unionism led to the establishment of *Zenkankōrō* (*Zenkoku Kanko Shokuin Rōdō Kumiai Kyōgikai*), or National Council of Governmental Employees Unions, in 1946 in order to achieve co-ordination among them. Three years later this council was reorganized to include almost all public worker groups, whether in *Sōhyō* or not. The new organization took the name of *Kankōrō* (*Nihon Kankōchō Rōdō Kumiai Kyōgikai*), or Japan Council of National and Local Government Workers Unions, and now has a membership of almost 2.5 million. Thus, there has been a need to structure intermediate bodies between the national labor center and constituent and nonconstituent government worker unions to achieve a semblance of industrial unionism.[11]

The one-third of *Sōhyō's* members who are private industry workers belong to national unions more clearly of the industrial type. However, even here the organizational distinction is blurred. Industrial jurisdictions are fragmented by the presence of government worker unions. They are also difficult to define because the enterprise entities which originally were established and integrated by the *Zaibatsu* cut across conventional industrial lines. Thus,

---

[8] Membership figures cited above and subsequently are approximate as of June 30, 1956. See *Year Book of Labor Statistics, 1956*, pp. 375-79. For more recent figures for *Sōhyō* unions, see *Sohyo News*, No. 92, December 25, 1956, mimeographed.

[9] Major *Sōhyō* constituents in the public worker field which more closely fit the industrial union classification are the Japan Teachers Union (membership 593,000) and All-Japan Local and Municipal Government Workers Union (membership 438,000).

[10] For an analysis of "departmentalism" in Japanese government, see Kiyoaki Tsuji, "The Cabinet, Administrative Organization, and the Bureaucracy," *The Annals of the American Academy of Political and Social Science*, CCCVIII (November, 1956), pp. 10-19.

[11] Still another co-ordinating council has been formed to include only the unions of workers in public corporations and government-owned enterprises.

Sōhyō's national unions for private industry workers tend to be clusters of worker organizations around key enterprises rather than organizational units with clearly staked out industrial boundaries.[12] Two *Sōhyō* unions divide the chemical industry. Communications is apportioned among national unions for workers in the postal service, domestic telephone and telegraph, international telecommunications, radio broadcasting, and radio wave control. Transportation is divided among marine, automotive, express, harbor, and the two railway unions.

Splits and defections have further served to reduce the status of industrial unionism in *Sōhyō*. A sharp blow came with the withdrawal of the long-established seamen's union in 1953 and shortly afterward the disaffiliation of the 300,000-member textile workers, then the largest private industrial union in *Sōhyō*. The split in the coal miners and electric power workers (the latter to disband altogether in 1955) also weakened the industrial union base among *Sōhyō's* private industry workers.

Zenrō Kaigi also departs from the ideal of industrial unionism which the center officially supports in principle. Two of its three major components, the textile workers and the seamen, are industrial organizations and together comprise about half the center's membership. The third, the *Sōdōmei* federation, however, combines both industrial and regional groups. For example, it includes national unions of coal miners, metal industry workers, shipbuilders, chemical workers, construction workers, food industry workers, transportation workers, and harbor workers, but it also embraces a number of prefectural federations that cut across industrial lines. In addition, smaller groups of near-industrial and enterprise types, such as portions of the independent electric workers union, national railway engineers union, theater employees union, and the broadcasting workers union, are directly affiliated with *Zenrō Kaigi*.

---

[12] The major private industry unions of *Sōhyō* are the following (approximate membership in parentheses): The Japan Coal Miners Union (200,000), Japan General Federation of Private Railway Workers Unions (134,000), Japan Federation of Iron and Steel Industry Workers Unions (121,000), All-Japan Express Workers Union (68,000), Japan Federation of Synthetic Chemical Workers Unions (98,000), National Metal Workers Union (84,000), and All-Japan Federation of Metal Mining Workers Unions (64,000). A large semi-private workers union is the All-Japan Garrison Forces Labor Union (82,000). Unions such as the coal miners, private railway workers, and the now-defunct electric power workers also have been closely allied with the public workers unions because of governmental controls exercised over these industries.

Because of their small size, little needs to be said of the organizational structure of *Shinsanbetsu* and *Sanbetsu*. Both have been ideologically dedicated to national industrial unionism. However, *Shinsanbetsu* counts as a substantial portion of its membership a separate oil enterprise union and a prefectural federation, while the three components of *Sanbetsu* resemble general unions more than industrial unions.

The thirty or more nonaffiliated national unions usually follow rough industrial jurisdictions. Yet, they have been reluctant to join the national centers, partly from a desire to avoid open ideological or political identification with the centers, and partly from a fear of jurisdictional conflicts and loss of independence. On the other hand, many of the independents have displayed sympathetic attitudes toward the centers. *Sōhyō* counts at least two-thirds of these national organizations as "friendly" unions; six or seven have participated regularly in the so-called Problem Consultative Association under *Sōhyō* sponsorship. Others, especially in the government, transportation, communication, and public utility fields, have formed various co-ordinating and planning committees on industrial or functional bases which cut across the national centers.

There is intense competition among the rival centers to win over the independents as permanent constituents. Several of the independents have attained considerable size: for example, the bank employees federation, until it split in two in 1956, had over 130,000 members; electric equipment workers, close to 120,000; electric power workers, more than 115,000; shipbuilding workers, about 60,000; and national railways locomotive engineers, at least 50,000.[13] Others are relatively small organizations spread through silk-reeling, department stores, insurance, newspapers, petroleum, rolling stock, cement, electric cable, printing and publishing, automotive transport, warehousing, hotel and restaurant, chemical, construction, ceramics, and government industries. As would be expected, secessions, affiliations, and reorganizations occur regularly among them.

The federations, whether they be national labor centers, affiliated

---

[13] The National Railway Locomotive Engineers Union lays claim to being the only sizable craft organization in Japan. Apparently, however, while operating engineers form the nucleus of this union, having broken away from the National Railway Workers Union in 1951, they have attempted to include other types of railroad employees in rivalry with their former parent union. In addition, the engineers union has confined itself exclusively to the government-owned railways.

or unaffiliated national industrial unions, prefectural or other types of organizations, are little more than loose co-ordinating bodies with relatively weak powers over their enterprise union constituents. It is probably correct to assume that only *Sanbetsu*, openly Communist and affiliated with the WFTU, has had highly centralized controls and, as part of the Japan Communist party, attempted to establish cells within each of the enterprise unions.

Among the national industrial unions, the seamen and textile workers of *Zenrō Kaigi* seem to have achieved a centralization not unlike that typically found in major American national unions. In part, this has beeen the result of the unusual characteristics of maritime and textile labor markets in Japan. Also, centralization is strong in some of the smaller national and regional federations, especially among the *Sōdōmei* units. This can be attributed to personal followings, some going back to the prewar period, rather than to any logically consistent organizing principle. However, in the national industrial unions of *Sōhyō* and in the independent group, the typical structure is a loose co-operative arrangement among the participating enterprise unions. Where control at the national level is strong, as in exceptional cases such as the National Railway Workers or the All-Japan Express Workers, the union's jurisdiction matches the virtual monopoly control of an enterprise.[14]

Zenrō Kaigi in fact plays down centralization by giving greater voting strength at conventions to smaller affiliates than does *Sōhyō*. This provision was a conscious choice at the time of *Zenrō Kaigi's* formation because of the complaint that the smaller private industry members of *Sōhyō* were outvoted by the larger and more unified government unions.[15]

---

[14] The express union represents the ultimate in equating an enterprise union with a national industrial union because the Japanese express industry is monopolized by a single company.

[15] The recent Ota-Takano conflict within *Sōhyō* arose in part from this situation. Ota's chief support appears to have come from the private industrial unions, while Takano drew his from the government workers. Not only has there been disagreement between the two blocs over voting strength, but also, as a result, on the question of tactics and strategy. The Takano group, stressing the leadership of the government workers unions, has advocated a "popular front" appeal, not unlike the Communists', which would bring all elements in the nation into labor disputes and demonstrations. The Ota faction has argued for concentrating economic and political activity only within the union membership with co-ordination between the private and public workers. In this respect, the Ota group more closely approaches the position of *Zenrō Kaigi*.

In the relationship between a national industrial union and its enterprise components the locus of economic power typically is concentrated among the latter. National union leaders are highly aware of the situation and would prefer to see less emphasis placed upon the existence of enterprise unionism. For example, the *Sōhyō* coal miners union has given no official recognition to affiliates organized on an enterprise basis. Each mine is considered a local branch of the national union, to which it is affiliated through regional and district bodies, not unlike the United Mine Workers of America. However, the fact of the matter is that the mines of each enterprise, such as the Mitsui or Mitsubishi, even though scattered throughout Japan, are invariably banded together into an enterprise federation, and it is through this organization that miners carry on their principal union activities. And the textile workers union, an organization modeled after the Textile Workers Union of America and therefore subdivided into cotton, wool, rayon, and other branches, is nonetheless essentially based on enterprise unions that correspond to managerial jurisdictions. Thus, when an enterprise has operations in all branches of the textile industry, the enterprise union usually has organized accordingly.

FUNCTIONAL DISTINCTIONS AT NATIONAL AND LOCAL LEVELS

The principal functional distinction between the national organization and the enterprise union is that the former largely looks after the political activities of the labor movement and the latter concentrates on the economic. This division has not been purposive but is the resultant of forces that have made Japan's postwar labor movement what it is.

Fundamentally, the explanation is that the postwar labor movement in Japan grew in two directions—from the top labor center down and from the enterprise union up. In effect, two loosely related movements converged at the national industrial union level, but in many cases failed to meet squarely and in some instances merely brushed past one another.

Concentration of the upper structures of the Japanese labor movement upon political functions should not come as a surprise. The initial drive to achieve wholesale reform of the Japanese society, the radical heritage of the prewar labor movement with its rival ideologies, and the realization that Japan's economic viability depended to a major extent upon central government policy drove the national organizations toward their preoccupation with political functions. At the same time the traditional concern with permanent attachment to enterprises meant a primary emphasis on economic activity at the local level.

Accordingly, the chief function of the national organization has remained a political one, evidenced in the fact that here most of the planning and organizing of political action takes place, almost to the exclusion of other activities. It is here also that rival ideological and political groupings contest to exercise control. When disputes occur at the enterprise level, much of the thinking at the upper levels is in terms of how they may be turned to one political advantage or another. Thus, the political emphasis of the national unions arises partly from the disinterest of the enterprise unions in using them for economic purposes, and partly from deliberate attempts by political groups to gain support from the enterprise unions.

One evidence of the failure of the enterprise unions to rely upon the national organizations and centers for carrying out economic functions is the latter's lack of personnel and funds. Financial support is meager due in part to the needs and expenses of the enterprise unions and in part to low local union dues, necessary because of low income levels.[16] Relatively little is left over for the parent bodies. In most cases the affiliated enterprise union retains well over half the money it collects and uses more than 25 per cent for wages and salaries of its own staff. Heavy staffing of the enterprise unions accounts for the relatively large proportion of the funds expended at the local level. For example, it is estimated that among the enterprise unions there is at least one full-time paid union official for every 150 members. Local groups rarely rely upon volunteer workers from among the rank and file.[17] These practices mean that not only do the federations have few resources for maintaining large staffs, but also that many of the service functions that they might provide to their constituents are already pre-empted by the enterprise unions. Because collective bargaining relationships are mainly at the enterprise level and therefore would require detailed

---

[16] Usually the rank-and-file member pays his dues as a flat sum per month or as a percentage of his monthly earnings. Two hundred yen or 1 or 2 per cent a month are not uncommon levies.

[17] See Y. Haraguchi, "The Free Trade Unions of Japan Democracy's Bulwark," *Free Labour World*, 61 (July, 1955), pp. 17-20.

supervision in negotiating and administering labor agreements, the national unions and labor centers are hardly equipped to carry out these economic functions.

Furthermore, a national union only rarely has authority to enter collective bargaining negotiations or to require national approval of local agreements or strike action. Representatives of the enterprise union use the national organization primarily to co-ordinate their activities and to render mutual aid, not to provide direction and leadership. Centralized strike funds are very small and usually are raised on an *ad hoc* basis. In general, the enterprise unions are reluctant to permit the national and central bodies to provide even limited research, financial, legal, and educational services. They prefer to retain bargaining-related activities for themselves.

The lack of collective bargaining leadership at the national levels stems to a considerable degree from the hesitancy of enterprise union leaders, especially the officials of the huge units which constitute an industrial union, to accept positions as national officers. They are often unwilling to exchange their powers for the relatively minor role that a national leader plays in enterprise union affairs. In addition, rivalries among leaders of the separate enterprise unions frequently produce stalemates which are resolved by agreeing upon less talented persons to head the national offices. Finally, conflicts within enterprise unions over ideological differences and, more important, clashes of diverse interests in the combined membership divert attention from any importance which the national organizations might attain.

In sum, what the national unions and centers are left with is leadership in political agitation. Leaders of the national organizations have tended increasingly to participate actively in the political parties of the left.[18] It is not uncommon for such leaders to run for public office. The restricted trade-union functions that remain for the national unions and federations to perform undoubtedly have continued to turn them to seek expression in the political arena.

---

[18] For analyses of the relationship between the trade-unions and the Socialist party, see George O. Totten, "Problems of Japanese Socialist Leadership," *Pacific Affairs*, XXVIII (June, 1955), pp. 160-69; Allan B. Cole, *Japanese Society and Politics: The Impact of Social Stratification and Mobility on Politics*, Boston University Studies in Political Science, No. 1 (Boston: The Graduate School of Boston University, June, 1956), especially Chapter VII; and Cecil H. Uyehara, "The Social Democratic Movement," *The Annals of the American Academy of Political and Social Science*, CCCVIII (November, 1956), pp. 59-60.

This tendency appears to be as much the result of the functional division within the postwar Japanese labor movement as of the ideological predilections of its national leaders.

Enterprise unions, on the other hand, have not been wholly apathetic to this politicalism. There is little doubt that the workers were aroused by the postwar events and that as a result their political consciousness was heightened. Rank and filers responded to political appeals made at the top of the labor movement, if for no other reason than that they experienced a catharsis from the tensions arising from their stringent economic lives and disturbed social relationships. Traditional conformity also was at work; the fact that a new supreme authority, SCAP, gave its approval, if not encouragement, to this behavior produced large followings among the workers for radical political leaders. As a result ideological rivalries spread into the enterprise unions and have occasionally led to shifting affiliations and splits among the unions at the enterprise level.

Nevertheless, even though the penetration of political consciousness among the rank and file has been much greater than it was in the prewar era, in most cases it appears to be momentary thrusts rather than deep anchorages. A basic weakness of political movement in Japanese trade-unionism lies in what may be described as the "flip-flop" nature of the enterprise unit, rising at certain points of time to a high pitch of politicalism and then reverting to quiescence or almost complete inactivity. The failure of the general strike attempt in 1947, of the *Sanbetsu*-led drives in 1949 to prevent revisions in the basic labor laws, of the *Sōhyō* political campaigns and coal and electric strikes of 1952, and of the protest stoppages in 1953 manifested this characteristic. More generally, the tendency often is seen in the sudden splitting in two of enterprise unions in the midst of ongoing disputes.[19] Its explanation becomes clear when we examine the nature of enterprise unionism more fully.

THE CENTRAL THEME OF THE JAPANESE LABOR MOVEMENT: ENTERPRISE UNIONISM

Even though almost every conceivable labor ideology from abroad—British Fabian socialism, Soviet communism, French syn-

---

[19] In the case of a split, so-called Number One and Number Two unions result. Under the law, both must be recognized as legitimate organizations provided they meet the legal requirements for internal procedures and independence from employers. See Chapter VI.

dicalism, German codetermination, American business unionism—
has been articulated within the Japanese trade-union movement
since the end of the war, just as the foreign "isms" competed in the
prewar movement, none of these philosophies has yet proved predominant in Japan. While it is true that the Japanese movement
has been identified primarily with the parties of the left, particularly
the Socialists, the Socialist hold has been far from complete. Driven
into disfavor by occupation, government, and management policy
and by trade-unionists themselves, communism has made even
fewer inroads. Japan's distinctive trade-union concept, if it can
be called that, is enterprise unionism. It appears to be an indigenous
product, whether for better or worse. Rarely voiced as the guiding
spirit for Japan's labor movement, nevertheless, enterprise unionism
has provided a dominant theme.

That traditional forces were subtly at work to produce enterprise
unionism was not easily recognizable in the chaotic rush of postwar
events. Immediate circumstances rather than deep-seated attitudes
could readily explain this structural form. Enterprise-wide organization seemed to evidence a burst of enthusiasm for complying with
the occupation directive to achieve a broad-based independent
labor movement. All workers, whether white-collar or production
employees, shared a common interest in protecting their incomes
against the rampant inflation. The enterprise basis of organization
was a logical means for venting protest against managements who
had long subjected the workers to abuse and degradation. White-
collar and intellectual employees, with their more advanced education and knowledge of enterprise operations, were "natural" leaders
for the industrial wage-earners in this drive "to set matters straight."

Only after the repulsion of communism, the Socialist splits, the
"red purge," the Dodge Plan retrenchment, the labor law revisions,
and the restoration of employer status did it finally become clear
that enterprise unionism provided the basic characteristic of the
Japanese labor movement rather than any form of unionism associated with foreign ideological concepts. The main interest of the
industrial workers now was seen as focused upon a unionism imbedded in the web of traditional Japanese culture. Up to this time
the trade-union movement seemed to bear all the earmarks of
Syndicalist industrial unionism. Actually, however, it was principally an evolutionary result of traditional relationships rather than
a rapid upsurge of a long-repressed ideology. Formation of com-

bined unions, including both the white-collar and production workers, did not necessarily come from a sudden emergence of a
common class consciousness; it resulted as much, if not more, from
an ongoing common identification with a management entity. Reliance upon white-collar, intellectual leadership did not spring mainly
from a drive to articulate the philosophy of trade-unionism for a
new society; it indicated rather the need for maintaining the integrity of enterprises when traditional management no longer exercised directive control and co-ordination. The swift, *en masse*
joining of unions was not merely an expression of relief from long-
standing police suppression; it was also a way for enterprise-
bounded groups to conform readily to the will of a new supreme
authority. Although on the surface foreign-inspired ideologies appeared to be prime movers, underneath home-grown Japanese
enterprise consciousness provided quick and easy impetus for
widespread unionism.

The fundamental pattern of Japanese industrialization had
shaped this trade-union response. The twin factors of industrial
structure and labor market organization channeled Japan's postwar
union movement along a distinctive, indigenous course. Unions
sprang up almost overnight, chiefly in that portion of the industrial
apparatus (the *Zaibatsu* and government-owned operations) which
was stable and permanent—where hard cores of the Japanese labor
force had become rigidly attached. Yet, each of these entrepreneurial units had played a specific role in developing an economy
precariously dependent upon foreign countries for raw material
supplies and finished goods outlets. Each had come to possess its
own distinct technology and organizational hierarchy. Among them
a separateness of identity, allied with traditional social verticalism
and abetted by management paternalism and ultranationalistic
ideology, had long thwarted the growth of craft, job, and class
consciousness among industrial workers.

The sudden opening of the gates to long-suppressed ideological
appeals imported from abroad was likely to engender sharp rivalries in the attempt to combat traditional attitudes. But because
sectionalism was so deeply rooted, there was no certainty that
any of these ideologies would clearly triumph. The struggle between *Sōdōmei* and *Sanbetsu*, especially the aggressiveness of the
latter, exemplified the intensity of this competition in face of obdu-
rate enterprise sectionalism. In the Japanese context, trade-unionism

found its most fertile soil for growth in its promise of assuring attachment to the enterprise and not of restructuring the society. It has been the phenomenon of enterprise orientation with which the postwar labor movement has had to cope from the beginning in its efforts to achieve unity and stability. The sheer size of the movement and its sudden emergence complicated the process of achieving these goals.

Nor did the operation of Japanese labor markets serve to undercut the tenaciousness of enterprise consciousness. Narrow channels of labor mobility had accompanied the development of Japan's industrial structure in order to assure a well-disciplined work force in an era of rapid transition. Despite the expansion of public employment exchanges and the prohibition of the labor "boss" system, the traditional constrictive arrangements were difficult to replace with open and free labor markets. Permanent attachment to specific enterprises of those workers wholly committed to industrial life made any horizontal movement among stable business units relatively insignificant. The very widespread practice of temporary employment buttressed the narrow labor market structures.

Despite the phenomenal population growth, the inability of agriculture to absorb the swelling labor force, and the overcrowding of the urban areas, temporariness remained a strong characteristic of a large segment of the industrial work force. The exclusion of temporary workers from membership in many of the enterprise unions and from benefits of collective bargaining agreements continued to confirm this labor market bifurcation. Although economic forces were making it more and more difficult for Japanese society to operate within its traditional framework, the temporary workers did not evidence, as yet, firm commitment to industrial work. If they did, at best they were characteristically ambivalent. Although only temporarily employed and in fact forced to move from one place of employment to another, often as day laborers, they too sought to identify themselves individually only with the one enterprise that afforded the possibility of permanent attachment. Barred from accession to the ranks of the permanent, they tended to float between the enterprise and their family farms and shops. They poured especially into the petty enterprises and into the tertiary occupations, which best preserved the traditional familial relationships. There was little success in inducing them to form strong and lasting unions.[20] They carried with them agrarian backgrounds and ingrained family traditions which they could not readily abandon in the type of labor markets afforded by the Japanese economic structure.

The swift growth of a broad-based movement of the proportions attained by organized labor in Japan rested on few possible alternatives to enterprise unionism. Given the specialized technologies and work hierarchies of each Japanese enterprise, craft unionism had little opportunity for success, simply because few distinct craft lines existed. Industrial unionism also was somewhat of a mere hope because historically there were no industrial groupings in the Western sense of common market competition and because it was uncertain what future development in this direction there would be. General unionism was a somewhat more feasible alternative for widespread worker organization, as some "professional" labor leaders and traditional labor "oyabun," particularly in Sōdōmei, found that they could disregard industrial, enterprise, and craft lines and build up personal followings from among smaller and financially weak enterprises in urban communities. However, this too had a limited potential. Because workers had become strongly and permanently attached to positions within the family-like social orders of their enterprises, the most "natural" units were the large enterprise entities. In fact, it had been this very tendency that underlay the organizational structure of the wartime labor front.

The paradox of postwar unionism in Japan is that the enterprise structure contributes both to its strength and weakness. On the one hand, enterprise unions assure a wide base for the development of a trade-union consciousness among workers. They have a potential for promoting worker solidarity and for mobilizing against threats to worker interests. In this sense, they provide institutionalized means to protect industrial wage-earners which previously did not exist in Japan.

On the other hand, the self-containment and inward focus of enterprise unions pull the labor movement apart. Alliances with other unions are sacrificed in order to achieve strong centralized organization only within the enterprise union itself. In itself, the

---

[20] Various attempts have been made to organize a federation of temporary workers unions. In 1955, Sōhyō launched the so-called All-Japan Coordinated Council of General Workers, which has succeeded in organizing only about 70,000 temporary workers.

enterprise union is often a cumbersome apparatus. Diversity of interests in its typical combined membership usually is a drag on its internal administration. The union is unlikely to cater to individual grievances or to propose changes that might upset long-established relationships within the work force of the given enterprise. It gains solidarity by stressing permanency of worker attachment. This emphasis leads to attempts to match the scope of management control in an enterprise entity. One union of all permanent employees in the enterprise is preferable to craft or occupational unions that run the risk of playing one group off against another. It is also preferable to industry-wide or general amalgamations in which separate enterprise identities may be lost and with them the guarantee of permanent attachment.

Nonetheless, the enterprise unions and the national movements do at times coalesce. The former's focus upon broad, generalized across-the-board demands for their diverse memberships often joins with the egalitarian political appeals of the national leadership. In actuality the objectives differ. The one seeks to enhance traditional security and identification by impressing upon management the needs of the permanent workers; the other aims for ideological fulfillment by taking over the entrepreneurial function. It is this difference in objectives, when they come in conflict, which gives to the Japanese unions their "flip-flop" nature.

No doubt enterprise unionism also subjects the Japanese labor movement to the danger of succumbing to employer domination. The national leadership of the labor movement strongly fears this possibility. On the other hand, enterprise unions have features of independent strength which in the Japanese context could not readily be duplicated by some alternative trade-union structure. Their large, all-or-none membership, their success in breaking down discriminatory treatment by despotically inclined managements, and their inclusion of white-collar workers with specialized knowledge of management operations and understanding of legal issues, all serve to make the enterprise unions something more than institutions that merely exist at the pleasure of employers.

That enterprise unionism exists to the extent that it does today represents a break from the past history of Japanese industrial relations, though perhaps not as sharp a one as the occupation originally contemplated in launching the postwar labor reforms. Worker consciousness, almost nonexistent in terms of a broad working class or labor movement, certainly supports unionism within the enterprise. Readiness of workers to pay dues—in contrast to the French situation, for example—is an indication of this.[21] When the time comes that the economic security of the permanent worker is relatively unthreatened, the Japanese unions may begin to release their energies on a sustained basis for broader economic and political purposes. In most cases, however, at least for the time being, enterprise unions are too completely absorbed in their own local situations to give any more than passing attention to such activities.[22]

---

[21] The Ministry of Labor recently reported that 95 per cent of all members pay their union dues. The check-off, however, is a common practice. See Haraguchi, p. 18.

[22] Recently, following its 1956 convention, Sōhyō has launched a program to organize Socialist party committees within each local union. Ostensibly, these are designed to combat the influence of Communist cells among the rank and file, but they are also aimed at promoting political consciousness among the workers and at building up the status of the national organizations. Zenrō Kaigi and the more moderate union groups, even though supporters of the Social Democrats, view this program as an unwarranted dilution of trade-unionism with political activity.

V

COLLECTIVE BARGAINING

AND LABOR DISPUTES

Collective bargaining over the terms of industrial employment is a distinctive function of trade-unions in free societies. Where the processes of autonomous collective bargaining, including the threat of and actual resort to work stoppages, fail to develop, the labor movement may well be jeopardized, for collective bargaining appears to preserve trade-union independence and to provide stability in union-management relations. Without it, the labor movement runs the danger of losing its identification with the interests of the industrial wage-earner, or, what may come to the same thing, of failing to achieve effectiveness as an institution acting in behalf of the workers. The purpose of this chapter, then, is to probe the extent to which collective bargaining has become established in Japanese industry during the past decade. In particular, we shall be concerned here with the machinery employed, issues covered, agreements arrived at, types of disputes that have arisen, and the manner of their disposal.

Because collective bargaining represented almost a wholly new and sudden departure for Japanese industrial relations in the postwar period, public policy affecting the relations between employers and workers has been intimately involved in its development. The Trade Union Law of 1945 set forth the legal basis for collective bargaining by declaring as its central purpose ". . . to raise the status of the workers and thereby to contribute to economic development through the guarantee of the right of organization and the encouragement of collective bargaining." [1] Thus, the law con-

---

[1] Quoted in Isao Kikuchi, "Freedom of Association and Unfair Labor Practices," *The Japan Annual of Law and Politics*, No. 2 (Tokyo: Second Division, Science Council of Japan, 1953), p. 62.

ceived of collective bargaining as a central activity for the newly forming unions.

Additional impetus for collective bargaining came a few months later with the enactment of the Labor Relations Adjustment Law in September, 1946. It stipulated that "nothing in this law shall be construed either to prevent the parties from determining for themselves their labor relations or from adjusting the differences of their claims concerning labor relations by direct negotiations or collective bargaining or to relieve the parties concerned with labor relations of their responsibility for making such endeavors."

These principles were set forth even more strongly in the 1949 revision of the Trade Union Law which provided:

The purposes of the present law are to elevate the status of workers by promoting that they shall be on equal standing with their employer in their bargaining with the employer; to protect the exercise by workers of autonomous self-organization and association in labor unions so that they may carry out collective action including the designation of representatives of their own choosing to negotiate the terms and conditions of works; and to encourage the practice and procedure of collective bargaining resulting in trade agreements governing relations between employers and workers.[2]

The legislation envisioned establishment of a widespread network of negotiating machinery through which employers and unions, acting independently, would make contracts of long enough duration to insure stability in industrial relations.

SCAP's educational activity in the labor field was directed largely to this end. Much of what was suggested and urged was drawn from American experience. Throughout the occupation period Japanese scholars and government officials aided in disseminating information to workers and employers on techniques of collective bargaining, contents of collective agreements, methods of contract administration, and so forth. The establishment of the Ministry of Labor in 1947 and the work of the labor relations commissions were part of this effort to bring about the spread of private collective bargaining.

COLLECTIVE BARGAINING MACHINERY

Private collective bargaining, of course, draws its vitality from actual practice rather than from public policy pronouncements.

[2] English translations of the laws quoted above and hereafter are found conveniently together in *Japan Labor Code, 1952* (Tokyo: Ministry of Labor, 1953).

Moreover, its successful implementation depends not only upon the establishment of negotiation machinery by the parties, but also upon the degree to which the machinery is used in the various phases of collective bargaining—the making, interpreting, and administering of labor agreements and the settling of disagreements—on a regular and sustained basis.

Japanese collective bargaining machinery, however, appears to fall short in both respects. The reasons lie in the decentralization of the labor movement in its economic function, the existence of competing decision-making machinery at the enterprise level, and the lack of traditions of horizontal contractual relationships.

No doubt widespread enterprise unionism and preoccupation of upper union organs with political action have contributed to the decentralization of negotiating arrangements in Japanese industrial relations. The locus of bargaining has been principally at the enterprise level. As a result, not only has there been lack of co-ordination in collective bargaining activity but also, especially in view of the absence of any historical tradition in the area, failure of what negotiating machinery there is to develop fully.

In only a few instances has the area of collective bargaining extended beyond the limits of the enterprise itself. The seamen, with a history of large-scale collective bargaining extending back to the prewar period, have successfully operated permanent industry-wide negotiating machinery with the major shipping companies. This, however, is a lone example. Other cases of industry-wide bargaining have been only temporary arrangements. An industry-wide setup in the coal industry resulted from governmental efforts to rehabilitate the industry on an over-all basis and continued through much of the occupation period and for a short time thereafter. However, by 1954 the situation had reverted largely to enterprise-by-enterprise negotiations. Multiple-company bargaining also has been carried on sporadically among the ten major enterprises in the cotton textile industry but is not firmly entrenched. Enterprise bargaining itself often takes on the appearance of industry-wide negotiations when a company which has far-flung operations throughout the nation—the Japan Express Company or the National Railways Corporation, for example—exercises a virtual monopoly in its field.

In contrast to the absence of centralized bargaining at national and industrial levels, all negotiations within the enterprise typically are conducted by top officials of both management and union. On the management side, responsibility for the planning and carrying out of collective bargaining as well as the administration of labor agreements is concentrated in the hands of the industrial relations specialists in the head office. Here, a specialized staff usually assists the responsible officials, and, in enterprises with several branches and plants, subsections of staff specialists study and report on local conditions and situations and execute the decisions made at the headquarters.

The enterprise unions have similar highly centralized mechanisms for collective bargaining. Although delegates from each of the union's branches usually participate in the union's bargaining committee, the top union officers elected on an enterprise-wide basis take the lead in planning and formulating demands. Staff assistants at union headquarters assist the top leaders in negotiating and executing labor agreements.

Bargaining machinery at the local plants and branches is not apt to be elaborate, since even variations needed for the local situations are usually decided upon at the top. Most negotiations are carried on at the enterprise headquarters in the major commercial centers, such as Tokyo or Osaka, even though much of the work force affected actually may be far removed. Management, in fact, is likely to provide office facilities to the union both at the enterprise headquarters and branches.

The presence of competing deliberative machinery in many Japanese enterprises, mainly in the form of joint worker-management councils and "productivity" committees, has contributed to the failure of collective bargaining machinery to develop more fully and more rapidly. Joint councils and committees were suggested initially to help meet the desperate problem of production rehabilitation after the war. Both SCAP and the Japanese government, pointing to the wartime experience in American industry, urged formation of joint councils both to promote union-management co-operation and to prevent resort to "production control," a dispute technique whereby workers actually take over operation of a plant.[3]

---

[3] In mid-1946, the Central Labor Relations Commission also called for the formation of such councils, suggesting that they be set up initially through collective bargaining, with the management and union reaching agreement upon the council's size, composition, manner of selection, and spheres of operation and authority. In its report, the commission characteristically urged that "neutrals" serve on joint committees in public utility enterprises.

On the other hand, the joint council resembled the prewar worker representation schemes which had been developed by the more patriarchal employers. Nevertheless, many unions sought to increase their influence in management operations through the joint councils, especially after their attempts at "production control" ran into both practical and legal problems.[4] Even though the councils presumably were to limit themselves to problems of improving production, at first it often was difficult to draw a line between this function and that of collective bargaining. The number of councils rose rapidly, and by mid-1946 they were operating in as many as a third of all unionized enterprises.

After the turnabout in political and economic conditions in 1948 and 1949, many of the councils came to resemble the American employee representation plans of the early 1930's. Now that the trade-union movement was placed on the defensive and management status was re-established, management began to dominate the joint councils. In recent years managements generally have favored the use of joint councils, and it is a fair guess that at least half of the unionized enterprises now possess such machinery in one form or another.

The combination of enterprise unionism and joint consultation now tends to restrict the scope of collective bargaining in Japanese industry. Each is concerned only with the internal affairs of a single enterprise. The union concentrates primarily on the issue of permanent attachment to the particular firm; the joint council serves principally to advise management on problems of internal personnel administration. The two functions are likely to complement rather than conflict with one another. But their narrow focus means that relatively little attention will be paid to broad issues which, if widely shared in numerous collective bargaining situations, often give the collective bargaining institution its vitality. The relationship among separate collective bargains is left to the national unions for political exploitation rather than economic co-ordination. In turn, negotiators gain limited bargaining experience in only a few problems and are not prepared to participate in the working out of many of the detailed elements of the terms of employment.

---

[4] "Production control" often resulted in improved production records. However, this technique ran into difficulties of procuring raw materials and selling in the market. By 1947, SCAP held that production control was an illegal invasion of private property rights, and a court ruling to this effect was made in 1950.

Not only is collective bargaining generally limited in scope, but the penetration of the process within the enterprise is not very deep. Vigorous contract administration with union and rank-and-file participation is often prerequisite for effective contract negotiation. In the United States well-developed procedures for processing individual complaints and grievances from the bottom up symbolize this relationship; however, the lack of grievance procedures in Japan is notable. Despite widely broadcast advice of SCAP labor officials and Japanese government agencies, neither unions nor management have given much attention to installing and promoting the use of grievance machinery. Even where the machinery is formally set up, it is seldom used.

The reasons for this failure are not difficult to find. The very fact that top union and management officials in the enterprise pre-empt what bargaining there is and do not decentralize the bargaining function reflects the tenaciousness of authoritarian organization in Japanese industry. Enterprise unions and management hesitate to introduce an idea which would promote individual and subgroup protest. The general orientation of the enterprise union toward the membership as a whole and the patriarchal role played by the managerial staff, especially industrial relations specialists, play down the desirability of individual expression.

Moreover, there is likely to be little pressure from below for systematic grievance processing. The dual position of the traditional first-line supervisor, identified with the working class yet intensely loyal to management, reduces his willingness to act as a spokesman for either side in a conflict over contract interpretation. Traditional subservience and group conformity of the workers are obstacles to voicing individual complaints in as blatant a fashion as the initial step in American grievance procedures requires. As a result, union representatives at the shop level resemble but little their shop steward counterparts in Western countries where one of their chief functions is to assist rank-and-file union members to pursue individual complaints through a grievance machinery. Theirs is mainly a "watch-dog" and reporting function, so that top-level negotiators will take up grievances only when they become widespread. Thus, dissatisfactions are likely to be presented in the form of generalized union demands with little opportunity for the aggrieved workers to become immediately involved in the bargaining process.

Still another aspect of the incomplete negotiating machinery in Japanese industrial relations has been the failure to develop arbitration systems. There is a general aversion to any type of arbitration, private or public, and what arbitration procedures do exist have been provided by law. Both management and enterprise unions seem unwilling to entrust decisions on matters concerning themselves to outsiders. In the context of American industrial relations, such attitudes could be considered a manifestation of autonomous and mature collective bargaining, but in the Japanese situation, they appear to reflect a lack of autonomy, as well as immaturity and a failure to establish meaningful collective contracts. The parties are likely to view arbitration as the submission of one side to the other rather than the affirmation of their independence of one another. In the event of disagreement, they tend to resort either to open warfare or to mediation and conciliation in which a third party takes no forthright stand. The function of the official labor relations commissions is of interest in this connection, for their principal role, even in protecting legal rights, has been largely to promote compromises by the parties themselves.[5]

The weakness of the Japanese collective bargaining machinery has also hampered efforts to bring unions and managements together for the discussion of and agreement upon procedures to meet problems of national concern. Except for the tripartite approach of the labor relations commissions, no other voluntary arrangement has met with singular success. For example, it was hoped that a SCAP-sponsored nationwide labor-management conference at the time of the institution of the Dodge Plan would lead to some permanent apparatus for negotiations over the impact of the retrenchment and disinflation programs. No visible results, however, were achieved. Also, when most of the major unions and the *Nikkeiren* in 1949 jointly established the Japan ILO Association for the purpose of securing Japanese readmission to this body and to deliberate problems arising under the Labor Standards Law, it was hoped that a basis for consultations on a nationwide scale would result. The management federation, however, withdrew its support early in 1955 and the organization soon collapsed. In turn, with the backing of the Japanese government and funds derived from the American Foreign Operations Administration (Point IV) program,

---

[5] See Chapter VI.

in March, 1955, *Keidanren* and other management groups proceeded to establish the Japanese Productivity Center and invited trade-unions to participate on an equal basis. The national unions and labor centers, however, have refused to join, fearing their participation would further undercut efforts at collective bargaining and would endorse a program they politically oppose.[6] If collective bargaining were more firmly rooted in Japanese industrial relations, arrangements such as these might have attained readier acceptance.

MAJOR BARGAINING ISSUES

Collective bargaining as the major institution in Japanese industrial relations has been hampered not only by weaknesses of the negotiating machinery, but also by limited subject matter. Both management paternalism and government regulation pre-empt much of what in other nations usually is the grist of collective bargaining. Moreover, there is relatively little in the actual substance of Japanese collective bargaining which is not closely related to one or the other of these factors. With a few notable exceptions, collective bargaining issues have revolved around either improvements (or prevention of retrogression) in long-established paternalistic practices or the protection and interpretation of benefits provided by law.[7] Negotiations between unions and managements in Japan have not as yet instituted any wholly new set of principles for setting terms and conditions of employment. Rather, they have dealt mainly with elements already rooted in law and management practice. Issues therefore have been relatively limited in scope. For the most part, they have been concerned with wages and job tenure. Of less central importance have been questions of union recognition and security, conclusion of fixed agreements, hours and working conditions, personnel administration, welfare facilities, union participation in management decision-making, and so forth.

---

[6] Recently, however, the seamen's union, *Sōdōmei*, and other right-wing unions, commonly at the enterprise level, have agreed to participate in the new center, but only upon gaining assurances that productivity increases would be shared equitably with the workers. In furtherance of the aim of the center, also, a few union-management agreements at the enterprise level have been made. Although both *Sōhyō* and *Zenrō Kaigi* are opposed on record to the productivity center, the latter has expressed some sympathy with its purposes.

[7] Since the latter are dealt with in Chapter VI, little specific reference to them is made in the present chapter.

With the rampant inflation of the early postwar years, the dis-inflation of the Dodge Plan, and later the rise in price levels during the Korean War, it is not surprising that wages have been a preoccupying issue in Japanese collective bargaining. While com-modity prices advanced at least 250 times between 1945 and 1949, unions constantly engaged in efforts to keep wage incomes abreast of living costs. Rates might be set on one day and remade the next. Advances secured in any one enterprise led to demands for com-parable increases in the others. Gains by workers in private indus-try promptly became the impetus for drives among the government workers, and vice versa. The disinflation following the Dodge Plan forced unions to protect workers against wage cuts, while renewed inflation after 1951 brought a repetition of wage rounds.

Moreover, the very nature of the Japanese wage system has absorbed the energies of negotiators. Because wages traditionally are computed on a monthly basis, the time dimension alone gives the wage issue special significance. Also, wage components are numerous, typically including a minimum rate, basic rate, family allowance, seasonal bonus, overtime payment, cost-of-living adjust-ment, regional allowance, transportation and housing allowance, skill and job-status premium, extra pay for hazardous and dirty work, and the like. Most of these have long existed in the wage system of any single enterprise. Age and sex differentials further complicate the various wage items. Each component has readily afforded a basis for collective bargaining demands by the unions.

In most cases there is a regular progression from one wage issue to another on a continuous negotiating basis, and usually negotiations do not take place at some stated period in the year, but are pursued on an around-the-year schedule. If there is any regularity in bargaining, it is the semi-annual negotiations over seasonal bonuses, paid traditionally at the time of the New Year's and summer Buddhist festivals, but these, too, are distinct com-ponents of the monthly wage rate. When unions fail to secure base-rate increases, they then attempt to seek larger seasonal bonuses or one-time payments as a substitute.

In other words, the large variety of wage components affords great flexibility in wage bargaining. Bargaining takes the common pattern of a series of spring, summer, fall, and winter wage "strug-gles" in which different aspects of the wage system become focal points. In turn, wage agreements are usually fixed for only very short periods of time.

The wage issue also gains primacy because it is tied to ideology stemming both from traditional Japanese paternalism and Marxist influence. During the inflation, this took shape in union campaigns to achieve the so-called "living-standard" wage, which for all practical purposes meant keeping worker incomes abreast of rises in living costs. More recently, especially as inflation subsided, union emphasis has been upon computing wages according to a "theoretical" living standard related solely to the minimum "needs" of the worker and his family. In its most concrete form this has been expressed in *Sōhyō's* "market-basket" formula. Although these positions are partly Marxist in inspiration in that they propose that all workers receive the same increases and benefits, that little recognition be given to individual differences in productive contributions, and that there should be a uniform minimum wage rate, enterprise unions, in catering to their combined memberships, have also lent support to this approach.

Accordingly, at both national and enterprise levels the unions have struggled for general wage increases but have shown relatively little interest either in revising the wage system itself or altering wage structures. With individual wage rates largely resting upon a host of personal factors, such as age, length of service, social status, schooling, work experience, family size, regularity of attendance, sex, and so forth, the trade-unions have refrained from insisting upon programs of wage rationalization, because they fear it would produce divisive effects. Thus, the demands put forth by the unions are egalitarian in that they attack management attempts at differential treatment. At the same time, however, the unions have made few onslaughts against the bases of the traditional wage system per se, although the net result has in fact been a percentage-wise narrowing of wage differentials within enterprises. In some cases the union simply demands an increment to the total wage bill and proceeds to divide any increase so granted among the various worker groups without further negotiations with management.

The traditional wage system has been of special concern to the more "modern" Japanese employers, who hope to institute "scientific" job classification and evaluation procedures which would relate worker effort to productivity and thus serve to systematize operations and reduce costs. Serious efforts in this direction were undertaken when the postwar inflation began to subside and employers regained status and power. Ignoring union demands for the "living standard" wage, managements began to institute payment of "efficiency" wages. In some cases, companies introduced job classification and revised their wage structures based on job evaluations. Some managements also expanded wage incentive plans. However, in many instances it is doubtful that these are anything more than the traditional wage system, in a new guise, for "merit," "loyalty," and "co-operation," which often are tied to length of service, have been used as major criteria for increases granted in this fashion.

Unions have reacted sharply to these attempts at "rationalizing" the wage system mainly because they fear that it might remove many of the wage questions from collective bargaining and might threaten to disrupt the union. The left-wing leaders in the national centers, of course, oppose their adoption on ideological grounds. On the other hand, most managements too have not proceeded hastily toward full-blown wage rationalization because of their own concern with preserving worker identity with the enterprise. They tend to continue to employ long-established factors such as length of service as the principal basis for individual wage increases. Where managements have been able to reject general, egalitarian wage demands of the union, the workers still gain solace in the recognition that individual wage benefits will be forthcoming for all as long as they retain their permanent status in the enterprise. As a result, while wages occupy the center of the collective bargaining stage, often the true significance of the issue is related to the question of job permanency.

The issue of the size and membership of an enterprise's permanent work force usually does not come to the fore except upon management initiative. This appears to be the case because of the well-entrenched patterns of permanent attachment throughout Japanese social and economic life. But discharge and dismissal programs have been occasions for the most bitter disputes in postwar Japanese industrial relations. Thus, when management undertakes retrenchments, as it did under the Dodge Plan and more recently under the government's austerity program, the issue becomes especially crucial in collective bargaining. Essentially the enterprise union is dedicated to preserving the permanent attachment of its membership, and in effect one concession it makes to secure this objective is to forego strong affiliation with other unions.

On the other hand, the demand for permanent attachment can serve to bring together the national trade-union leadership and the enterprise union, especially in a time of crisis. Political aims of the national organizations and economic functions of the enterprise union clearly may coalesce whenever there is a threat of discharging permanent workers. In order to strengthen the bonds between the national and enterprise organizations, the national leaders stress the need to enforce the daily and weekly hours provisions of the Labor Standards Law and to reduce the legal maximum hours of work.[8] By seeking to spread the work through hours reduction, the national unions essentially cater to the sentiment for permanent attachment at the local level. However, the enterprise unions appeal to the nationals for bargaining assistance only when management actually threatens a reduction of the enterprise's permanent work force. If management avoids taking such a step, the enterprise union is not likely to lean heavily on the national organizations for protecting the permanent worker's job security.

The guiding principle in Japanese enterprise unionism has been the effort to secure permanent attachment of workers regardless of changes in business activity. The means for protecting the permanent workers in their employment is the existence of buffer groups of temporary employees. It is this which largely explains why the Japanese unions have not attempted to institute seniority systems, so common in American industrial relations as a method of meeting the problem of job security. Seniority has been rejected because of the implicit recognition it gives to management's authority to reduce or otherwise manipulate the work force in the face of economic changes without regard to traditional obligations to employees. Management, too, has not been insistent upon displacing the permanent-temporary worker system with job seniority procedures, because of its own sense of paternalistic responsibility toward the permanent workers and because of the flexibility of operations afforded by the employment of temporary workers. As a result, even when there is not enough productive work available for the permanent workers, normally they will be retained on the payroll and will continue to receive all the benefits to which they are entitled. In most cases only natural attrition has been effective in

---

[8] Recently *Zenrō Kaigi* has embarked on an intensive campaign for a forty-two-hour week rather than the present legal forty-eight-hour week. *Sōhyō*, similarly, has pressed for a maximum forty-hour-week under the law. *Zenrō Kaigi*, however, hopes to achieve a reduction of hours through collective bargaining as well as through legislation.

whittling down the size of the permanent work group. On the other hand, in some industries such as coal mining, where distress has been especially serious, managements have made deliberate and successful attempts to reduce the permanent work force. But even in these cases the blow of unemployment has been softened by cash inducements for voluntary quits and by sizable displacement and retirement allowances for those who must be separated.

As the proportions of temporary workers have increased in some enterprises, the permanent hard core has become even more intent upon its attachment to the enterprise and has sought to strengthen its identification with the enterprise union in order to protect its favored position. By agreeing with management not to extend benefits to the temporary workers and by withholding union membership from them, the union gains security and acceptance within the enterprise. But even though permanent attachment is as crucial if not more crucial a matter than wages, it has not become an issue for constant rounds of collective bargaining. The enterprise unions have not continually pressed for maintaining or expanding the hard core of permanent workers through negotiations, except in emergency situations. It is more likely that the question of where to draw the line between permanent and temporary is taken up in the relatively quiet joint committees, for the system of job tenure cuts two ways as a bargaining issue. On the one hand, it gives rise to a touchy political problem within the enterprise union, where the membership usually prefers to avoid upsets in established relationships. The union will vigorously press a case if a permanent employee is actually discharged or laid off, but because of the risk of internal divisions will avoid raising the issue of extending permanent status. On the other hand, the employers are also likely to be cautious, for dismissal of permanent workers, individually or on a wholesale basis, is certain to evoke unanimous support for a strike. Since the concept of permanency is so widely accepted and respected, the likelihood of finding enough willing and able replacements, even from among the temporary group, is minimal. In other words, while the issue of job tenure is central in bargaining relationships, it is a hazardous one for either side, for once raised it is likely to involve the most bitter of struggles. The longer practices such as these continue, the more ingrained the permanent worker system becomes and the greater is the resistance to changing it.

Other issues in Japanese collective bargaining are in effect tangential. With unionism formed largely on an enterprise basis, there has been very little bargaining over union recognition and jurisdiction, although to some extent bargaining has been related to the scope of the union's membership, particularly the question of whether it should extend into the lower levels of management. The problem of jurisdiction has been largely removed from collective bargaining through revisions of the Trade Union Law in 1949, dealing with examination of trade-union qualifications and unfair labor practices.

The issues of union security and union participation in management take on their own peculiar twists in Japan. Neither has reached the proportions of cruciality, although considerable theoretical debate over these matters has been carried on by unions, management, and government agencies. Union security, in the form of the "full" and the "modified" union shop, is widespread in Japanese industrial relations. The closed shop and the open shop are relatively infrequent. Indeed, with enterprise unionism as the prevalent form, union security is largely an academic question. Written contracts, however, usually include union security clauses for their symbolic value in order to denote the acceptance of the enterprise union. In most cases, the union's jurisdiction is equivalent to the permanent work force cadre in nonmanagement categories. A worker does not join the union before hired, as would be required by the closed shop, simply because usually there is no union for him to join. After he is hired, his membership is virtually automatic as a condition of permanent attachment to the enterprise. Japanese union shop provisions out of context appear to say that all workers must join the union once they are employed, but in actuality they are more likely to mean that a member of the union must first become a permanent employee of the enterprise. Managements have not resisted this type of union security arrangement.[9]

In the same vein, unions have achieved the dues "check-off" with little struggle. Employers are not likely to fear a check-off when they know that the funds for the most part will be used at the enterprise union level for officers' salaries and membership welfare

---

[9]A Labor Ministry Survey in 1951 reported that in a sample of 1,075 agreements, 942 had some type of union security provision; 81 per cent were "union" or "modified union" shops, while only 5 per cent were "open" shops and 12 per cent had no clause whatsoever. See *Industry and Labor*, X (November 1, 1953), pp. 348-49. For the first time in Japan, an industry-wide union shop agreement was won by the seamen's union in 1954.

rather than in support of national union activities. Nor does the check-off appear to arouse any great resentment among workers. Such practices have been common, going back to the days when the wages of girl textile workers were withheld until they had completed their employment periods or a portion of their wages was paid in advance to their peasant parents.

The issue of union participation in management has already been touched upon earlier in connection with joint councils, and it, too, has its deceptive aspects in the context of Japanese industrial relations. Some right-wing unions, especially the *Sōdōmei* group, have endorsed wholeheartedly efforts to achieve participation in management and are willing to co-operate in arrangements such as the recently established Japanese Productivity Center in order to reach this goal. On the other hand, experience with joint councils has led many national unions in *Zenrō Kaigi* and *Sōhyō* to reject such a program on the grounds that, given the enterprise union setup, unions which "participate" in management too easily tend to fall under employer domination and control. However, even among the *Sōhyō* unions, attitudes vary considerably. For example, the Mitsui enterprise union of the *Sōhyō* coal miners and the National Railway Union, one of the major *Sōhyō* constituents, look to participation as a means of achieving a West German type of codetermination. So far, however, this question has proved to be more of an issue for debate among the unions themselves rather than in collective bargaining with employers.

With the exception of retirement provisions, welfare benefits have been matters of relatively little concern in collective bargaining and have been left largely in the hands of employers or the state. Among the large enterprises, for example, the cost of voluntarily provided private welfare programs is estimated to be at least equal to the payments required of these employers by law.[10] Many of the welfare benefits, particularly those pertaining to the provision of meals and housing (worker dormitories, for example),[11] are

---

[10] See *Wages in Japan* (Tokyo: The Daily Labour Press, Inc., 1954), pp. 23-25.

[11] A Labor Bureau Standards survey in 1947 reported that there were over 11,000 enterprise-supported dormitories, housing 450,000 workers. Eighty-three per cent were in the cotton spinning industry, and 53 per cent of the residents were female. See Masaichiro Ishizaki, "The Legal Status of Female Laborers in Japan," *The Japan Annual of Law and Politics*, No. 1 (Tokyo: Second Division, Science Council of Japan, 1952), p. 53.

now subject to governmental regulation under the Labor Standards Law of 1947. Because the law also permits workers and management to form mutual benefit associations to set up and operate welfare programs, the role of the union has been reduced from what it otherwise might have been.

The major exception has been in the field of retirement and old age benefits. Here, the traditional underlying sentiment that management is responsible for providing for the whole life of employees remains especially strong and prompts enterprise unions to use the issue as a rallying point for their members, especially as the senior workers have begun to reassert their influence. The possibility that management will abdicate its traditional responsibility in this area in favor of state welfare programs arouses the workers' fear that the concept of permanent attachment will also be weakened.

By and large, the function of the union in these matters has been to police administration of the programs in order to assure that legal rights and regulations are not violated. Except for benefits such as retirement and severance allowances, unions have not made great use of collective bargaining to seek improvements in the welfare provisions. Similarly, social insurance schemes for unemployment, pensions, health and accident, and so forth, are more closely tied to legal requirements and traditional practice than to collective bargaining. The scope of Japanese collective bargaining is thus hemmed in by employer paternalism on one side and welfare stateism on the other.

COLLECTIVE BARGAINING AGREEMENTS: EXTENT AND CONTENT

Collective bargaining agreements in Japanese industrial relations had only the scantiest prewar history. Employers opposed them, the government suppressed them, and the left-wing unions were disinterested. However, in 1928 the seamen's union and several shipping companies concluded the first known written wage agreement. It dealt only with minimum wages. The Japanese government reported that forty-nine minimum wage contracts, covering about 110,000 workers, mostly seamen, existed in 1930. Six years later as many as 135,000 wage-earners were covered by 122 agreements in the metal, machinery, tool, chemical, textile, and transport industries.

Some unions had succeeded in achieving recognition by agreement. As early as 1926 the Tokyo Seiko Company agreed to recog-

nize a *Sōdōmei* union, which had organized its workers, and to
follow a system of preferential hiring. The company further promised to raise worker living standards and maintain working conditions equal to those in other parts of the industry. The union, on
its part, agreed to co-operate in promoting efficiency and to clean
out subversive elements. Some sixty or seventy similar agreements
were reached with various companies. Beyond this limited experience, there is little evidence of prewar collective bargaining.[12]

The postwar period saw a wildfire spread of written labor agreements (see Table VII). By July, 1948, there were contracts covering

Table VII. LABOR AGREEMENTS IN JAPAN, 1947-54

Year[a]	Unions Covered		Union Members Covered	
	Number	Per Cent[b]	Number (in thousands)	Per Cent[b]
1947	5,591	23.9	—	—
1948	20,301	62.8	3,922	79.0
1949	14,099	50.4	3,745	65.5
1950	9,746	45.1	2,553	58.8
1951	10,329	50.5	2,646	61.8
1952	11,054	54.4	2,970	69.4
1953	13,538	59.4	3,348	71.6
1954	14,226	60.7	3,507	73.7
1955	16,182	64.9	3,817	78.2
1956	17,095	63.7	3,856	77.1
1957	18,370	64.2	4,042	77.7

[a] As of June of each year.
[b] Percentage of only those eligible by law to conclude labor agreements.
Source: *Labor White Paper, 1957* (Tokyo: Division of Labor Statistics and Research,
Ministry of Labor, 1957), p. 278; and Division of Labor Statistics and Research, Ministry of Labor, news release, December 4, 1957.

more than 20,000 of the trade-unions, almost 63 per cent of the total
number, and close to 4 million workers, nearly 80 per cent of the
union membership. Because of the prevalence of enterprise bargaining, the number of contracts was not much less than the number of unions included in the coverage.

After 1948, however, a "no-contract" era set in which reduced
the number of agreements by almost half and the workers covered

[12] See Martin T. Camacho, "The Administration of the SCAP Labor Policy
in Occupied Japan" (unpublished Ph.D. thesis, Harvard University, 1954),
pp. 406-7.

by more than one-fourth. By this time, managements had stiffened against union demands and began to refuse to renew contract provisions which earlier they had accepted without resistance. In addition, the revision of the National Public Service Law and adoption of the Public Corporation and National Enterprise Labor Relations Law in 1948 removed a considerable portion of the labor unions from eligibility to bargain for contracts. The 1949 amendments to the Trade Union Law also made it easier for management to refuse to bargain with unions which were unwilling to submit to the new tests for determining their qualifications as bona fide trade-unions. Finally, the disinflation accompanying the Dodge Plan and the disappearance of many small and medium firms obliterated many unions which had held contracts.

Since 1952, there has been a slow recovery in contract-making. More than 18,000 unions had agreements as of June, 1957, accounting for almost 65 per cent of the unions eligible to conclude labor agreements. Membership coverage exceeded 4 million, or about 77 per cent of the eligible membership. Thus, despite the curtailment which occurred between 1949 and 1951, contracts have remained fairly widespread.[13] The single plant and enterprise-wide agreement by far has remained the predominant form.[14]

The substance of the labor agreements serves to correct any impression that horizontal contractual relationships have taken firm hold in the dealings between unions and management in Japan. At best, in the typical set of circumstances, a collective bargaining contract is little more than a confirmation of rights already provided by law, and the major problem facing unions with respect to these

---

[13] The industries in which written labor agreements are widespread in terms of union and membership coverage (more than 65 per cent in both) include agriculture and forestry, metal mining, coal mining, textile mill products, petroleum and coal products, finance and insurance, land transportation, communication, heat, light, and power, and garrison force installation. Relatively low rates (less than 30 per cent of the unions and members) are found in construction, amusement and recreation, personal services, and education. In the middle range are such groups and industries as fishing, paper printing, chemicals, rubber, primary and fabricated metals, electrical and other machinery, transportation equipment, wholesale and retail trades, motion pictures, and government. See *Labor White Paper, 1955* (Tokyo: Division of Labor Statistics and Research, Ministry of Labor, 1955), pp. 261-62.

[14] In 1955, there were only 636 contracts which had been made in the name of union federations. These covered about 250,000 workers. *Labor White Paper, 1956*, p. 331.

contracts is to prevent their subtle deterioration. It has been difficult for workers and their unions to consider the development of
collective bargaining contracts as a primary goal in dealing with
management. Aside from traditional habits of verticalism, which
have impeded bargaining on equal terms, the chief issues in industrial relations have not been suitable for making fixed contracts
of any long duration.

That contracts have been limited means for developing a new
system of industrial jurisprudence in Japan is the result of the
narrow scope of collective bargaining. The chief issues, as already
noted, have not been amenable to contractual resolutions. Wage
bargaining is in constant flux. Job tenure is subject to protest, not
negotiation. Other terms of employment are resolved by carrying
over past practice, by legal enactments, or by implicit understandings. Accordingly, bargaining has been largely on an *ad hoc* basis
and results in temporary understandings rather than lasting principles contractually spelled out. Moreover, the widespread use of
joint councils and reassertion of employer power hold back the
development of labor agreements. For example, in the contracts
that have been renewed, clauses which do provide job or work
rights to the union membership are now frequently hedged by
clauses recognizing management prerogatives.

As a result, agreements are likely to be concerned principally
with defining the respective rights of union and management and,
to a lesser extent, the actual conditions and terms of employment.
In this context, the contract, like the law, serves as the legitimation
for carrying on collective negotiations and using coercive weapons
in the dealings between management and union, rather than the
embodiment of the substantive terms of employment. It has not
become the ultimate objective for collective bargaining, but a basis
on which bargaining begins. Thus, recognition of the union and
its right to strike and definition of management prerogatives and
the right to lockout are central provisions. Accordingly, the duration of the contract, although limited by law to three years, is of
small significance; in fact, many contracts extend to this limit
and are automatically renewable.[15] That labor agreements have
developed in this way is not surprising in view of the absence of

---

[15] Sakurabayashi Makoto, "*Rōshi Kankei No Nihonteki Seikaku*," ("Characteristics of Japanese Labor Relations"), *Seni Keizai* (*Textile Economy*), No. 21
(December, 1953), p. 20.

contractual traditions based on legal theories of equal bargaining parties. The whole concept has been utterly foreign to the traditional Japanese way of life, so that headway toward Western types of agreements has been necessarily slow. Perhaps it has been too much to expect the spelling out of terms of employment, the meaning of which may be distorted easily in actual practice.

Japanese unions, in their present stage of development, especially those under radical ideological influences, are reluctant to run the risk of concluding firm long-run agreements which may prove too rigid on the one hand or too flexible on the other. In numerous cases workers have been disappointed to find provisions negotiated and made part of a fixed contract turn out differently in actual administration, and they have turned away from or lost interest in the union. Labor leaders, therefore, often consider detailed labor agreements as a device which might weaken rather than strengthen the unions. Where such contracts have been agreed to, they are likely to have come about at the insistence of management, especially the industrial relations executives, rather than the union.

Basically, then, the absence of stable labor agreements stems from ingrained traditions of vertical relationships in Japanese society and from the present precarious state of the Japanese economy. Because the concept of horizontal contracts premised on equal rights of the parties has had only the scantiest history in Japan, it should come as no surprise that Japanese labor agreements are substantively shallow despite their widespread numbers. Similarly, even when agreements are detailed, procedures for their day-by-day administration are seldom adequate to assure that they are carried out. The flux and instability of economic conditions, of course, also detract from achieving lasting contracts. As a result, if new changes are to emerge in Japanese industrial relations, they are likely to come about more readily in the direct conflicts between unions and management rather than through the instrument of collective bargaining agreements. It is for this reason that labor disputes in Japan take on added significance.

LABOR DISPUTES: INCIDENCE AND TYPES

The statistical record of labor dispute activity in Japan must be viewed with caution. Although dispute statistics can be utilized to appraise the degree of conflict existing between workers and management, low indexes of dispute activity are not necessarily a reflection of their ability to accommodate their conflicting claims without resort to industrial warfare. Low indexes may indeed indicate that the parties are equal or nearly equal in bargaining power and, therefore, avoid dispute action except as a very last resort. But low figures may also indicate the inability of one or the other party to engage in disputes either because of the dominance of one over the other or because of regulation by government. Also, the full meaning of the statistics is not likely to be clear without examining at the same time the tactics employed and the results obtained.

The postwar statistics certainly indicate a resort to dispute weapons in Japan to a degree not uncommon among other industrialized nations of the free world. On the other hand, analysis of the disputes which the figures represent produces reservations about the vigor with which claims are asserted, particularly on the part of the trade-unions.

One difficulty of measuring the incidence of labor disputes lies in the problem of defining what a dispute is. Another is the problem of collecting statistics relevant to the definition decided upon. For lack of better measurements, therefore, most dispute figures relate only to those conflicts which involve actual work stoppages, mainly strikes, lockouts, and slowdowns, although it is to be recognized that many disputes do not necessarily end in any stoppage at all or that they are accompanied by changes in production which are not readily identifiable as to cause.

As in most other countries, statistics on the number of disputes resulting in work stoppages, the number of workers involved, and the number of workdays lost are available for Japan. In addition, the Japanese Ministry of Labor publishes statistics on disputes which do not result in actual work stoppages, but are known to have occurred because of assistance of third parties in their negotiation or settlement. It is probable that both sets of statistics cover most labor disputes of any significance in Japan.

The number of disputes with or without work stoppages has not been alarmingly high during the postwar period, although some have had serious economic impacts. As shown in Table VIII, the number of disputes in process year by year from 1946 to 1956 has varied from about 900 to about 1,500; the number beginning in each year, as a rule, has been slightly less than the number already in process. On the average, about half of them have eventuated in work stoppages; all but a very few have been strikes rather than lockouts. Despite the phenomenal growth of postwar unionism, however, the annual number of labor disputes in the past decade has not exceeded those recorded in the years around the end of World War I or during the first half of the 1930's when a trade-union movement barely existed. Also, compared to the dispute experience in other industrialized countries over the last ten years, the numbers with or without stoppages have not been unusually high, even when one takes into account the relative size of labor movements and proportion of industrial workers in the labor force.[16]

In terms of the number of workers involved, however, the incidence of disputes in postwar Japan has been considerably higher than that for any of the prewar years. Japan ranks high in international comparisons. Whereas before the war fewer than 350,000 workers were involved in disputes in any one year, the annual postwar totals have ranged from 2.3 million to more than 6.7 million. In most years the number was between 3 and 4 million. The year 1948, which was marked by numerous sporadic strikes on the part of the government workers and by the disintegration of *Sanbetsu*, was the highest in the postwar period in the number of workers involved. Up to 1956, the low year in this respect was 1950, when, of course, the trade-union movement actually declined in size and was engaged in reorganization. The drop in 1954 after two fairly active years is accounted for in part by *Sōhyō's* failure to repeat its widespread political strikes. Actually, the number of workers involved in work stoppages has been a minor proportion of the total involved in all disputes. The ratio has been between one-third and one-half of the total each year. On the other hand, there has been a growing use of slowdown tactics, so that by 1954 the number of workers involved in slowdowns actually exceeded the number involved in stoppages.

A more critical index for labor disputes, the number of man-days lost through work stoppages, has ranged from 4 to 7 million per year, except in 1952 when prolonged strikes, notably in coal and electric power, resulted in more than 15 million man-days lost. Yet

---

[16] See "Industrial Disputes, 1937-54," *International Labour Review*, LXXII (July, 1955), pp. 78-91, and *Year Book of Labor Statistics, 1956* (Tokyo: Division of Labor Statistics and Research, Ministry of Labor, 1957), pp. 416-17.

Table VIII. LABOR DISPUTES IN JAPAN, 1946-56

Year	All Disputes		Work Stoppages[a]			Slowdowns	
	No.	Workers Involved (in thousands)	No.	Workers Involved (in thousands)	Man-days Lost (in thousands)	No.	Workers Involved (in thousands)
1946	920	2,723	702	517	6,266	130	75
1947	1,035	4,415	470	220	5,036	141	63
1948	1,517	6,715	750	2,306	6,995	136	302
1949	1,414	3,307	564	1,124	4,321	100	129
1950	1,487	2,348	611	788	5,486	267	409
1951	1,186	2,819	599	1,165	6,015	184	362
1952	1,233	3,683	605	1,632	15,075	241	617
1953	1,277	3,399	629	1,357	4,279	261	732
1954	1,247	2,635	655	937	3,836	271	968
1955	1,345	3,748	678	1,038	3,467	310	1,000
1956	1,330	3,372	675	1,122	4,562	310	737

[a] Strikes and lockouts.
Source: *Labor White Paper, 1957* (Tokyo: Division of Labor Statistics and Research, Ministry of Labor, 1957), pp. 282-83.

for the same period in the United States, with roughly twice the number of workers involved, man-days lost were three to ten times as many as in Japan and, despite a much smaller industrial labor force and labor movement, India also has frequently surpassed Japan in the number of man-days lost from disputes during the postwar period.[17] Finally, to make a prewar comparison, in 1929 the man-days lost in Japan exceeded one million, although fewer than 200,000 workers were involved in some 2,289 disputes. Thus, both in comparison with the prewar period and with other countries during the postwar era, the extent of labor disputes in Japan on the average does not appear inordinately great.

One reason for this is that widespread stoppages lasting over long periods of time have been relatively infrequent. Long strikes like those experienced in the coal and electric power industries in 1952 have been exceptional. Short stoppages explain why in 1948, despite a record high of 1,517 disputes, the number of days lost was less than half the number lost in 1952, even though the number of workers involved was almost twice as many. The duration of dis-

---

[17] *Ibid.*

putes which do not result in stoppages also seems relatively short. In 1956 one-third of all the disputes settled lasted less than five days, and about one-half less than ten. How many of the remainder were continuing stoppages is not known, but in view of the widespread use of the one- or two-day strike as a dispute tactic, it is unlikely that the incidence of long stoppages has been very great.

Moreover, dispute proneness has tended to be strong only among a certain few industrial sectors. Until restrictions were placed upon government employees in 1947 and 1948 and upon miners and electric workers in 1953, these groups principally accounted for man-days lost through work stoppages each year. Between 1948 and 1953, mining alone had both the majority of workers involved and man-days lost, although the number of strikes and lockouts in this industry did not exceed 108 in any one year. Elsewhere, the incidence of stoppages, however measured, has been considerably less.[18]

The short duration of most disputes in Japan is to be explained by numerous factors, not the least important of which is the dislike of both unions and management of confronting one another in open conflict. This aversion to confrontation has its cultural roots in the socially required appearance of harmony within the traditional family system, long-established vertical relationships, and general tendencies to gain permanent group membership. Open clashes within such a social system run the risk of unbearable loss of face before one's most intimate associates.[19]

It seems likely therefore that many potential disputes in Japanese industrial relations never come to a recognizable head or that they are avoided through the use of third party intermediaries. Again this probably represents more the continuation of traditional forms of relationships between employers and workers than any "maturity" in their collective bargaining dealings with one another. Thus, the statistics on disputes without resort to stoppages take on additional significance, because the element of conciliation is exceptionally strong. Furthermore, even when strikes occur, management often displays conciliatory attitudes illustrated, for example,

[18] See *Year Book of Labor Statistics, 1956*, pp. 385-86.

[19] In industrial relations, a not uncommon occurrence in the game of "saving face" is for the labor leaders to resign their posts when management turns down the union's demands. The resignations are usually accepted, but the leaders are then voted back into office.

by its common practice of paying special bonuses to workers after returning to work, both as a means of making up losses suffered by the employee and as a symbol of re-established harmony in the enterprise, by management's reluctance to bring in strike-breakers, by continuation of welfare services and provisions for workers,[20] and in some cases by actual payment of wages or granting of "loans" by management. In turn, such practices serve to continue obligations felt by workers toward the enterprise.

Other reasons, of course, explain the short duration of stoppages in Japan. Strike funds are limited and workers are likely to have few cash reserves. With the system of enterprise unionism and the rivalry of labor centers, only in exceptional instances will a strike be supported in any substantial way by contributions from other unions.[21] The risk of a long strike lies in the breakup of the union as funds run out and feelings of loyalty to the enterprise begin to predominate. The coal and electric power stoppages in 1952 and the Nissan auto strike of 1953 demonstrate this point.

The ever present threat of government intervention is still another discouragement to the long stoppage. Because of the very precariousness of the Japanese economy, with its highly interdependent industrial structure, a prolonged strike or lockout could produce a national crisis. Almost from the beginning of the occupation, therefore, it was clear that emergencies created by labor disputes would not long be tolerated by the ruling authorities. Throughout the occupation period, the powers of the government to intervene steadily increased. Initially, the 1946 Labor Relations Adjustment Law restricted stoppages in public utilities. In 1947 prohibition of the scheduled general strike was the first major in-

---

[20] For example, during the prolonged Omi Silk Mills strike of 1954, management refused to permit the workers to remain in the company-owned dormitories or to provide the usual meals. In conciliating this dispute the Central Labor Relations Commission held that the workers, even if on strike, were entitled to these benefits because of long-established practice in Japanese industry and because the workers were still technically in the employ of the enterprise. See Ichiro Nakayama, "Japanese Labor Trends," *The Oriental Economist*, XXIII (February, 1955), p. 79.

[21] Of increasing importance, however, has been the growth of labor banks to provide loans to workers and unions during stoppages. Operated by union groups, these banks have been increasingly patronized by unions. Only one such bank existed in September, 1950, but by 1955 there was a labor bank in almost every prefecture and a federation of labor banks had been established. Management groups have begun to seek increased government regulation of these banks. See *The Oriental Economist*, XXIII (April, 1955), p. 192.

stance of interference by SCAP in labor dispute activities. A year later, when the government workers resorted to a series of localized, sporadic walkouts, legislation prohibiting strikes of public employees followed. With the Dodge Plan and later the outbreak of the Korean War, the occupation forced the calling-off of some stoppages and warned that it would intervene where necessary to prevent interference with its economic and military objectives. As the occupation period came to a close, the powers of SCAP in the area of labor disputes at least in part were transferred to the Japanese central government with the enactment in 1952 of the "emergency" provisions of the Labor Relations Adjustment Law. Soon afterwards the threat to apply this power brought a halt to the coal and electric power strikes. Thus, by the beginning of the period of independence, the authority of the government to intervene was firmly established,[22] and ever since there has been a good deal of speculation about the desirability of enacting special legislation prohibiting or controlling labor stoppages in vital industries such as textiles and shipping.

Unless stoppages are kept fairly localized and of short duration, the pressure for increased government intervention is likely to grow. In view of this likelihood, unions often adopt strike strategies which avoid the appearance of large-scale prolonged walkouts. For example, after the passage of the coal and electric power strike control legislation, the coal miners and other unions began to use so-called "partial" strikes, whereby only key personnel would leave their jobs in specific enterprises at specific times. Another technique commonly employed has been the so-called "piston" strike in which short walkouts follow one another in rapid succession among the different enterprises of an industry. These strategies and tactics indicate that unions are reluctant to carry on full-fledged assaults partly out of fear of government reaction.[23]

Lastly, another factor contributing to the shortness of disputes is the concept of the strike function itself. Both for reasons of tra-

---

[22] See Chapter VI.

[23] The government workers also resort to various dilatory tactics that border on the illegal. Refusal to work overtime, mass furloughs, and menstrual leave-taking, strict observance of safety regulations, and so forth are common devices. The government, in turn, may take punitive action, illustrated, for example, in the discharge and disciplining of almost 50,000 workers, including the union officers, during the national railways dispute in the spring of 1957.

ditional relationships and of ideological influences, the strike is not necessarily conceived of as a test of strength over some given bargaining issue. It appears reasonable to state that most Japanese strikes are carried out chiefly to dramatize some widespread grievance within an enterprise or to achieve a political purpose. As such, strikes and other dispute tactics are not essentially the result of breakdowns in collective bargaining, but rather a stage in the negotiations themselves. Very often the union will announce in advance when walkouts will occur regardless of the progress in bargaining. For these reasons the half-day, one-day, or two-day stoppage occurs frequently and is considered a "normal" stage in collective bargaining procedure. Where there are strong ideological influences, strikes are likely to be demonstrations to manifest working class solidarity and therefore are not usually concerned with any specific controversy with the management involved. Rather, they are expressions of protest against governmental policy. The walkouts in the campaign against the labor legislation revisions of 1952 and 1953 are major examples.

Most strike tactics in Japan take simple and direct forms. The workers either leave their jobs or do not show up for work. Usually there is picketing, including mass "squatting" in front of plant gates. Demonstrations are common. More "sophisticated" forms, such as consumer and production boycotts, secondary strikes, sympathy walkouts, and general strikes have been exceptional.

The first prominent case of the boycott, for example, occurred only as recently as October, 1955, when, during a strike of the textile workers, the seamen's union agreed not to load aboard ship any products of the ten major cotton spinning companies.[24] In addition to legal obstacles which might deter the use of the boycott, unions have not considered it a practical economic weapon. This attitude partly arises from reluctance of enterprise unions to concern themselves with disputes in other enterprises, partly from lack of union organization in the small firms which supply or serve as outlets for the struck enterprise, and partly from the fact that major enterprises usually are vertically integrated from the stages of raw material supply to consumer sales. For many of the same reasons, sympathy, secondary, and general strikes for economic purposes

---

[24] *Japanese Trade Union Congress Report*, I, Nos. 14 and 15 (Tokyo: *Zenrō Kaigi*, October 15 and November 1, 1955), mimeographed. Actually, the boycott did not take place as the strike was settled before action was taken.

have been infrequent, although political strikes when timed with economic stoppages often take on the appearance of these types of strike tactics.

Dispute actions distinctive of Japan include "partial" walkouts, "piston" strikes, series of short stoppages, tactics obstructive to production while at work, mass leave-taking, and "production" or "business control." All of these, it should be noted, avoid complete breaks between the workers and management and seek to maintain the identity of the employees with their enterprises. The most notable examples in this vein were the instances of "production control," which in the context of the postwar situation, were not necessarily revolutionary measures with Leninist or anarchist inspiration.[25] Mixed in were motivations of providing work and rehabilitating the enterprise where impasses between union and management had developed or where management did not appear to be exercising managerial functions with efficiency. In some "production-control" cases during the inflation, management motives often were suspect in that there was evidence of companies hoarding raw materials and holding back production in order to profit from rising prices and black-marketeering.[26] The fact that production control often resulted in improved productivity led both the government and the occupation to go slow in taking steps to outlaw this type of dispute activity. Actually, even before SCAP and later the courts declared production control illegal, disputes involving this tactic had not become widespread.[27]

As in the United States, the use of these various techniques has raised numerous legal questions, particularly whether "neutrals" have the right of access to struck establishments, whether there is a distinction between "peaceful persuasion" and "coercion," and whether there are illegal invasions of property. On the theory that a legitimate dispute must be confined to the employer and his own

---

[25] Production control, however, had a prewar history. As early as 1921, strikes at the Kawasaki and Mitsubishi dockyards, involving 35,000 workers and lasting forty-five days, involved the seizure of plants by the workers. These strikes were crushed by army troops.

[26] Iwao Ayusawa, *Post-War Developments in Organized Labor* (Tokyo: Foreign Affairs Association of Japan, 1953), p. 27.

[27] In 1946, there were 170 "production control" cases, involving fewer than 150,000 workers. Since then, they have steadily declined in number and in extent of workers involved. In 1956, there were five such disputes with 209 participants. See *Labor White Paper, 1957*, p. 344.

workers, especially when outsiders who are not employed at the enterprise join in, management is likely to charge that the strike is no longer legal. Unions, on their part, usually defend their strike tactics on the grounds of the broad guaranties provided in the postwar constitution and trade-union legislation.

Thus far, however, although numerous cases have found their way into the courts, there has been no definitive resolution of the legal principles involved. In the latter part of 1954, the Ministry of Labor expressed the position of the central government by advising the prefectural governors to take steps which would restrict picketing to "peaceful" persuasion, permit free entry and exit, and assure that control of the strike remains in the hands of the disputing union. The labor centers, as would be expected, protested that the interpretation was an unconstitutional abrogation of rights to strike and act collectively.[28]

To sum up, the whole question of the form and legitimacy of dispute activity in Japanese industrial relations closely depends on the one hand upon the degree to which horizontal collective bargaining becomes institutionalized and replaces the concept of enterprise consciousness, and, on the other, upon the extent to which government pre-empts the making of decisions affecting terms of industrial employment. With respect to the former, it is evident that collective bargaining in Japan is still in an incipient stage; the latter is explored further in the chapter to follow.

---

[28] *The Oriental Economist*, XXII (December, 1954), p. 612. The general restrictive attitude of the government is expressed in a circular issued in January, 1957. See *Industry and Labour*, XVIII (August, 1957), pp. 120-22.

VI

GOVERNMENT REGULATION

OF INDUSTRIAL RELATIONS

One of the occupation's principal objectives in restructuring Japanese society, was to reduce, if not eliminate, governmental controls over the daily life of the people. The preferred arrangement was to establish democratically operated private institutions, which would work out their mutual relationships with a minimum of direct governmental regulation. It was to this end that trade-unionism and collective bargaining received enormous encouragement and at least at first were subject to few restrictions. Yet, since the early days of the occupation there has been a steady regression from these principles, as it became manifest that collective bargaining was not achieving the orderly industrial relations sought for the New Japan. Accordingly, government intrusion gradually has grown in at least two ways—regulation of the form of collective bargaining itself and stipulation of the substantive conditions and terms of employment. Both have contributed to the decreasing importance of private negotiations. Each shall be treated separately in the pages that follow, but here it should be noted that the tendency toward government intervention in both forms has led to increasing emphasis on the political aspects of Japanese industrial relations.

INITIAL POLICY: VOLUNTARISM AND DECENTRALIZATION

The original Trade Union Law and its companion piece, the Labor Relations Adjustment Law, placed few restrictions on freedom to organize and bargain collectively, including the right to engage in work stoppages.[1] Employers were expressly forbidden

---

[1] Later, in 1947, the new Japanese constitution also guaranteed these rights as basic law of the nation, especially in Articles 21, 25, 27, and 28. For the

to discriminate against workers who exercised their trade-union rights.

This legislation was all-embracing. Only groups employed in public safety work, such as policemen and firemen, were excluded from some of these privileges. Although denied the right to strike, government employees in administrative and judicial agencies were still free to organize and carry on collective bargaining. Otherwise, strikes were limited only in public utility industries (specified as transportation, communication, power, water, and public health facilities), where the parties were required to wait thirty days before resorting to stoppages. During this period a labor relations commission would conduct a fact-finding inquiry and offer a recommendation for settlement. The law, however, stipulated that in order for a workers' organization to gain legal status as a trade-union, it had to behave principally as an autonomous economic institution, rather than as a political or social movement or a mutual aid society, and had to avoid reliance upon employer financial aid. Since a main objective was to prevent the transformation of the wartime industrial patriotic associations into alleged unions, labor relations commissions with equal representation for labor, management, and the public were established at prefectural and national levels [2] to handle charges of employer discrimination; unions were to register with the prefectural governments within a week after formation to ascertain whether they were in fact autonomous organizations. Both steps aimed at promoting trade-union independence rather than restricting collective bargaining.

In order to promote a private collective bargaining system that would result in orderly and peaceful settlements, the Labor Relations Adjustment Law provided voluntary conciliation, fact-finding, and arbitration procedures through the newly established tripartite commissions. As a further impetus, the Trade Union Law required that contracts be written and signed by the parties and that the duration of any collective agreement be limited to three years. All such agreements would supersede individual employment contracts. Finally, agreements covering three-fourths of workers of a

full text of the constitution and all labor laws cited in this chapter, including amendments through 1952, see *Japan Labor Code, 1952* (Tokyo: Ministry of Labor, 1953).

[2] A central commission was established at the national level, with one local commission in each of the forty-six prefectures. In addition, maritime labor relations commissions—one central and twelve regional—were provided exclusively for the maritime industry.

"similar kind" in one establishment would extend automatically to all, while agreements covering a majority in a given locality could be widened to include all relevant workers in the locality at the request of either management or union, or both, upon approval of the appropriate labor relations commission.[3]

Despite the fact that occupation authority continually hovered in the background until the general strike ban of 1947, intervention occurred in only a few unimportant instances, when disputes directly interfered with army operations. Initial occupation policy was to give almost complete leeway for the exercise of the new labor rights and to leave the interpreting and administering of the new laws largely to the Japanese. The Japanese governmental authorities also leaned over backwards in their liberalism. Only the grossest abuses—usually involving physical violence—were brought into the slow processes of the court system, itself undergoing drastic revisions. Police action was tightly restrained lest the occupation crack down upon what had been a chief symbol of military dictatorship. The labor relations commissions attempted to draw no hard and fast principles for collective bargaining or criteria for discriminatory practices, on the grounds that such rulings might rigidify the situation and impede rapid trade-union growth.

This approach placed greatest emphasis upon education and experience to be gained from the voluntary dispute adjustment procedures administered by the tripartite labor relations commissions.[4] The Labor Relations Adjustment Law stressed conciliatory methods and, except for a few amendments to be noted later, has essentially retained this principle intact up to now. The commissions have no power to compel binding arbitration. Arbitration in which the award must be made formally and must be accepted, and mediatory fact-finding investigation including commission recommendations for settlement are performed only upon request of both parties or of one party in accordance with terms of an existing agreement.[5] However, in the case of a public utility, the formal

---

[3] The commission, however, was empowered to amend clauses of the agreement which appear "inappropriate." Actually, neither of the extension provisions has been of significance, and in only a few cases have they been applied. The prevalence of enterprise unionism probably accounts for this.

[4] Even these, however, the left-wing unions opposed as too much interference by government in labor relations.

[5] In the original law, arbitration was to be conducted on a tripartite basis. An amendment in 1949 changed the arbitration board to include only public members of the commissions.

mediation procedure may be used upon the request of one party, the Labor Minister, or prefectural governor, or upon a commission's own motion. The commissions may undertake conciliation quite freely—formally or informally, individually or on a bipartite or tripartite basis, at the request of one or both parties, or upon the initiative of the commission itself. Any one of these procedures, of course, does not preclude the use of the others.

In order to accumulate experience at the local level and to avoid centralization, the commissions were made fairly independent of one another in administering their jurisdictions.[6] For dispute adjustments, there are no provisions for appeal from the prefectural or local commission to the central body. Only in the semi-judicial activities of the commissions—nomination of commission members, union qualification examinations, unfair labor practice cases, applications for juridical person status, extension of contracts, filing of dispute notices and prosecution for failure to file such notices in public utility industry disputes—does the central commission supervise the local commissions and serve as an appeal and review board. This, in fact, was a change initiated in 1949 as a means for strengthening new provisions relating to the clarification of employer unfair labor practices and to the eligibility of unions to use commission procedures.[7]

CONTROL OF TRADE-UNIONS AND COLLECTIVE BARGAINING: PUBLIC WORKERS

The turnabout in East-West relations brought an abrupt end to this initial "free-for-all" policy. By 1947, the emphasis of the American occupation began to shift toward achieving Japan's economic rehabilitation and gaining assurance that Japan would ally with the Western world. Accordingly, pressure was applied to secure a greater degree of certainty and order in Japanese industrial relations. The general strike prohibition of February 1, 1947, was the

---

[6] The commissions, also, were made semi-independent agencies within the government. Except for budgetary purposes, they are subject to none of the governmental ministries or agencies in their operations. On the other hand, the members are appointed for a year's term only, and control over appointments is shared by government, management, and the qualified unions. For a full treatment of the development of the labor relations commissions, see Solomon B. Levine, "Japan's Tripartite Labor Relations Commission," *Labor Law Journal*, VI (July, 1955), pp. 462-82, 490. See, also, *Labor Relations Commissions of Japan* (Tokyo: Central Labor Relations Commission, March, 1956).

[7] See below pp. 145-48.

first step in the direction of controlling union activity and collective bargaining.

At the time, the most troublesome spot in the Japanese labor picture was the government workers, 2 million of whom had been organized. Severe difficulties arose from a sharp lag of public workers' wages behind those in private industry during the spiraling inflation. Grievances over this issue also opened the door to extremely radical union leadership in these unions. Stalemates in bargaining inevitably occurred as government budget deficits mounted. In turn the government workers unions increasingly resorted to political activity. When the entire governmental apparatus was threatened with near-paralysis by a widespread series of localized, sporadic strikes among government workers during the "March offensive" of 1948, SCAP felt it could sit by no longer. It believed it could not continue to depend heavily upon an unstable Japanese government bureaucracy for effective execution of the new occupation policies. In July, 1948, General MacArthur put forth his proposals to delimit the trade-union rights of the public employee.

In response to SCAP's suggestion, the legislation relating to government workers adopted in the latter part of 1948 distinguished between public employees engaged in the civil service and those employed in government-owned industrial enterprises. The former, under the revised National Public Service Law, were now removed from the jurisdiction of the Trade Union Law and were expressly denied any rights to make collective bargaining agreements or to strike. The National Personnel Authority, composed of three commissioners appointed by the Cabinet with Diet confirmation, was given sole authority to determine all terms and conditions of employment in the central government's civil service. Moreover, while the new act continued to permit civil servants to form their own associations, they could negotiate conditions of work only with the permission of the Authority.

Workers in government-owned industries, which included the national railroads, printing office, mint, and the alcohol and tobacco monopolies, were dealt with in a new act, the Public Corporation Labor Relations Law.[8] In 1952 the Diet adopted a similar

---

[8] In 1952, this act was retitled the Public Corporation and National Enterprise Labor Relations Law, when the telegraph and telephone corporation was established as an enterprise separate from the Postal Ministry of which originally it was a part. Workers in this corporation had been under the

enactment to cover local government enterprise employees.[9] This legislation continued their right to organize and to bargain collectively but denied their right to strike. In addition, provisions of the new act introduced for the first time the concept of "appropriate" bargaining units as a means both to decentralize bargaining and to eliminate outside labor leadership from the public workers unions. Unions of public corporation employees were now limited only to the workers in a single enterprise, and each of these unions had to choose its officers from its own membership. The unions also were required to meet the qualifications stipulated in the Trade Union Law. The legislation further provided that, while employees could

---

jurisdiction of the National Public Service Law, but now were transferred to the Public Corporation and National Enterprise Labor Relations Law. Similarly, employees of the state-owned forestries were also made subject to the latter act. Until 1951, moreover, the electric power industry was entirely under government operation pending SCAP's decision on its disposition. In 1951, the industry was divided into nine separate companies and returned to private ownership, thus placing the electric power workers under the jurisdiction of the Trade Union and Labor Relations Adjustment laws with the latter's restrictions on public utility stoppages.

[9] The National Public Service Law and the Public Corporation and National Enterprise Labor Relations Law both apply only to employees in the national government. Laws for local governments, corresponding to each of these enactments, were adopted in December, 1950, and July, 1952, respectively. Until their passage, the local government workers technically were still under the Trade Union Law and the Labor Relations Adjustment Law, although virtually banned from carrying on collective bargaining and engaging in work stoppages under SCAP prohibitions and Cabinet enforcement orders. The Local Public Service Law of 1950 established civil service commissions in each of the local government units with powers parallel to the National Personnel Authority within their respective jurisdictions. Thus, local civil servants were permitted to form unions to negotiate for wages, hours, and working conditions, but were prohibited from engaging in work stoppages or concluding collective bargaining agreements. Unions of local government workers also were allowed to form federations among themselves, but each union was required to register with its local personnel commission. The Local Public Enterprise Labor Relations Law, adopted in 1952, separated workers in local government-owned corporations from regular civil servants. These operations for the most part are railways, tramways, bus service, electricity, gas, water, and so forth. As under the Public Corporation and National Enterprise Labor Relations Law, these workers may organize and bargain for collective agreements on certain specified issues, but they are prohibited from striking, and agreements necessitating funds beyond budgetary allowances are not valid without legislative approval. On the other hand, while this act provides for joint grievance machinery in these local operations, no special conciliation or arbitration commissions have been established. Collective bargaining disputes remain in the jurisdiction of the regular labor relations commissions, but as in the national act their arbitration may be made compulsory.

freely form unions as they chose, persons in managerial or supervisory posts engaged in confidential work were not permitted to join. The Cabinet itself was empowered to designate the ineligible personnel.

In each government-owned enterprise, negotiations were to be carried out by one committee representing management and another the employees of the enterprise. The Cabinet was empowered to fix the maximum size and method of internal administration of each committee. As a first step these committees were to agree upon the appropriate bargaining units in the enterprise, and designation of the units had to be submitted to the Labor Minister before January 31 of each year. Then, by February 25, in each unit the unions representing the organized workers and delegates elected by the nonunion workers were to appoint a committee to carry on the actual negotiations. A list of committee members was to be submitted to the Minister of Labor. If the February 25 deadline was not met, the Labor Minister could then designate the appropriate bargaining units, the unions eligible to participate in selecting the workers' negotiating committee, and the voting procedures for electing the committee members. In either case, bargaining committees remained in office for a year beginning April 1.

The act also restricted bargaining to specified subjects—wages and other forms of remuneration, hours, rest periods, vacations, promotion standards, demotion, transfer, discharge, suspension, seniority rights, discipline, safety and sanitation, accident compensation, working conditions, and grievance machinery. Explicitly excluded were "the management and operation" of the enterprise, while any agreement requiring expenditures not available in the enterprise operating budget or reserves would not be considered binding upon the government unless the Diet also gave its approval.[10]

In removing the public corporation workers from the jurisdiction of the Labor Relations Adjustment Law, the act set up special machinery, separate from the labor relations commissions under the Trade Union Law, to handle grievances and disputes. It provided that for each bargaining unit, joint grievance boards at national and local levels would be established through the collective bar-

---

[10] If the Diet is in session, agreements must be submitted to the Diet within ten days after they are reached. If the Diet is not in session, they must be submitted within five days after the Diet reconvenes.

gaining machinery to process complaints arising from day-by-day operations. Collective bargaining disputes, however, were to be adjudicated first by equally tripartite, nine-man mediation commissions, also set up at both national and local levels, with the management and employee members appointed by the Prime Minister upon the recommendation of the respective bargaining agents, and the public members designated with the consent of the partisan members. The term of the commission was one year.

Conciliation and mediation procedures identical to those of the labor relations commissions under the Trade Union and Labor Relations Adjustment laws were to be followed. A commission was to attempt conciliation either on its own initiative or at the request of one or both parties. Also, it was to conduct fact-finding inquiries and issue recommendations (1) at the request of both parties, (2) at the request of one party as permitted by an existing collective bargaining agreement, (3) when the commission itself deemed it necessary regardless of contract provisions, or (4) when requested by the appropriate government minister.

Departing from the "voluntarism" of the LRAL, the new public corporation law provided compulsory arbitration of disputes in the event that conciliation or mediation failed to secure agreement. The act established in the Labor Ministry an arbitration board of three members appointed by the Prime Minister from among persons recommended by the chairman of the national mediation commission. However, it did provide that both management and worker representatives would select ten-man committees for the purpose of designating which of the persons recommended by the mediation commission chairman should serve as the arbitrators. If these committees failed to designate their preferences within thirty days after the recommendations were made, the Prime Minister then could choose freely among those recommended. Members of legislatures, political party officials, those who did business with public corporations, and officials and employees of these enterprises were declared ineligible to serve. The term of the board was set at three years.[11]

---

[11] Under the act, arbitration is restricted to issues defined as bargainable, to interpretation of existing agreements, and to certain matters regulated by the Labor Standards Law, such as the extension of working hours. Awards are binding, but the Diet must give its consent if funds to be drawn upon are beyond the budget allowance or reserve of the enterprise involved. The pro-

The effect of the special legislation dealing with public workers was to remove almost one-fourth of all the unions and about one-third of the union membership from the coverage of the Trade Union Law. Close to one million union members were affected by the acts relating to public corporations and enterprises. More than 1.3 million union members now fell under the jurisdiction of the national and local civil service laws. Table IX provides a breakdown of coverage by each of the laws of union organizations and union membership.

Table IX. NUMBER OF UNIONS AND UNION MEMBERSHIP BY LEGAL COVERAGE, 1955 AND 1956

	1955		1956	
Law	Number of Unions	Membership (in thousands)	Number of Unions	Membership (in thousands)
Trade Union Law	14,375	3,980	15,182	4,096
Public Corporation and National Enterprise Law	28	884	25	899
Local Public Enterprises Law	269	91	295	102
National Public Service Law	308	255	300	259
Local Public Service Law	3,033	1,076	3,133	1,107
Totals	18,013	6,286	18,935	6,463

Source: *Labor White Paper, 1957* (Tokyo: Division of Labor Statistics and Research, Ministry of Labor, 1957), p. 275.

CONTROL OF TRADE-UNIONS AND COLLECTIVE BARGAINING: PRIVATE INDUSTRY

In 1949, soon after the restrictions were placed upon the government workers, the Diet, with SCAP approval, tightened provisions of the Trade Union Law and the Labor Relations Adjustment Law

---

cedure is voluntary when both parties request arbitration or one does so under the terms of an agreement. But it is compulsory (1) when a majority of a mediation commission requests arbitration in a dispute being conciliated or undergoing fact-finding, (2) when two months have elapsed after a fact-finding recommendation has been issued without subsequent agreement, or (3) when an appropriate government minister makes a request for arbitration. The arbitration board also has authority to direct management to cease any unfair labor practice, although it does not have the power to seek enforcement of these orders.

relating to labor unions in private industry. The principal amendments aimed at promoting democratic procedures among the trade-
unions, making employer unfair labor practices more specific, and
systematizing the functions of the tripartite labor relations commissions. Their chief purposes were to encourage autonomous collective bargaining and to reduce the influence of both political
parties and management in union affairs. To achieve these ends,
however, meant that in certain respects trade-unions would be subject to increased government surveillance.

Although compulsory registration was dropped, unions now had
to pass a qualifications examination in order to utilize and participate
in the activities of the labor relations commissions. They could not
admit to membership any supervisory employees, defined as those
who hire, fire, promote, or transfer workers, have access to confidential information regarding employer labor relations plans or
policies, or represent the interests of management. Unions were
forbidden to accept from employers any financial support for meeting operating expenses, although a company could provide minimum office space for a union and workers were not to lose wages
and benefits for time consumed in negotiations and conferences.

Positive requirements written into law dealt with internal union
procedures. Union constitutions now had to provide rights of equal
participation and equal treatment for all members. Workers could
not be disqualified for membership because of race, religion, sex,
social status, or family origin. Local union officials were to be
elected by direct secret ballot of the membership. In the case of
federations and national labor organizations, officials could be
elected in the same manner. However, the law also provided that
the members of each affiliated local could elect delegates by secret
ballot, and in turn these delegates were to elect the national and
federation officers by secret ballot. A union had to hold at least one
general membership meeting each year and to provide the membership with an annual financial report certified by professional
auditors selected by the members. Strike action could be initiated
only upon approval of a majority of the members voting in secret
or, in the case of a federation or national union, of a majority of
the delegates voting by secret ballot. To revise a local union's constitution, the majority of the membership had to approve in a secret
vote. To revise the constitution of a federation or national union,
either a majority vote of the membership or of the elected dele-

gates was required. Finally, the act specified that a union could dissolve itself only by following procedures in its constitution or by the resolution of three-fourths of its membership.

If a union fulfilled these requirements to the satisfaction of the appropriate labor relations commission, it then was entitled to receive protection against employer unfair labor practices, to utilize dispute adjustment procedures, to participate in selection of commission members, and to seek status as juridical persons. The examination of union qualifications was required every time a union desired to utilize or participate in the commissions. This requirement, however, placed a heavy load on the commissions and hampered their work, especially in the many cases which needed quick processing to achieve effective results. An amendment in 1952 dropped the qualification examination for dispute adjustment procedure.

By meeting the new qualifications under the 1949 revisions of the TUL, a union was assured of greater protection against employer unfair labor practices. Although the original act prohibited discrimination against workers for union activity, the provisions proved obscure and suffered from inconsistent interpretation. The new clauses were made considerably more specific by following the wording of the Wagner Act almost to the letter. Employers were expressly prohibited from discriminating against or discharging workers for union activity, refusing to bargain, controlling or interfering with the union, and discriminating against workers for testifying before a labor commission.[12] However, it should be realized that the prior requirement of a qualifications examination poten-

---

[12] Highly similar to the Wagner Act, the text of the law reads as follows: "(1) To discharge or impose discriminatory treatment upon a worker by reason of his being a member of a trade union, for his having tried to join or organize a trade union or for his having performed proper acts of a trade union; or to make it a condition of employment that the worker must not join or must withdraw from a trade union. . . . ; (2) To refuse to bargain collectively with the representative of the workers employed by the employer without fair and appropriate reasons; (3) To control or interfere with the formation or management of a trade union by workers or to give financial support to it in defraying the trade union's operational expenditures. . . . ;(4) to discharge or give discriminatory treatment to a worker for his having filed a complaint with the Labor Relations Commission that the employer has violated the provisions of this Article, . . . or of his having made testimony at the investigation or hearing conducted by the Labor Relations Commission in regard to such complaint or request or at the adjustment of labor disputes provided for in the Labor Relations Adjustment Law. . . ."

tially constitutes a greater barrier to a union seeking to utilize these provisions than does the representation election procedure under the Wagner Act or even the non-Communist affidavit and financial report requirements of the Taft-Hartley Law.

Other steps toward containing organized labor were the 1949 revisions of the Labor Relations Adjustment Law increasing the power of the government over work stoppages. The principal amendment authorized the Prime Minister, with the prior approval of the Diet, to extend the list of industries already specified as public utilities in the law to include those in which stoppages would "seriously affect the national economy or seriously endanger the daily life of the general public." A one-year limit was placed on such additions. In view of the precarious structure of the Japanese economy, this provision meant that compulsory mediation with its mandatory thirty-day cooling-off period could now be applied very widely.

The cooling-off technique proved of dubious effectiveness, paralleling the experiences of other countries. Often the thirty days provided merely a "warming-up" period for labor disputes. As long as the occupation was in effect, the procedure was retained because the supreme authority of SCAP could be relied upon to avert and control "emergency" strikes. But, in 1952, soon after the occupation ended, the Diet abandoned the cooling-off period and in its stead required that the parties in public utility industries must file notice with the appropriate labor commission ten days in advance of committing an "act of dispute."[13] Failure to comply could bring labor commission prosecution and court penalties.

At the same time, the Diet enacted an "emergency adjustment" provision which enabled the Prime Minister, if he believed a stoppage would seriously threaten "national economic activities, or daily life of the nation," to declare a state of emergency and to obtain a fifty-day court injunction against acts of dispute. However, he had to seek the opinion of the CLRC before taking this action. During the injunction period, the CLRC was to use whatever dispute adjustment procedures it felt would achieve the quickest settlement. The

---

[13] "Acts of dispute" in the Labor Relations Adjustment Law are defined as strikes, soldiering, lockouts, and "other acts and counteracts hampering the normal course of work of an enterprise, performed by the parties concerned with labor relations with the object of obtaining their respective claims." Prohibited as acts of dispute are those which "hamper or cause the stoppage or maintenance of normal operations of safety accommodations at factories, mines, and other places of employment." See *Japan Labor Code.*

amendment, however, expressly prohibited compulsory arbitration, and the parties were free to carry on their dispute at the end of the injunction period.

Although the "emergency adjustment" provision has not actually been utilized, the experience of the coal and electric power strikes late in 1952 led the government to adopt still another restrictive measure. A special act passed in 1953 outlawed stoppages specifically in these two industries on any but a local scale. This legislation was to remain in effect for three years. After heated debate, it was renewed in December, 1956.

EXPERIENCE WITH GOVERNMENT DISPUTE MACHINERY

Government-sponsored machinery has provided a major stage for negotiations between unions and management. Most crucial bargaining decisions, whether concerning government enterprise or private industry workers, have been reached through the procedures provided by the various labor relations commissions. However, government enterprise negotiations have tended to rely upon the formal procedures of fact-finding and compulsory arbitration, while private bargaining has leaned toward the informal conciliation process. Of less significance has been the use of legalistic arrangements, such as adjudication of unfair labor practice cases.

Given the nature of Japanese collective bargaining, with its unceasing series of demands, continuing negotiations, and absence of detailed contracts, the various dispute adjustment agencies are likely at some point to be drawn into active situations. This partly reflects the failure of autonomous collective bargaining to develop, and partly the attempt by the parties, particularly the unions, to strengthen their bargaining positions through use of government-sponsored procedures. Thus, the commissions do not appear to function only at the point where the parties exhaust the collective bargaining process; in addition, a major role of these agencies has been to provide an integral intermediate step in collective bargaining dealings.

Few disputes escape some form of "intervention" by the commissions, and it is likely that even a major proportion of union-management negotiations which do not end in officially recognized disputes also involve some modicum of commission activity. What happens, of course, is that the commissions not only enter the collective bargaining process when sought out by the parties or under the conditions specified in the laws, but also continually survey and keep watch over developing situations which may eventually require their formal participation. In one sense, this represents an attempt to "put the fire out" before disputes occur; in another sense, especially in view of the tripartite composition of the commissions, it often injects still another group into the bargaining.

Where compulsory dispute settlement procedure applies, almost inevitably the outcome of bargaining is a dispute and resort to further government intervention. Before enactment of the National Public Service Law and the Public Corporation Labor Relations Law, most negotiations involving government or public utility workers turned to the mediation procedures of the labor relations commissions for a formal recommendation for settlement. Since the passage of these laws, those government workers unions still eligible to negotiate agreements still tend to bring collective bargaining issues almost immediately before the specially established public corporation commissions for mediation and then move as quickly as possible to arbitration. Between 1949 and 1956, 365 cases involving in the aggregate about 27 million workers were brought before the mediation and arbitration boards. Of these cases less than one-third were first subjected to conciliation, while about half went directly to fact-finding with recommendation and seventy were arbitrated. The remainder were withdrawn, settled without formal participation of the commissions, or not acted upon.[14]

The high rate at which these formal procedures under the public corporation law have been used is probably an indication of an equally high number of incomplete bargaining efforts by management and union. Since most government enterprises have been operating under stringent budgets within the framework of an anti-inflationary governmental fiscal policy, often the unions, and sometimes management, attempt to get the bargaining problems before the Cabinet or Diet for decision. The surest route has been through fact-finding recommendations and arbitration awards, which are likely to go beyond budgetary allowances in compromising union demands and management offers. In addition, because they are denied the right to strike, and because their members are intimately involved in the governmental process, public workers unions are prone to conduct their struggles in the political arena. They are

[14] *Year Book of Labor Statistics, 1956* (Tokyo: Division of Labor Statistics and Research, Ministry of Labor, 1957), p. 394.

likely to reject the offers made in direct negotiations and to protest against the awards made in the dispute adjustment machinery. In some cases, at least, it is probable that the compulsory procedures actually are turned to the unions' advantage.

It has also been rare in the privately owned public utility industries for unions and managements to reach settlements through their own efforts at direct collective bargaining. While the thirty-day cooling-off provision was in effect, the parties typically went through the motions of negotiating but actually were making ready for a work stoppage while awaiting a fact-finding recommendation for settlement. In only relatively few cases did the parties agree immediately to accept the recommendation, although frequently after a protracted dispute they used the award as a basis for agreement. Abandonment of the thirty-day waiting period and the substitution of the ten-day notification provision were attempts at inducing the parties to exhaust their own collective bargaining efforts before turning to the labor relations commissions for fact-finding investigations. Although the ten-day notification did succeed in stimulating fuller collective bargaining, resort to commission fact-finding inquiries has remained normal procedure, with the unions initiating the preponderance of cases.[15] But, in contrast to the experience with the government enterprises, exceedingly few cases have gone to arbitration for binding decisions. The explanation for this appears to be that, while arbitration in the government corporations is a step to further consideration of the issues, it is a final step in the case of the public utilities. On the other hand, the parties, particularly the unions, are willing to go to formal fact-finding in order to garner outside support and to bring pressure upon government agencies that regulate privately owned utility industries.

Paradoxically, where mediation procedures are available, dispute adjustment in Japan has tended to follow the least formal paths. By far the great bulk of labor relations commission activity has been in the area of conciliation, the most informal procedure available. Of the 10,392 disputes recorded as handled by the commissions between their establishment in 1946 and March, 1956, almost 80 per cent utilized conciliation. Seventeen hundred and thirty-three cases went to fact-finding, and a mere twenty-four

---

[15] See *Tenth Annual Report of Labor Relations Commission, Fiscal Year April, 1955-March, 1956* (Tokyo: Central Labor Relations Commission, August, 1956), p. 81.

to arbitration.[16] Most cases, usually in the neighborhood of 75 per cent each year, were initiated by unions. The preponderance of settlements came either through conciliation or after disputes were withdrawn at this stage. Very few went into the formal fact-finding process, and most of these were public utility disputes where fact-finding was required.

Over the years, moreover, the commissions have encouraged reliance upon informal procedures which would stimulate collective bargaining and at the same time help the parties to exhaust all bargaining possibilities before resort to the dispute adjustment provisions in the law. To accomplish these goals they have provided an extra-legal technical service manned by their members and staff personnel. From April, 1952, to March, 1956, almost 4,500 "cases" found their way into this service. Probably one-third to one-half were settled at this stage. An additional 20 to 30 per cent were withdrawn and there is no record of their disposition. In all likelihood many were settled by the parties themselves. Only about one-fourth actually went on into formal conciliation procedure, and only a handful ended with recommendations based on fact-finding.[17]

This penchant for conciliation and informal intervention generally in Japanese industrial relations seems to derive from several sources. It was previously mentioned that social custom in Japan abhors direct conflict, or confrontation, especially in relationships between superiors and subordinates. Accordingly, the use of intermediaries has been a time-honored device. Undoubtedly, this has carried over to the new field of Japanese industrial relations, facilitated by the ready availability of numerous postwar mediatory agencies such as the labor relations commissions. In this sense, then, the commissions have assumed an important traditional function. Other conciliators, notably elected government officials, have also at times performed in this role, but none has gained the significance which the commissions have come to possess. Unions and managements themselves have developed but little formal private machinery for third-party participation. For example, private arbitration is almost unknown.

More than any alternative arrangement, the commission system offers a flexibility which can be tailored to individual cases, because

---

[16] *Ibid.*, p. 80.
[17] *Ibid.*, p. 88, and Levine, p. 480.

the commissions are independent of one another and because they offer a wide range for choosing conciliation services. Cases may be handled on a local, regional, or national level,[18] and the third-party conciliator may range from an individual to a tripartite group, appointed either on an *ad hoc* or permanent basis. Except where it is clear that fact-finding and arbitration procedures are fully sanctioned by law and are likely to advance the position of the parties (particularly the union as in the case of government and public utility workers), the use of outsiders to make decisions runs the risk of loss of face for one or the other party, especially after it has taken a firm stand in the argument. Thus, also, in the Japanese context the failure to resort to private arbitration does not reflect any sure growth of "mature" bargaining relationships; on the contrary, heavy reliance on conciliation is more a manifestation of inability of the parties to bargain strictly on their own, to make clear-cut issues dividing them, or to arrive at firm and lasting collective agreements. Conciliation is highly amenable to traditional indirection in social relationships.[19]

The commissions themselves also are reluctant to push vigorously for the use of formal fact-finding and arbitration procedures. The tripartite structure of these agencies accents the informal approaches of negotiation and conciliation, and the commissions have realized that formal procedures are likely to short-cut efforts to settle by inducing rigidity on both sides. As a result, if for no other reason than to preserve their existence, they are likely to seek "backstage" compromises between disputing parties, even in the formal fact-finding and arbitration proceedings. This concern becomes most apparent whenever, as commonly happens, a commission recommendation or award is rejected.[20]

---

[18] Up to March, 1956, more than 95 per cent of all disputes processed were handled at the local level. See *Tenth Annual Report of Labor Relations Commissions,* p. 76.

[19] That, in the experience of the labor relations commissions, unions initiate three out of every four dispute cases probably reflects management reluctance to negotiate and traditional worker aversion to confront employers with bargaining demands.

[20] Still another reason why the commissions are reluctant to go beyond conciliation arises from the lack of unity within the labor movement, so that compromises must be sought among the various unions and union leaders who may be involved as well as between the unions and managements. Relationships are often too delicate and complicated to leave to the inflexibility of firm commission decisions.

Thus, the commissions have wended a highly pragmatic path in their role of promoting collective bargaining and have preferred to avoid imposing rigidities in Japanese industrial relations. They have formulated few criteria for guiding autonomous negotiations or determining the scope of agreements, and in this sense have not served to institutionalize rapidly the type of collective bargaining so firmly established, for example, in the United States.

Similarly, by stressing the informal approaches, the commissions have not rigorously pursued their quasi-judicial functions. What few rules and regulations have been made are important, but they have accumulated only slowly. Sensing this approach, many unions have not sought to utilize the commissions for regulatory purposes. Only a minority of the eligible unions have petitioned for certification of their qualifications.[21] While this lack of response is due partly to aversion to outside surveillance, partly to fear of employer retaliation, partly to time and expense involved in litigation, and partly to probable failure to qualify, another explanation is that unions do not anticipate any recourse to the commissions except for conciliation purposes. Most of the unexamined and uncertified organizations are probably among the independent or loosely affiliated enterprise unions in the smaller firms where enterprise consciousness of the workers is apt to be especially strong. Among them there is likely to be but a weak desire to secure their status through the regulatory processes of the commission. Moreover, those unions which do obtain certification seem to be interested principally in participating in the nomination of commission members. Their chief interest appears to lie in influencing the conciliation and other dispute adjustment activities of the commissions rather than in defining precisely the law-given trade-union rights through their regulatory functions. A low rate of unfair labor practice cases reflects this motivation.

At first glance it is surprising that there have been few unfair labor practice cases brought either by individuals or unions, in view of the long history of worker subjugation and union opposition by employers. However, a chief reason is that many charges do not become formal cases simply because they are conciliated or compromised out of existence beforehand. In this way, embarrassing

---

[21] On the average, each year three to four thousand qualification certifications have been granted. For the most part, these have been repetitions. See Levine, pp. 470-75.

confrontations are avoided. Informal conciliation also is not likely to absorb the time and expense it takes to process a formal case, especially if it has to go through the mechanics of appeal and review procedures of the Central Labor Relations Commission and the courts. Evolution of clear-cut administrative law for these cases is apt to be painfully slow because in the traditional Japanese context many uncertainties surround the interpretation of the new unfair labor practice clauses. Finally, since few employers overtly resisted formation of unions, charges of employer discrimination have been relatively rare. At the same time, compulsory registration of unions and, later, qualification examinations served to reveal whether company domination or interference in fact existed.

Disposition of the relatively few cases also reveals the desultory record of the unfair labor practice provisions. Prior to the revision of the Trade Union Law in 1949, only sixty-two of several hundred cases of employer discrimination were referred by the commissions to the public procurators, who at that time were responsible for enforcing the law. Only eleven cases resulted in actual findings of punishable violations. Since the 1949 amendments and up to March, 1956, less than 2,900 unfair labor practice cases were filed with the commissions, or an average of only about 400 each year. However, even though case processing under the new provisions was made more systematic, only about 20 per cent of all the cases have ended with commission decisions, with cease-and-desist orders, back-pay awards, and so forth. The large majority still have been settled at earlier stages, often before any formal charge is actually issued. It seems reasonable to conclude that the factors which lend emphasis to the heavy reliance upon conciliation in Japanese industrial relations also account for the sparse use of the unfair labor practice procedures and the slow development of administrative law in this area.

Analysis of the charges themselves further indicates the lack of deep penetration by commission regulation into the various phases of the collective bargaining relationship. At least two-thirds of all the cases since 1949 involved discrimination pertaining largely to individual rather than institutional problems. In the first two years after the revisions, in fact, cases involving "red purge" discharges, which were brought by individuals and received little union support, predominated. Charges of union interference have run a poor second, while only a handful of cases each year concerned employer refusal to bargain. In addition, only in the most recent years has the majority of cases been brought in the name of unions rather than by individual workers.[22]

On the other hand, the fact that conciliation is frequently an integral part of collective negotiations in Japan provides a degree of stability and serves to dispose of issues as they arise. Moreover, the entire conciliatory process underpins the continued existence of unions, for, while not immediately achieving the firm horizontal relationships envisaged by long-term detailed collective agreements, it grants continuing recognition and outside support to unions in their function of challenging management on matters affecting wage-earners—in this sense, an important departure from Japanese industrial history. As a means for clarifying union rights and the procedures of collective bargaining, it has frequently been proposed in Japan that the dispute adjustment and regulatory functions of the commissions be divided between two separate agencies as in the case of the American National Labor Relations Board and Federal Mediation and Conciliation Service. While the 1949 amendments of the TUL made a concession in this direction by allowing only public members of the commissions to make decisions in the quasi-judicial cases, at present neither the Japanese unions nor employers appear eager to go further for the very reason that such steps would rigidify their relationships to the possible disadvantage of one group or the other. Development of clear-cut relationships has been sacrificed in order to provide continuous participation for each institution at every important stage of the decision-making process.

Compromises and "deals" may be the result of this pragmatism, but the risk of a sudden decline and possible extinction of private negotiations has been thereby lessened. This indefiniteness and indecisiveness eventually could provide an accumulation of experience upon which autonomous and independent collective bargaining could become firmly institutionalized in Japan; on the other hand, in times of great stress, they could invite direct government intervention, as we have seen in the cases of the civil servants, the public corporation employees, and the coal and electric power workers. The extent to which government already controls the terms of employment, directly or indirectly, would bear upon this eventuality.

---

[22] *Tenth Annual Report of Labor Relations Commissions,* pp. 28-35.

GOVERNMENT REGULATION OF TERMS OF EMPLOYMENT: LABOR STANDARDS

The subject matter of collective bargaining may widen or narrow in scope depending upon what issues are pre-empted by government regulation. In free nations where living standards are low and inter-relationships among economic sectors are precarious, as in Japan, extension of the welfare state is likely to reduce the vigor of private collective bargaining and to intensify the competition of group interests within the governmental apparatus. Collective bargaining, in turn, tends to become an ancillary activity—a means for affecting the political process and for implementing rather than expanding upon governmental enactments.

Even before the surrender, the role of the government in setting terms and conditions of industrial employment was extensive. Factory regulations were first adopted before World War I,[23] and, of course, the government was directly involved through its own industrial operations. During World War II, the government imposed almost totalitarian control of industrial work through conscription, wage and hour regulations, and "labor front" activity.[24]

Despite its intention to minimize government regulations, actually the occupation required the Japanese government to assume more direct responsibility for the protection of working conditions than it had before the war. This policy was understandable on the grounds that, since Japan's belligerency was attributed in part to her intense effort to compete successfully in world markets with little regard for worker interests, governmental measures were needed immediately to stamp out vestiges of militarism in industrial relations. To accomplish this, there was an attempt to bring Japanese employment practices abreast of the free West virtually in one leap. ILO conventions were used as a model.[25] However, these

---

[23] Foremost and first of these was the Factory Law of 1911, which principally dealt with the working hours of women and minors. Actually, this legislation did not go into effect until 1916 and its provisions abolishing night work for these groups were not applied until 1929. Adoption of the Factory Act was partly in response to the demands of the early Japanese labor movement and to international pressures, but more likely it was a means for attracting workers into the expanding industrial enterprises.

[24] See Jerome B. Cohen, *Japan's Economy in War and Reconstruction* (Minneapolis: University of Minnesota Press, 1949), pp. 271-352.

[25] During her membership in the interwar period, Japan adopted few ILO conventions.

steps meant that private collective bargaining would not be used to deal with a whole range of issues which in the industrial relations history of other countries often provided the core of union-management negotiations long before they were adopted as law. Perhaps, unwittingly, the heritage of prewar state welfareism had actually been strengthened.

The most important direct governmental measures to regulate terms of employment were the Labor Standards Law, Workmen's Accident Compensation Insurance Law, Employment Security Law, and Unemployment Insurance Law—all of which were adopted in 1947.[26] Other leading enactments expanded and liberalized old age and health insurance provisions, legislation first established in the prewar period. Brief summaries of these laws indicate the areas of governmental responsibility for determining terms and conditions of employment.

The Labor Standards Law (LSL) provides the foundation of the postwar protective labor legislation. Beginning with the fundamental principle that "working conditions must be those which should meet the need of the worker to live the life worthy of a human being," the content of the act is comprehensive. The government is responsible for supervising private procedures for setting minimum standards of work as well as enforcing numerous substantive provisions. But, because coverage of the law is limited to enterprises which are not household or family undertakings (domestic servants are also excluded),[27] the regulations apply only to about one-third of all industrial establishments and two-thirds of the industrial labor force. This means in effect that independent collective bargaining weakly supplements the regulatory functions of the government, especially when conditions of severe economic stringency turn legal minima into economic maxima. As a result, there is a tendency for dealings between unions and management, at least among the weakest enterprises, to be concerned mainly with the interpretation of the law. If they do not reach satisfactory understandings, they are likely to concentrate their energies upon

---

[26] Although amended on various occasions, these acts have remained virtually intact since their adoption. The most important revisions were made in 1952 following General Matthew Ridgway's earlier suggestion that occupation reforms be re-examined. See *Japan Labor Year Book for 1952* (Tokyo: Ministry of Labor, 1953), especially Parts III, IV, and V.

[27] Seamen also are not protected by the Labor Standards Law but receive almost identical coverage under the Seamen's Law of 1947.

pressuring for revisions in the law rather than bargaining with one another. With so many enterprises very close financially and organizationally to the uncovered groups, the locus of decision-making in industrial relations tends to shift to the government agencies rather than to remain confined to the immediate parties.

Although the law stipulates that workers and employers are to reach agreement upon working conditions on an equal and voluntary basis [28] and that they must abide by their negotiated collective agreements, employment rules, and individual labor contracts,[29] the government has a direct hand in the procedure. An employer of ten or more workers in a covered establishment must submit general rules of employment to the Labor Standards Bureau of the Labor Ministry for examination in regard to compliance with the law and consistency with any labor agreements in the enterprise.[30] As a minimum, the rules must specify beginning and ending hours of work, time for recess, holidays, vacation periods, and change of shifts, and they must clearly state the method of deciding, computing, and paying wages, the date of wage payment, and the explanation of wage increases. In addition, employers have to include the rules that are made for systems of retirement and other allowances, the payment of bonuses and minimum wages, provision of food and equipment, safety and sanitation, accident compensation, relief of injuries and illnesses at work, application of penalties [31] and

---

[28] The law also specifies that in respect to wages, hours, and working conditions, all workers are to be treated equally without regard to nationality, creed, or social status, and without regard to sex in respect to wages.

[29] Long a source of pre-occupation abuse, individual labor contracts now must not contain working conditions below the standards of the law and of the rules of employment for the establishment, and except under certain conditions are limited to a year's duration. An individual contract must clearly specify wages, hours, and working conditions and may be cancelled without notice if these are not met. Indemnities for breach of contract are not to be fixed in advance, while deductions from wages in repayment of money advances to the worker are prohibited. Unless agreed to under a collective agreement, employers are not allowed to hold wages on deposit; if there is such an agreement, the going rate of interest is to be paid and the savings are to be available upon demand. Individual contracts also must not allow the dismissal of injured or ill workers while under medical treatment and for thirty days thereafter as long as the enterprise is a going concern.

[30] This procedure must also be followed whenever the rules are altered.

[31] The law specifies that monetary penalties must not exceed half a day's wages for a single violation or 10 per cent of the total wages for all violations during the day period.

rewards, and so forth. Although it is not required that these rules
be bargained out with the unions in the enterprise, the employer
must seek the opinion of any union which represents a majority of
the workers and submit documentary evidence to the Labor Standards Bureau that he has done so. If there is no union, the employer
has to obtain the opinion of a person representing the majority of
the workers.

Substantive provisions of the LSL deal with a vast honeycomb
of regulations covering wages, hours, rest, holidays, vacations, safety
and sanitation, employment of women and children, dormitories,
apprenticeship and skill training, accidents, and dismissal.

Sections regarding wages made some of the worst practices of
the past illegal. Regular wages must be provided in full and paid
directly to the workers on a fixed date at least once a month, and
in emergencies accruals are to be paid upon request without delay.
Days not worked because of reasons for which the employer is
responsible must be compensated by at least 60 per cent of the
worker's average day wage. Under a piece rate system, the worker
is to be guaranteed a fixed hourly compensation.

However, much to the chagrin of the labor movement, the law
fixes no set minimum wage as in the American Fair Labor Standards Act. Instead, like the British system, the Labor Standards
Bureau is empowered to set and administer wage minima locally
and nationally upon investigation and recommendation of a tripartite wage council.[32] To date, despite this enabling provision, the
Bureau has not placed a single minimum in effect, although in
May, 1954, after prolonged study of several years, the central wage
council proposed that there be two kinds of minimum wages, one
of a general type and another for "low-wage" industries. This plan
called for beginning first with only a small portion of the latter—
parts of the silk, rayon, furniture, and hand-made paper industries—
and gradually extending the system to additional sectors of the
economy as experience is accumulated.[33] With government and
management fearing inflation and fostering a policy of economic
austerity, concrete action has been postponed. This, of course, has

[32] Wage councils are established at the national level and in each of the prefectural offices of the Labor Standards Bureau. Appointments are made by the
competent office, with the labor and employer members recommended by their
respective organizations.

[33] *The Oriental Economist*, XXII (July, 1954), p. 358.

provided organized labor with a major rallying point for political activity.

The law is more specific in the matter of hours, rest, holidays, and vacations, and these provisions represent vast improvements over pre-occupation practice. It sets a maximum eight-hour day and forty-eight-hour week, which may be extended only under special circumstances with sanction of the government administrative agency. Forty-five minutes of recess must accompany every six to eight hours of work, and one hour must be allowed for more than eight hours of work, with no restrictions upon the workers' personal freedom in the time allotted. One day off in seven is required. A premium wage of at least 25 per cent must be paid workers for overtime, work on rest days, or work between the hours of 10 p.m. and 5 a.m. Finally, there have to be annual vacations with pay— six days where a worker has been employed continuously for a year and absent less than 20 per cent of the working days, and one extra day of paid vacation for each additional year of employment up to a maximum of twenty days.

Standards for safety and sanitation, the employment of women and minors (those under eighteen years of age), and the operation of company-owned dormitories are spelled out in full detail both in the LSL and in special enforcement and interpretative ordinances, making these provisions among the most advanced codes of factory law in the world. In sum, employers are required to take steps to prevent accidents and disease, provide safety equipment, avoid the use of harmful substances, restrict dangerous work to experienced workers, offer safety education, prevent ill employees from working, provide health examinations, and engage safety and health supervisors. Children under sixteen may not be employed except under certain specified conditions, while additional recess and restrictions on working hours and types of hazardous work apply to women and minors. Pregnancy leaves and benefits and menstruation time off also are provided. In the regulation of worker dormitories, an important aspect in that three-fifths of all industrial enterprises with more than thirty employees furnish housing facilities, special stress is laid upon guaranteeing the freedom of the worker residents. While the law permits the employer to make dormitory rules, the consent of the residents must be obtained and there must be no interference in their self-organization. Also, management must meet specified standards for equipment, furnishings, facilities, space, safety, sanitation, and so forth, set by the dormitory ordinance.

In regulating apprentice training, the LSL expressly prohibits exploitation and places the training of skilled labor directly under the surveillance of the Bureau's offices. An equally tripartite apprenticeship council appointed by the Labor Ministry undertakes the study of, and makes recommendations pertaining to the development of, these training programs. The Ministry through ordinance regulates the period of training, rates of minimum compensation, the nature of instruction, and the types of work to be performed by apprentices.

Although workmen's compensation is treated separately by the Workmen's Accident Compensation Insurance Law, the LSL provides that the employer furnish all necessary medical treatment and expense for workers injured or falling ill at work. An employee is entitled to at least 60 per cent of his average wages if he is unable to work while undergoing this medical treatment. If he is permanently handicapped, he receives compensation in accordance with the type of disability. In case of the death of the injured or ill worker, the employer must compensate the worker's family in an amount equal to 1,000 times the worker's average daily wage plus funeral expenses up to 60 times the average daily wage. These payments, however, are not made if the injury or illness is due to the personal fault of the worker.

Finally, in dismissing workers, generally the employer must give at least thirty days notice or else pay the equivalent of thirty times the average daily wage, unless the enterprise is forced out of business for reasons beyond its control or unless the discharge is due to reasons for which the worker himself is responsible. The thirty-day dismissal notice, however, does not apply to temporary workers, defined as those employed on a daily basis for less than a month consecutively, on a regular basis for less than two months, on a seasonal basis for less than four months, or on a probationary basis for less than fourteen days.

In administering the LSL, the Labor Standards Bureau employs a large army of factory inspectors in offices maintained at the Labor Ministry and in each of the prefectures. In addition, attached to each of these offices are tripartite labor standards councils which carry on studies and make recommendations; within the Ministry there is a Women's and Minors' Bureau with its own separate powers of enforcement. Various parts of the law provide appeal and review machinery where appropriate. Fines and imprisonment as well as payment of back wages may be levied as penalties for violations.

Ever since the LSL was enacted, there has been considerable controversy over how effectively the government has carried its provisions out. Not only has the government failed to set up any system of minimum wages, but also it is dubious whether the government has vigorously enforced the act in general. Twenty to thirty thousand establishments are inspected each month, most of them on a regular basis. However, as many as 10 per cent of the inspections result from complaints. In 1954 alone, when nearly 300,000 inspections were made, almost 50 per cent of the establishments were reported in violation on one score or another, about one-third involving the provisions on wages. Yet, only an insignificant number of these violations reached the stage of formal prosecution. In 1953 and 1954, for example, a total of 1,038 cases were referred to the public procurators for legal action. Even then, only about half of these ended in prosecution with a mere fifty-one cases in 1953 and eighty-one in 1954 resulting in actual fines or imprisonment.[34]

This relatively low proportion of formal actions is no doubt related in considerable measure to attempts at overcoming ignorance of the law by educational methods, to the making of compromise settlements, and to the securing of informal assurances for compliance. But it is also suspected that many violations continue to exist without anything being done or that they are again committed after inspection and supposed correction. This is probably especially true among the large mass of smaller enterprises which fall in the twilight zone between family and non-family operations. The trade-union centers, of course, have demanded far more vigorous enforcement of the law, but management groups and some government officials hold that except in large establishments the law is essentially unenforceable, or even if it could be enforced anywhere, it imposes unrealistic and inequitable burdens on many sectors of the economy.

Probably the pressure of foreign opinion, which has long inveighed against "social dumping" of Japanese goods in world mar-

---

[34] *Year Book of Labor Statistics, 1954*, pp. 325-26.

kets, has been as effective as any factor in preventing any whole-sale attempt at a scaling-down revision of this law; it is also likely that, except in the large enterprises, compliance with the law is largely a matter of employer decision. Trade-unionism, even on an enterprise basis, appears effective as a policing device, but, where workers do not have a truly autonomous "outside" union, enforcement is likely to be sporadic and incomplete. This means, however, that in many cases collective bargaining often gets diverted to arguments over legal matters that usually are highly technical.

LABOR MARKET REGULATION AND SOCIAL SECURITY: THE WELFARE STATE

Government responsibility for ordering labor markets and pro-viding wage-earners with social security also developed rapidly in the immediate postwar period.[35] The new constitution pointedly stressed these obligations in Article 25:

All people shall have the right to maintain the minimum standards of wholesome and cultural living.
In all spheres of life, the State shall use its endeavors for the promotion and extension of social welfare and security, and of public health.

Laws since enacted have dealt with employment exchanges, un-employment insurance, unemployment relief, accident, health and old age insurance, housing, food and clothing rations, and family assistance. Below are discussed only those that exclusively affect industrial wage-earners.

In compliance with the constitution, two pieces of legislation were enacted in 1947 to deal directly with the labor market and unemployment. The first of these, the Employment Security Law, expanded and promoted the use of public employment labor ex-changes in order to wipe out the pre-occupation "labor boss" and similar labor recruiting systems, to bring about a balance between labor supply and demand, and to "make the most effective use of the nation's manpower resources." Administered by the Employment Security Bureau of the Ministry of Labor, the Employment Secu-rity Law established a wide network of public employment ex-

---

[35] For an incisive review of the social security developments, see George F. Rohrlich, "War and Postwar Developments in Japanese Social Security," *Bulletin of the International Social Security Association*, III (July, 1950), pp. 1-13.

changes.[36] For advisory purposes, tripartite councils, each with at least one woman member, were set up at both prefectural and national levels. The exchanges were opened to all workers and employers [37] with special programs for day laborers, physically handicapped, school graduates, and seasonal and harbor workers. Referrals, however, were not made where a strike or lockout was in progress, and, if a dispute was threatened, referrals were made only up to the number which would maintain the size of the work force. Private employment agencies were placed under strict regulation. Recruitment which required workers to change residence could be carried on only with government permission. Local recruitment was to be encouraged, and so-called "labor supply" projects— the supplying of the work force by a single agent (once a prevalent labor market operation in Japan)—had to be authorized by the Labor Minister.

The magnitude of the employment exchange operation may be seen in that there were almost 10.6 million job applications filed in 1956. Over 4.2 million referrals were made for continuing jobs, while almost 103 million man-days were made available for casual work. Placements reached over 2.2 million continuing jobs and nearly 99 million man-days of casual labor.[38]

The second act, the Unemployment Insurance Law, was a companion piece and introduced unemployment insurance to Japan for the first time. It established a compulsory system for all enterprises with five or more workers, except for those which have no juridical status in agriculture, education, medical services, social work, and the like. Excluded enterprises, however, could join the system on a voluntary basis. Government workers were covered if they were ineligible for equivalent retirement and unemployment benefits under the civil service laws, but day laborers, seasonal workers, probationary workers, and workers in enterprises having no fixed location received coverage only if they met qualifications

---

[36] Officially these are called Public Employment Security Offices, commonly referred to as PESO. In addition to 426 PESO's and 144 branch offices throughout Japan, there are 304 vocational training centers. See Akira Nakahara, "Employment Security Service in Japan Today," *Employment Security Review*, XXIV (January, 1957), pp. 3-7.

[37] Similar provisions for seamen were embodied in the Seamen's Employment Security Law of 1948.

[38] *Year Book of Labor Statistics, 1956*, pp. 68-69.

similar to those required for their protection under the Labor Standards Law.[39] As of March, 1957, nearly 9 million workers in over 260,000 establishments had obtained unemployment insurance coverage. In addition, more than 100,000 seamen were protected by their own separate system.[40]

A worker receives unemployment benefits beginning one week after dismissal if he has been insured for six months in the year preceding unemployment and if he applies for work at an employment exchange at least twice a week. Daily benefits are paid according to wage classes, decided upon periodically by the Labor Ministry in consultation with the central employment security council. These are set at 60 per cent of the average daily wage of workers in the particular class, but cannot exceed 460 yen per day. Benefits continue for a maximum of 180 days in one benefit year, provided the recipient does not earn wages which, combined with the benefit, exceed 80 per cent of his daily wage; if he does, the benefit is scaled down accordingly. If the recipient refuses suitable employment offered through an employment exchange or does not accept its offer for vocational training, benefits are denied for a month. Workers who are discharged for cause or who quit their jobs upon their own request without suitable reason must wait one to two months, as determined by the employment exchange, before receiving benefits. The national treasury finances one-third of the insurance payments and also bears the total expense of administering the system. To finance the remainder, a premium rate of 1.6 per cent is applied to the total monthly payroll of an insured enterprise and is shared equally by employers and workers.[41] However, special benefits and premiums are set for insured day laborers.

A third act dealing with unemployment, the Emergency Unemployment Countermeasures Law, was adopted in 1949 primarily to meet the unemployment problem arising from the disinflationary Dodge Plan. This law provided for work relief through public projects. Wages, however, were not to exceed 80–90 per cent of

---

[39] An amendent adopted in 1949 provided that day laborers may be covered if employed in certain "covered areas" designated by the Labor Ministry. It is estimated that half a million day laborers now are "insured."

[40] *Year Book of Labor Statistics, 1956,* pp. 348, 353.

[41] Financing has proved successful. Originally, the premium rate was set at 2.2 per cent, but in April, 1952, was lowered after several reductions to 1.6 per cent. Benefits also have been expanded. See *Japan Labor Yearbook for 1952,* p. 142.

the going rates in the community, while the workers hired first had to be those unemployed registered at the public employment exchanges. The majority of day laborers seeking work at the public employment exchanges have been employed in government projects under this act. On the average, unemployment relief projects have been expected to provide 250,000 jobs a day.[42]

The accident insurance law of 1947 made workmen's compensation compulsory for enterprises employing five or more wage-earners and voluntary for non-covered employment.[43] Compensation, of course, varies with the type of incapacity, and a sliding scale operates when the price level changes. By March, 1957, the law applied to over 585,000 establishments embracing almost 10.8 million workers.[44] Premiums are collected from employers, while rates are determined on the basis of industry-by-industry experience. "Merit-rating" provisions apply to enterprises with more than 100 employees. The Labor Standards Bureau is charged with enforcement and an equally tripartite council advises on policy and administration.

In the fields of health and old age, social insurance for industrial workers was carried over and expanded from systems developed before and during the war.[45] The Health Insurance Law,[46] which dates from 1922, provides protection for industrial workers and their families against the cost of sickness, injury, and death caused

[42] Nakahara, p. 7.

[43] Seamen are covered by a separate but comparable act, while government workers are separately protected by the Government Employees Accident Compensation Law of 1951.

[44] *Year Book of Labor Statistics, 1956*, p. 354.

[45] As early as 1871 a pension system for selected military and civil service officials had been developed by the government. All public workers were included in a mutual aid association system beginning in 1905. See Rohrlich, p. 1.

[46] This is not to be confused with the National Health Insurance Law of 1938, still in force and also broadened during the occupation, for the general population. Financial difficulties were experienced with the latter scheme in the early years of the occupation. Whereas in 1946 nearly 43 million people were covered by National Health Insurance, less than 33 million were covered a year later. The system has been gradually rebuilt, however, and full coverage is planned by 1960. See George F. Rohrlich, "Social Insurance Coordination: Some Observations Based on Japanese Experience with Health Insurance," in *Proceedings of the Third Annual Meeting of the Industrial Relations Research Association* (Madison: The Association, 1950), pp. 359-68; and *Industry and Labour*, XV, No. 8 (April 15, 1956), p. 345.

outside of employment. Coverage extends to all industrial employees, managers and workers, and their dependents, in enterprises regularly employing five or more persons, except seamen, who receive similar protection under the Seamen's Insurance Law, various types of temporary workers, and employees of health insurance associations and commission salesmen of life insurance companies.[47] Employers of non-covered enterprises, however, may apply for admission of their workers. The Ministry of Welfare administers the program.

Insurers may be either the government itself or health insurance societies, the latter being formed by employers and employees in establishments with at least 300 regular workers or in two or more establishments which together have more than 300 workers.[48] As of December, 1956, the government-managed programs covered over 255,000 establishments with almost 5.8 million participants, while the health insurance associations numbered 925 with nearly 3.5 million members.[49] Benefits are all-inclusive—medical examination, medical supplies, treatment (including maternity care), hospitalization, nursing, transportation, and funeral expenses. A partial charge is imposed upon the beneficiary equal to the amount of the first consultation fee according to a schedule drawn up by the Welfare Ministry. In cases where medical treatment does not permit the insured to work he receives as a sickness allowance 60 per cent of his standard daily wage for each day after four days and up to six months. Dependents, however, are covered only to the extent of one-half the cost. Societies may grant additional benefits beyond those provided in the law. The national treasury bears all the administrative expenses of the programs, including subsidies for operating the health insurance societies. Premiums are shared equally

---

[47] Also excluded are government workers who are members of Mutual Aid Associations set up under the National Public Service Mutual Aid Association Law of 1948.

[48] In forming a health insurance society, the consent of at least half the insured in each establishment must be obtained, and the society's constitution and bylaws approved by the Minister of Welfare. The Minister, however, may order the formation of a society in any enterprise with more than 500 regular employees. Federations of the societies also may be organized under supervision of the Minister.

[49] In addition, by December, 1956, nearly 175,000 seamen received similar benefits under the Seamen's Insurance Law. See *Year Book of Labor Statistics, 1956,* pp. 355, 362.

by employers and employees.[50] The law has set a premium rate of 6.5 per cent of the insured's monthly wages in the government-managed programs, although the Welfare Minister, after obtaining the opinion of an advisory social insurance council, may vary this rate from 5.5 per cent to 6.5 per cent depending on whether there are shortages or surpluses in the fund. Society health insurance rates may range from 3 per cent to 8 per cent of monthly pay, but the amount set must be approved by the Ministry. The maximum charged to the employee must be no more than 3.5 per cent. Any increase in the rates is to be borne solely by the employer.

Old age benefits are provided in the Welfare Pension Insurance Law, first enacted in 1941 but revised and expanded during the occupation. After the program suffered financial difficulties, major amendments were adopted in 1954. The law is administered by the government through the Welfare Ministry and covers virtually the same groups as the Health Insurance Law. In December, 1956, more than 8.9 million were insured in over 275,000 establishments.[51] Benefits include old age pensions usually obtainable at age 60, invalidity pensions and allowances, survivor pensions, retirement allowances usually obtainable at age 55, and miscellaneous welfare services. Workers qualify after twenty years of service (fifteen years for miners). The formula for remuneration provides a lump-sum payment and an amount which varies with the length of time the insured has participated and with his average monthly wages during the period. A person with twenty years coverage would receive an annual pension of about one-third of his average annual standard wages. Benefit payments are financed in part by the government, 20 per cent for miners and 10 per cent for nonminers. The remainder is financed by a premium of 3 per cent (3.5 per cent for miners) shared equally by the insured worker and his employer. The national treasury meets all administrative expenses. Unlike the health insurance scheme, there are no provisions for insurance societies, and administration of the program is entirely within the Ministry of Welfare.

Despite this seeming network of social insurance and other social security arrangements for industrial workers, the proportion of na-

---

[50] Insured persons severed from employment may continue to participate by paying the full premium.

[51] *Year Book of Labor Statistics, 1956*, p. 359.

tional income or of the central government budget going to their support is relatively small compared to the percentages expended by other industrialized nations. Since 1952, only about 1.6 per cent of Japan's national income has been expended for social security payments. This is about equal to the American percentage, but only about one-third of Norway's, one-fifth of France's, one-sixth of West Germany's, and one-twelfth of Great Britain's. In the trillion yen annual budget held to by the national government in the most recent fiscal years, total expenditures on social welfare have consumed about 17.5 per cent and the various types of labor insurance and government employee pensions account for most of this. The total of social security payments has been only 6–7 per cent of all government expenditure, national and local,[52] as compared to 17 per cent in the United States, 18 per cent in Britain, 29 per cent in Sweden, 37 per cent in West Germany, 15 per cent in France, and 13 per cent in Italy and Norway.

Low actual coverage explains the comparatively limited amount of resources devoted to the Japanese social security system. The 30 per cent of the industrial workers found in the small shops with fewer than five workers obtain none of the government social welfare benefits, except as they may qualify under the poor relief laws.[53] Otherwise, they must seek relief, along with the large mass of farmers and small individual proprietors, in the traditional family system. By and large, the groups which already receive the higher and steadier wages and benefits are those which also obtain the social security protections. In other words, the benefits go largely to the workers who are already organized.

Accordingly, as in the case of the Labor Standards Act, much energy of the trade-unions is absorbed in policing the administra-

---

[52] Hiromi Arisawa, "Level of Living in Japan," Economic Series No. 5 (Tokyo: The Science Council of Japan, Division of Economics and Commerce, March, 1955), p. 43. Adding in relief for families of war dead, the total would reach about 9 per cent. See, also, "Social Security in Japan," *The Oriental Economist*, XXV (August, 1957), pp. 399-402.

[53] The major relief legislation is the Daily Life Security Law, first adopted in September, 1946, and considerably revised in May, 1950. This act provides livelihood, educational, housing, medical, maternity, occupational, and funeral assistance for families who fall below minimum living standards set by the Minister of Welfare. The annual number of recipients has ranged from 1.7 million (in 1949), to 2.8 million (in 1947). See Arisawa, p. 44; Yoshitome Ushimaru, "Progress in Social Security," *Contemporary Japan*, XXIII (1955), pp. 693-99; and *Japan Report*, II (June 15, 1956), pp. 9-10.

tion of this system. Continual union pressure upon the government to raise the benefits and extend the coverage accentuates the state's welfare role, which in the pre-occupation era was performed largely by management. At the same time, it detracts from efforts at private collective bargaining, and there have been few significant attempts, except perhaps in the area of retirement, to supplant this approach with a privately bargained system.

Even the area of nonmonetary welfare benefits is not likely to fall within the purview of private collective bargaining. For the most part, these benefits—housing, personal financing, health facilities, educational and recreational programs, and so forth—fall within the tradition of paternalism. And, in fact, employer expenditures for the nonmonetary benefits have been equal to if not greater than those required under the laws. In most cases they average at least 10 per cent of the payrolls.

It thus would appear that the scope of collective bargaining is limited by the combination of benefits provided by employer paternalism and by welfare stateism, although neither by itself is an overly impressive amount. Few of these provisions may readily become issues at the bargaining table without sacrificing the major issues upon which trade-unionism in Japan has fed—wages and job tenure. Moreover, what business is transacted at the enterprise level in the social security and welfare areas usually is conducted outside the realm of union-management bargaining by coexisting institutions such as insurance societies, dormitory clubs, mutual aid associations, and joint councils. These institutions are likely to operate independently of the unions, even though in many cases their officers are union leaders; where the employer participates, management tends to predominate as a matter of paternalistic tradition. Enterprise unions have not made great efforts to compete with these welfare-oriented groups but confine their activities to assuring the job tenure of their members. It is at the national labor centers that one hears the greatest demands for an expanded social security program with increased benefits, but even here the argument is advanced in terms of reducing other major items in the national budget, in particular expenditures on armaments, rather than curtailing employer-provided welfare. Thus, social security and welfare have become primarily matters of political concern rather than questions to be decided through collective bargaining.

Wages, too, are limited as subjects of collective bargaining by governmental policy, giving further impetus to activity at political levels. Even though political expediency permitted wages to rise under the rampant inflation of the early postwar years and later during the Korean boom, there have been constant efforts by the government, through fiscal and monetary policies, to hold back increases in the general money wage level. At the end of 1948, the Dodge Plan warned against wage increases which could not be justified by advances in productivity. Its so-called three principles on wages prohibited commodity price rises, deficit financing, and government subsidies for private industry—all devices that had been used to up money wage rates. These principles have been the policy of the conservative governments which have been in power ever since. As a result, they have been a brake on the amount of money wage increases obtained through collective bargaining.[54] In addition, especially since the inauguration of its austerity program in 1953, the government has advocated the "pegging" of wages at some "standard" level rather than making any serious proposal for establishing minimum wages. While no enactment has been made, wage surveys have been carried on for the purpose of ascertaining the standard wage in various industries which would serve as a guide for making wage decisions, particularly in collective bargaining and in labor commission dispute adjustment. In March, 1955, the Labor Minister again proposed that wage increases be tied specifically to enterprise productivity, both for general wage increases and in individual cases.[55] Although the trade-union centers have vigorously protested this type of indirect pressure by the government, the effect of these administrative policies has been to diminish the role of private collective bargaining and to stress that of the state.

In general, government regulation and control, even though originally conceived of as an important means for elevating the economic status of the Japanese wage-earner, have detracted from the effort to institutionalize an effective private collective bargaining

---

[54] For example, while the "spring" wage drive of 1953 resulted in an average increase of 10 per cent, only 7 per cent was gained in 1954 and less than 3 per cent in 1955. See "Labor Front Today," *The Oriental Economist*, XXIV (August, 1955), pp. 390-91. Japan's economic expansion finally reversed this trend in 1956.

[55] See "Economic and Social Situation in Japan," *Industry and Labour*, XIV (October 15, 1955), p. 351.

system. The wage issue does not yet provide a rigorous basis for its growth. Should the government further pre-empt the wage area, collective bargaining is not likely to find an adequate sustaining outlet, even in fringe benefits.

VII

SUMMARY AND CONCLUSIONS

In the decade since V-J Day industrial relations in Japan have undergone significant developments. Despite the turbulence and uncertainties of these years and despite the brevity of the period, the character of Japan's postwar industrial relations has begun to crystallize along recognizable dimensions. What has emerged at once reflects the tenuous fastening of Western democratic institutions upon Japan and the ineluctable hold of her own historical traditions. The resulting amalgam partakes of each, yet is distinctive of both.

First we shall undertake to summarize the major characteristics of Japan's postwar industrial relations; later we shall seek to clarify the implications for the future of the Japanese nation. There are serious hazards in both tasks in view of the great flux that still remains in Japanese society, the continuing instability of Japan's economic position, and the dynamics of East-West conflict in general. While we are able to outline the principal trends, there are enough exceptions and contradictory tendencies to signal caution against accepting simplifications. These concluding observations then should be viewed as bench marks for guiding future analyses rather than sweeping generalizations that will hold inevitably and in every case.

1. In general, a new set of decision-makers has grown up in the system of industrial relations as in other sectors of postwar Japanese life. The traditional triumvirate of the military, *Zaibatsu*, and political bureaucracy has been replaced by a more democratic combination of professional management, organized labor, and representative government. Although one cannot pretend that each group shares equally in determining the "web of rule" in industrial life, that there is a sharing of this sort for certain issues and in certain sectors represents a distinct alteration contributing to the

New Japan. How far this actually has gone may be perceived more readily by examining the internal workings of each of these institutions and the relationships among them.

One should not overplay the present role of the new institutions as something more than formal entities existing on the Japanese scene. Ingrained traditions of authoritarianism in superior-subordinate relationships, harmony of the family system, group conformity, deprecation of individualism, intense personal loyalties, acceptance of the inevitable, and the like still are tenacious aspects of Japanese society and thus also permeate the industrial relations system. The point is, however, that within the traditional institutional context, these values received almost sole emphasis, but under the new set of arrangements they are accommodated along with competing values.

In the restructuring of industrial relations in postwar Japan, the logics of her industrialization process could not be disregarded. The existence of a wide agricultural base, proliferation of small and petty enterprises, superimposition of large modern undertakings, and government's pivotal role in economic policy, all had evolved in the spirit of an ultranationalism awakened by fear of foreign invasion. Limited resources, growing population, and dependence upon overseas trade intensified the ultranationalistic aspects of industrialization. This was hardly the setting for the emergence of Western-type institutions in any phase of life, let alone industrial relations.

Even though the occupation set forth to alter the purpose of the system and actually succeeded in removing the worst trappings of militarism and feudalism, it was not immediately feasible to change the basic forces that the process of Japanese industrialization had rapidly generated. The fundamental economic framework remained. There was little prospect for immediate alteration, except to reduce the Japanese nation to a level of abject poverty, which was neither desirable in terms of Western ideology nor politic when the East-West conflict ripened into cold war. As a result, the structure that had evolved was retained, although this meant that many elements of the industrial relationships which had been part and parcel of its original development were also likely to be carried forward. Within this context, it would have been surprising that a wholly new system of industrial relations could emerge except at a very slow pace.

Yet, despite drifts away from the concepts envisioned in the occupation reforms, enough was removed, enough was instituted to give rise to innovations in Japanese industrial relations that probably will prove durable. These may be seen in changed management, labor, and government roles.

2. It seems fair to conclude that the contemporary managerial system in Japanese economic enterprise has escaped rigidities from which it suffered before the surrender. The emphasis upon a specialized industrial relations function within the managerial hierarchy has tended to redistribute management's policy-making procedures and to break down the vertical relationships, narrowness of focus, and constricted access which once served to promote efficiency in an industrialization process geared to ultranationalism. This new infusion with its faith in the democratic responsibility and responsiveness to rank-and-file pressures now appears secure within many modern Japanese managements. Moreover, it seems compatible with the aims of Japanese recovery and is likely to release the entrepreneurial energy upon which Japan's economic viability eventually must depend. Management has thus accommodated to the forces unleashed by military defeat and occupation reform.

On the other hand, traditional methods of management are still attractive. With nationalism regaining strength, especially since the conclusion of the peace treaty and, more recently, the Soviet-Japanese settlement, the old tested approaches are inviting as a secure way toward Japan's re-emergence as a major power of the world. As a result, even the new elements in postwar management are caught in a dilemma of risking success of their enterprises by instituting unfamiliar procedures identified with group self-dependence in Western democratic nations or by falling back upon traditional relations between management and the work force. While a way has been opened to a new type of managerialism, there is at the same time a strong tendency to continue to stress paternalisim, albeit now emphasizing patriarchal humanitarianism. This approach is in keeping with a facet of Japanese culture that pervades small industrial enterprise, family farm, and village community.

Despite the importance of agriculture and medium and small enterprise for sustaining the Japanese economy, it is the performance of large modern industry which will be key to the solution of Japan's economic problems. Management in the larger and more basic industries is more apt to be conscious of the role it plays toward this end. In fact, this has been its traditional *raison d'etre*, and it may be said that the Japanese people, except for a minority of revolutionaries, accept this functional leadership provided it seems to maintain their cultural integrity. Thus, large enterprise management hesitates to experiment with concepts which could upset the very system of social relationships which it is supposed to preserve. It accepts trade-unionism as long as it is essentially conservative. It accepts government regulation and welfare stateism as long as they serve to promote identification of worker and enterprise. However, in going no further, these managers are also likely to place restraints upon dynamic entrepreneurship.

While modern management seeks out techniques which have successfully accompanied industrial expansion in the free West, such as autonomous collective bargaining, decentralization of authority and responsibility, matching of men to jobs rather than to social organizations, training supervisors in the "human relations" approach, and so forth, it proceeds but gradually to select only those features that square with traditional approaches. In other words, large enterprise management does not as yet perceive the course of industrialization to have ripened to the point where paternalism has lost its usefulness and must be replaced by devices that have worked out effectively elsewhere.

Given the stringent position in which Japan now finds herself in world trade and politics, this cautious approach may be justifiable for the time being. The problem, however, is whether the approach will harden and follow the tradition of despotic control or whether it can set loose its inherent tendencies to support democratic relationships. In great part, the test will come whenever the opportunity for Japanese economic viability, independence, and growth presents itself. Until then, and especially if the situation deteriorates, the present balance between the two is likely to remain precarious.

3. The growth of postwar trade-unionism undoubtedly exceeded the expectations of the most hopeful prophets. Organized labor has gained access to realms of decision-making which were once the exclusive province of the totalitarian elite. On the two major scores of job tenure and wage benefits, unions have successfully invaded management's reservation, and in supporting the new political parties of the left, particularly the Socialists, they have strengthened the bulwarks against the return of the old political configuration. It seems likely that these are enduring functions of the labor movement of the New Japan.

Yet, in pursuing these roles, organized labor is fractionized and its efforts are thus attenuated. For this institution, like management, contains strong elements of the past, which dilute the new set of values it was supposed to represent. It possesses distinctive Japanese characteristics which place the impressive statistics on membership and growth in a light somewhat different from that conventionally assigned to trade-unionism in countries of the free West. Although the movement has the imprint of foreign ideology and structure, it is not a reproduction of either the economic or political models which Western industrialization has furnished. This has come about not so much by conscious design as it has by the conjuncture of underlying forces. There has been a continuing struggle, especially at the top leadership levels, over which of the foreign models to follow. Underneath, and most subtly, the Japanese unions have cut out their major role. What has resulted is almost a dual movement—a smaller upper level engaged in political and ideological struggle and a larger lower level focused on select day-by-day economic issues. The interaction between the two is of a tenuous sort and, of course, varies in different unions, industries, and enterprises. At some points, the two movements coalesce; at others, they are widely divergent. This does not mean that they are necessarily incompatible; it merely signifies that different functions have been allotted to almost separate institutions and that their respective effectiveness depends upon arousing worker consciousness for different purposes.

Enterprise unionism has become the hallmark of the Japanese labor movement. Through this device has been mobilized the principal economic interests of the wage-earner in modern Japanese industry. It has two principal functions. The first is to secure the attachment of those who are committed for life to industrial work. The second is to provide equal treatment for the members of these permanent groups as they pursue their careers. Enterprise unionism therefore makes the underlying assumption that Japan's industrialization is built upon a carefully articulated set of specialized enterprise units performing distinctive roles in Japanese economic development. Accordingly, it is through these entities that the permanent wage-earner must seek his integration into the ongoing Japanese culture. Unionization, coming on a large scale so long after industrialization began and at a juncture where the very existence of the industrial structure was threatened, principally provided an opportunity for the industrial workers to secure their status in

Japanese society, rather than to attempt to build a wholly new set of relationships. Even when management regained its authority and after the occupation and government shifted its emphasis, the unions proved to have a considerable staying power, for within the Japanese context their function for this end was still widely regarded as legitimate.

In a sense, the character of the enterprise union is not unlike the Gompersism of American craft unionism. But the analogy actually is weak. Enterprise unionism draws heavily upon the values of traditional village and kinship structure, best seen in its "combined" membership, its inclusion of the permanent workers alone, and its heavy reliance upon white-collar leadership. It is not the outgrowth of a "craft" or "job" consciousness. In spite of its formal structure, moreover, the Japanese trade-union movement has but a slight semblance of either industrial or class-conscious unionism, for the process of industrialization avoided the creation of labor markets which would produce such horizontal bonds among the workers. This, of course, helps to explain the loose relationship between the basic enterprise units and the national labor organizations.

The enterprise union, by tying together the concepts of group self-interest and traditional patterns of industrial relations, does not as yet constitute the challenge to the industrial society that unionism has meant in the United States or Western Europe. Essentially, it plays a passive role in Japanese economic development, leaving management and government to take the initiative. Its chief function is to make sure that managements live up to their traditional responsibilities to the permanent workers. In its preoccupation with the enterprise, the enterprise union also does not press for political change as long as the government extends the benefits of a welfare state largely to the organized workers.

It would be, of course, an oversimplification to say that enterprise unionism is all that characterizes the postwar labor movement of Japan. The national organizations undoubtedly reflect an awakening of worker consciousness of both the advantages of a widespread, close-knit movement and the right to a voice in over-all political and economic processes. However, for the time being, these interests seem remote from the preoccupation of workers with permanent attachment to the enterprise and expectation of paternalistic benefits. With a great mass of the labor force unassailable by trade-unionism and wedded to familialistic small and medium enterprises, or at best moving within restricted labor market channels, enterprise unions perceive that they have a greater stake in the fortunes of their respective enterprises than in the prospect of a political or ideological movement which in the end might fail to alter the basic economic processes. Moreover, the success of such a movement might serve only to threaten the present security of the union membership. The problem for the national organization is how to mobilize enterprise consciousness to serve long-range social and political aims.

Lacking strong rank-and-file support, excluded from economic functions at the enterprise level, and inheriting the radicalism of the prewar era, national labor organizations have tended to increase their political vociferousness, concentrating where possible, as in the conspicuous case of the public workers, upon the coalescence of the egalitarianism present in enterprise union functions and in radical ideology. Even here, they have not been overly effective when there is too great a dilution of both elements. The recent shift to the Ota strategy in *Sōhyō*, the emergence of a more moderate *Zenrō Kaigi*, and the reunification of left and right wings of the Social Democratic party, for example, reveal the need for a careful merging of the two approaches. But this is likely to take considerable time and experimentation.

Failure to weld together a unified trade-union movement, either horizontally or vertically, is an obstacle to developing wholly new patterns of industrial relations in postwar Japan. Yet, the lack of unity does not foredoom the organized labor movement. True it is that sectionalism weakens the effectiveness of unions and opens the door to competition for the worker's loyalty either from paternalistic employers on the one hand or from political extremists of the right or left on the other. But even in its limited role Japanese trade-unionism can well be a portent of a future in which there is greater unity and forcefulness than at present. The enterprise unions could constitute building blocks for an independent, unified labor institution, as they acquire experience and discover their mutual interests, provided that in the interim Japan can enjoy a modicum of economic and political stability. Without this, the unions are likely to remain weak and divided and to stand on a narrow precipice between company domination and political subversion.

4. In light of these management and union developments, it is

not surprising that independent collective bargaining has yet to become the central channel for industrial relations decision-making. Collective bargaining has been hemmed in and restricted by traditional paternalism, government regulation, state welfare programs, and various co-operative arrangements which represent worker interests outside the unions. This has been due in part to the nature of the institutions on the postwar scene, but it also arises from a lack of bargaining tradition and long dependence upon central governmental agencies to define what is right and wrong in industrial relations. Although reliance upon conciliation keeps the peace, it is not apt to provide strong impetus for independent dealings between union and management. This is not to say that conciliation has no place in labor relations (indeed, it may be highly desirable), but that in the Japanese framework it is likely to be an impediment to, rather than a confirmation of, horizontal relationships.

Again, it should not be concluded that collective bargaining has been a failure in postwar Japan. In some instances, such as the maritime industry, it is well entrenched. Collective agreements have spread with surprising rapidity. This represents a considerable departure from pre-occupation Japan, for these labor agreements do provide an opportunity for a widening of the collective bargaining function.

Up to now, however, collective agreements principally have furnished a means for legitimizing disputes and for sharpening issues where interests of workers and employers conflict. Substantively, they are for the most part shallow and are little more than affirmation of legal rights gained through occupation reform. Although there have been a number of serious work stoppages, largely of a political nature, dispute action has not been highly instrumental in promoting the collective bargaining function. Continued immaturity of the collective bargaining processes may invite further worker reliance on employers and union reliance on political parties. Fundamentally these tendencies, too, may be traced to the lack of self-dependence in Japanese traditions and to the precariousness of Japan's economic and political situation.

5. Despite the occupation's desire to eliminate central political control, government intrudes heavily upon the industrial relations system of postwar Japan. The net effects of its enactments have been to throw roadblocks in the way of independent collective bargaining or to substitute traditional conciliatory and backstage

techniques that at times undermine efforts at independent collective bargaining. In one fell swoop, the occupation pre-empted large areas for direct government regulation—to be sure, a step necessary to provide workers with protections long since gained in other countries. In doing so, however, it sliced off many issues upon which independent institutions in the industrial relations experiences of other countries had nurtured and grown. Given the low economic level of Japan, this was an important slice, for it left to collective bargaining lean pickings and placed a premium upon political activity. By adding government responsibility to employer paternalism, these policies tended to shift the focus away from independent dealings between workers and management. Government intrusion, of course, grew even more with the later restrictions upon organizing, collective bargaining, and work stoppages.

The tendency toward welfare stateism, however, has not grown greatly since the initial occupation requirements were imposed. Increasing coverage has largely been the result of Japanese economic recovery and growth following the devastation of the war and chaos of the early occupation period. Despite pressure of the parties of the left and the national labor organizations, there has been little extension of benefits beyond the groups of workers which are already the best off. Reliance for security in many sectors is still left mainly to the workings of traditional social relations found in the Japanese culture, such as the local community, neighborhood, and family. And probably the organized industrial worker is apathetic about the problem because he sees in the welfare programs a means for maintaining his own status in Japanese society. Thus, the welfare state as it is practiced in Japan may be cutting two ways. In the event of economic or political upset, large masses of people who are now unprotected may arise to protest against intolerable conditions. At the same time, organized labor, lacking in unity and in the exercises that secure its independence, could lose the leadership it might otherwise hold among the laboring classes by taking refuge behind a governmental and employer paternalism. Such a course would be reminiscent of the 1930's. On the other hand, until the economic situation shows notable improvement, an extension of social security and protective labor measures, even if administrable, not only would seriously divert critical resources essential for needed capital development, but also might bring about an end to private efforts at controlling and regulating industrial relations.

Present arrangements may be a reasonable, even though unstable, compromise.

Perhaps the tempering forces in this situation are degrees of self-dependence, low as they may be, emerging in the form of trade-unionism, professional management, and the parties of the democratic left. These strains in contemporary Japanese society have an impact upon the conservative groups by pulling them back from reactionary temptation. What is demonstrated is that within the context of the Japanese cultural tradition and processes of industrialization there is room for independence of action. At the moment, this is a confined area, threatening to constrict even more.

What of the future? Is it likely that Japanese industrial relations have reached a point of equilibrium, unstable though it may be; that they will develop toward a more pluralistic form of decision-making which is identified with the Western democracies; or that they will revert to a monolith of totalitarianism? The whole world shares in providing answers to these questions. Yet, it is only the Japanese themselves who can translate them into concrete action.

The choices presented internationally are crucial for the future course of Japan's industrial relations. In the prewar past, the Japanese seized the opportunities made available by structuring an economy which fed upon and strengthened the values of individual subservience. What has been left by a disastrous war again tempts some Japanese to follow a similar course to escape from Japan's dilemma of too few resources and too many people. The neighboring example of Communist China and the overtures of Soviet Russia are no doubt playing upon these backward-looking sentiments. But any such bargain is not likely to achieve national independence whatever reversions to traditionalism are permitted, and it is clear that Communist party activity in Japan aims to develop a passion for a satellite future. An economically weak Japan, of course, plays into the hands of these elements.

A real choice for the Japanese lies in how they will go about managing the opportunity for economic development. Full revival of the *Zaibatsu* combines, a tendency for which there is some evidence, is likely to recast the process of industrialization into its old mold, giving rebirth to managerial despotism, constriction of entrepreneurial effort, and annihilation of worker self-dependence. A resurgent militarism, without broad concomitant economic opportunity for the nation as a whole, would also facilitate such a process

—a danger to be watched as America increases pressure for Japan to shoulder her share of Western defense burdens.

On the other hand, the dynamics of the postwar decade have produced a new set of incipient institutions which can lead Japan to a prominent place among the democratic nations. Some of these are to be found in her system of industrial relations. The nurturing of these institutions will require a slow, patient, and often agonizing approach. Ascendency of unified independent trade-unionism, democratic professional management, and autonomous bilateral collective bargaining will not occur suddenly. It is likely that for a long time to come the type of industrial relations which now exists in Japan will continue. But even this should represent considerable progress in the eyes of the free world.

Although the choice resides in Japanese hands, it is the responsibility of the free nations to make the opportunity meaningful. It is beyond the scope of this study to explore the alternatives available for promoting international trade in which Japan would find an equitable share or for developing international relationships which would enhance her dignity as a sovereign nation. But it would seem that still there is hope for structuring situations which would enable Japan to escape from her present economic strait jacket. For one encouraging aspect of what otherwise appears to be a dismal set of circumstances is that the Japanese are possessed of much imagination and entrepreneurship. Throughout her history, Japan has constantly adapted to new influences largely made in contact with or brought from abroad. One may be confident that the Japanese will succeed in seeking out and adopting profitably those technological changes, those institutions, and those concepts which blend the old and new in a successful mixture. The postwar developments in Japanese industrial relations are an indication of this process and provide stepping stones in this direction. Fortunately, despite the backward pull of the past, despite the economic and political diversions of the present, they give promise of improving the lot and dignity of the common man in Japan's industrial society.

Selected Bibliography

BOOKS, PAMPHLETS, AND ARTICLES

GENERAL

Allen, G. C. *Japanese Industry: Its Recent Development and Present Condition*. New York: Institute of Pacific Relations, 1940.

———. *A Short Economic History of Japan, 1867-1937*. London: Allen and Unwin, 1946.

Bisson, T. O. *Zaibatsu Dissolution in Japan*. Berkeley: University of California Press, 1954.

Cohen, Jerome B. *Japan's Economy in War and Reconstruction*. Minneapolis: University of Minnesota Press, 1949.

Cole, Allan B. *Japanese Society and Politics: The Impact of Social Stratification and Mobility on Politics*. Boston University Studies in Political Science, No. 1. Boston: The Graduate School of Boston University, June, 1956.

Colton, Kenneth E., Hattie K. Colton, and George O. Totten, (eds.). "Japan Since Recovery of Independence," *The Annals of the American Academy of Political and Social Science*, CCCVIII (November, 1956), vii-ix, 1-174.

Dull, Paul S. "The Japanese General Election of 1952," *American Political Science Review*, XLVII (March, 1953), 199-204.

Fearey, Robert A. *Occupation of Japan; Second Phase, 1948-1950*. New York: Macmillan, 1950.

Grad, Andrew J. *Land and Peasant in Japan, an Introductory Survey*. New York: Institute of Pacific Relations, 1953.

Henderson, A. M., and Talcott Parsons, trans., *Max Weber: The Theory of Social and Economic Organization*. New York: Oxford University Press, 1947.

Hewes, L. I., Jr. *Japan—Land and Men: An Account of the Japanese Land Reform Program, 1945-51*. Ames: Iowa State College Press, 1955.

Ike, Nobutaka, *Japanese Politics: An Introductory Survey*. New York: Alfred A. Knopf, 1957.

Japan as It Is Today. Tokyo: Ministry of Foreign Affairs, August, 1953.

Japan in Industry, 1954. Tokyo: The Oriental Economist, 1954.

Levy, Marion J., Jr. "Contrasting Factors in the Modernization of

China and Japan," *Economic Development and Cultural Change*, II (October, 1953).

Lindstrom, David E. "Outlook for the Land Reform in Japan," *Contemporary Japan*, XXIV, Nos. 1-3 (1956), 88-100.

Lockwood, William W. *The Economic Development of Japan, Growth and Structural Change, 1868-1938*. Princeton: Princeton University Press, 1954.

Martin, Edwin M. *The Allied Occupation of Japan*. Stanford: Stanford University Press, 1948.

Noda, Tetsugoro. "Agriculture: Its Recovery and Development," *Contemporary Japan*, XXIV, Nos. 1-3 (1956), 47-54.

Norman, E. Herbert. *Japan's Emergence as a Modern State*. New York: Institute of Pacific Relations, 1940.

Ohkawa, Kazushi. "Economic Growth and Agriculture," *The Annals of the Hitotsubashi Academy*, VII (October, 1956), 46-60.

Okazaki, Ayanori. "The Present and Future of Japan's Population," *Japanese Paper No. 4*, 12th Conf., Institute of Pacific Relations, Kyoto, September-October, 1954. Tokyo: Japan Institute of Pacific Relations, 1954.

Orchard, John E. *Japan's Economic Position, The Progress of Industrialization*. New York: McGraw-Hill, 1930.

Political Reorientation of Japan: September 1945 to September 1948: Report of Government Section, Supreme Commander for the Allied Powers. Washington: Government Printing Office, 1949.

Quigley, Harold S., and John E. Turner. *The New Japan: Government and Politics*. Minneapolis: University of Minnesota Press, 1956.

Rosen, George. "Japanese Industry Since the War," *Quarterly Journal of Economics*, LXVII (August, 1953), 445-63.

Scalapino, Robert A. *Democracy and the Party Movement in Prewar Japan, The Failure of the First Attempt*. Berkeley: University of California Press, 1953.

Schumpeter, E. B. (ed.). *The Industrialization of Japan and Manchukuo, 1930-1940: Population, Raw Materials and Industry*. New York: Macmillan, 1940.

Schwantes, Robert S. *Japanese and Americans, A Century of Cultural Relations*. New York: Harper & Bros., 1955.

Taeuber, Irene B. "Recent Population Developments in Japan: Some Facts and Reflection," *Pacific Affairs*, XXIX (March, 1956), 21-36.

Textor, Robert B. *Failure in Japan*. New York: John Day, 1951.

Totten, George O. "Problems of Japanese Socialist Leadership," *Pacific Affairs*, XXVIII (June, 1955), 160-69.

Tsuji, Kiyoaki. "The Cabinet, Administrative Organization, and the Bureaucracy," *The Annals of the American Academy of Political and Social Science*, CCCVIII (November, 1956), 10-17.

Tsuru, Shigeto. "Internal Industrial and Business Trends," *The Annals of the American Academy of Political and Social Science*, CCCVIII (November, 1956), 85-94.

Wildes, Harry Emerson. *Typhoon in Tokyo.* New York: Macmillan, 1954.

Yanaga, Chitoshi. *Japanese People and Politics.* New York: John Wiley & Sons, 1956.

LABOR AND INDUSTRIAL RELATIONS

Annual Reports of Labor Relations Commission. Tokyo: Central Labor Relations Commission, 1946-1956.

Arisawa, Hiromi. *Level of Living in Japan.* Economic Series No. 5. Tokyo: The Science Council of Japan, Division of Economics and Commerce, March, 1955.

Ayusawa, Iwao. *Post-War Developments in Organized Labor.* Tokyo: Foreign Affairs Association of Japan, 1953.

Camacho, Martin T. "The Administration of the SCAP Labor Policy in Occupied Japan." Unpublished Ph.D. thesis, Harvard University, 1954.

Colbert, Evelyn S. *The Left Wing in Japanese Politics.* New York: Institute of Pacific Relations, 1952.

Daya, E. "Freedom of Association and Industrial Relations in Asian Countries," *International Labour Review*, LXXI (April, 1955), 364-93; and (May, 1955), 467-97.

Farley, Miriam S. *Aspects of Japan's Labor Problems.* New York: John Day, 1950.

Galenson, Walter, (ed.). *Comparative Labor Movements.* New York: Prentice-Hall, 1952.

Haraguchi, Y. "The Free Trade Unions of Japan Democracy's Bulwark," *Free Labour World*, 61 (July, 1955), 17-20.

Harbison, Frederick H., and Eugene Burgess. "Modern Management in Western Europe," *The American Journal of Sociology*, XL (July, 1954), 15-23.

Industrial Labour in Japan. Studies and Reports, Series A (Industrial Relations), No. 37. Geneva: International Labour Office, 1933.

Ishino, Iwao. "The *Oyabun-Kobun* Institution: An Introductory Analysis of a Ritual Kinship System in Japan." Unpublished Ph.D. thesis, Harvard University, 1954.

Ishizaki, Masaichiro. "The Legal Status of Female Laborers in Japan," *The Japan Annual of Law and Politics*, No. 1. Tokyo: Second Division, Science Council of Japan, 1952, 45-55.

Japan Federation of Employers' Association. *Constitution, Officers, Items of Work, Outline of the Development of Employers' Association in Japan, the Structure of Japan Federation of Employers' Association.* Tokyo: The Federation, 1951.

———. *Analysis of Personnel Practices in the Principal Industries in Japan.* Tokyo: The Federation, 1953.

Japan Labor Code, 1952. Tokyo: Ministry of Labor, 1953.

Japan Labor Year Book for 1952. Tokyo: Ministry of Labor, 1953.

Kerr, Clark, Frederick H. Harbison, John T. Dunlop, and Charles A. Myers. "The Labour Problem in Economic Development: A Framework for Reappraisal," *International Labour Review*, LXXI (March, 1955), 223-35.

—— and Abraham Siegel. "The Structuring of the Labor Force in Industrial Society: New Dimensions and New Questions," *Industrial and Labor Relations Review*, VIII (January, 1955), 151-68.

Kikuchi, Isao. "Freedom of Association and Unfair Labor Practices," *The Japan Annual of Law and Politics*, No. 2. Tokyo: Second Division, Science Council of Japan, 1953, 57-80.

Kishimoto, Eitaro. "A Short History of the Labour Movements in Japan," *Kyoto University Economic Review*, XXI (April, 1951), 39-56.

Kublin, Hyman. "The Origins of Japanese Socialist Tradition," *The Journal of Politics*, XIV (May, 1952), 257-80.

Labor Relations Commissions of Japan. Tokyo: Central Labor Commission, March, 1956.

The Labor Union Movement in Postwar Japan. Tokyo: The Daily Labor Press, Inc., 1954.

Levine, Solomon B. "Japan's Tripartite Labor Relations Commissions," *Labor Law Journal*, VI (July, 1955), 462-82, 490.

——. "Prospects of Japanese Labor," *Far Eastern Survey*, XXIII (May, 1954), 65-70; and (July, 1954), 107-10.

McPherson, William H. "Industrial Relations in Occupied Japan," in *Labor in Postwar America*, ed. Colston E. Warne. Brooklyn: Remsen Press, 1949, 623-42.

Minobe, Ryokichi. "A Statistical Survey of Japan's Poverty," *Contemporary Japan*, XXIII, Nos. 1-3 (1954), 193-99.

Morita, Yuzo. "The National Income and the Standard of Living in Japan," *Japan Quarterly*, III (January-March, 1956), 107-17.

Nakahara, Akira. "Employment Security Service in Japan Today," *Employment Security Review*, XXIV (January, 1957), 3-7.

Nakayama, Ichiro. *Japan's Labor Problems*. Tokyo: Ministry of Foreign Affairs, Public Information and Cultural Affairs Bureau, 1956.

——. "Japanese Labor Trends," *The Oriental Economist*, XXIII (February, 1955), 79-83.

Noda Nobuo and Mori Goro, *Rōmu Kanri Kindaika no Jitsurei (Examples of the Modernization of Labor Administration)*. Tokyo: Daiamondo-sha, 1954.

Okochi Kazuo. *Nihon Rōdō Kumiai Ron (On Japanese Trade Unions)*. Tokyo: Yuhikaku, 1953.

——. "Rōdō" ("Labor") in *Gendai Nihon Shoshi (A Short History of Modern Japan)*, Vol. II, ed. Yanaihara Tadao. Tokyo: Misuzu Shobo, 1953, 111-215.

Perlman, Selig. *A Theory of the Labor Movement*. New York: Augustus M. Kelley, 1949.

——. "A Theory of the Labor Movement." (February, 1949), mimeographed.

Rōdō Hakusho. (Labor White Papers). Tokyo: Division of Labor Statistics and Research, Ministry of Labor, 1953-1957.

Rōdō Kumiai Chōsa Hōkōku (Report on the Survey of Labor Unions), July, 1952. Tokyo: Ministry of Labor, April, 1953.

Rohrlich, George F. "Social Insurance Coordination: Some Observations Based on Japanese Experience with Health Insurance," *Proceedings of the Third Annual Meeting of the Industrial Relations Research Association,* 359-68. Madison: The Association, 1950.

————. "War and Postwar Developments in Japanese Social Security," *Bulletin of the International Social Security Association,* III (July, 1950), 1-13.

Sakurabayashi Makoto. "Rōshi Kankei No Nihonteki Seikaku" ("Characteristics of Japanese Labor Relations"), *Seni Keizai,* (*Textile Economy*), No. 21 (December, 1953), 4-20.

Suehiro Izutaro. *Nihon Rōdō Kumiai Undō Shi (History of the Japanese Labor Union Movement).* Tokyo: Kyodo, 1950.

Tsuru, Shigeto. "Employment in Japan: Problems and Prospects," *Far Eastern Survey,* XXVI (July, 1957), 97-103.

Ushimaru, Yoshitome. "Progress in Social Security," *Contemporary Japan,* XXIII, Nos. 10-12 (1955), 693-99.

Uyehara, Cecil H. "The Social Democratic Movement," *The Annals of the American Academy of Political and Social Science,* CCCVIII (November, 1956), 54-62.

Wages in Japan. Tokyo: The Daily Labour Press, 1954.

Yamanaka, Tokutaro. "On Latent Unemployment: An Interpretation as an Economic Problem," *The Annals of the Hitotsubashi Academy,* VI (April, 1956), 1-11.

Yane, Boris S. "Wages in Japanese Mining and Manufacturing," *Monthly Labor Review,* LXXVIII (May, 1955), 547-52.

Year Books of Labor Statistics. Tokyo: Division of Labor Statistics and Research, Ministry of Labor, 1952-1956.

JOURNALS, NEWSPAPERS, AND REVIEWS

Information Bulletin. Brussels: International Confederation of Free Trade Unions.

Industry and Labour. Geneva: International Labour Office.

International Labour Review. Geneva: International Labour Office.

JTUC Report. Tokyo: *Zenrō Kaigi (Japanese Trade Union Congress).* Mimeographed.

Japan Information. Washington: Embassy of Japan. Mimeographed.

Japan Report. Washington: Embassy of Japan. Mimeographed.

The Oriental Economist. Tokyo.

Sohyo News. Tokyo: *Sōhyō* (General Council of Trade Unions of Japan). Mimeographed.

Index

Abe Isoo, 61

Agricultural workers, unionism among, 68

Agriculture, 4, 7, 11, 16, 17-18, 21, 23. *See also* Land reform

Akahata, 28, 73

Alcohol and tobacco monopolies, 141

All-Communications Employees Union, 94

All-Japan Coordinated Council of General Workers, 105n

All-Japan Express Workers Union, 95n, 97

All-Japan Federation of Metal Mining Workers Unions, 95n

All-Japan Garrison Forces Labor Union, 95n

All-Japan Local and Municipal Government Workers Union, 94n

American Federation of Labor (AFL), 61, 62

Antisubversive legislation (1952), 78, 79n

Arbitration, 25, 114, 138, 151-52, 153; compulsory, 139, 142n, 144, 150; voluntary, 25, 151, 152, 153. *See also* Labor Relations Adjustment Law, Public Corporation and National Enterprise Labor Relations Law

Assistance to Japan, American, 15, 83

Association for the Study of Social-

ism. *See Shakai Shugi Kenkyūkai*

"Austerity" program, 11, 15, 83, 118, 160, 172

Automobile workers, 82, 88n, 95, 132

Bolshevists. *See* Communism, Communists

Boycotts, 134

Buddhism. *See* Religions

"Business" unionism, 26, 61, 62, 102. *See also* Gompersism

Central employment security council, 166. *See also* Unemployment insurance

Central Labor Relations Commission (CLRC), 73n, 80, 111n, 132n, 148. *See also* Labor relations commissions

Chemical workers, unionism among, 69, 82, 83, 95, 123

Civil servants. *See* Government employees

Codetermination, 102, 122

Cold war, 23, 26, 29, 48, 72, 80, 175

Collective bargaining, 58, 85, 99-100, 108-27, 157, 158, 171, 180-81, 184; among government employees, 27, 125, 140-45; "appropriate" units for, 142-43; industry-wide, 51, 110; issues in, 115-23, 126, 171-73; ma-

191

ICFTU (International Confederation of Free Trade Unions),
74-75, 81, 82, 83, 85, 86-88
"Imperial Polity." *See* Emperor
system
Individualism, 36, 175
Industrial relations, definition of,
vii; method of analyzing, viii-x
Industrial relations specialists, in
management, 31, 43n, 46-53, 54-
55, 56, 57, 176; relations with
unions, 55, 111, 113, 127. *See
also* Management
Industrial structure, 6-9, 102
Industrial Workers of the World,
62
Industrialization, 1, 16-21, 32-35,
36, 40, 44, 46, 47, 57, 102, 103,
175, 176
Inflation, 10-11, 27, 48, 63, 75,
102, 116, 117, 135, 160, 172.
See also "Austerity" program,
Dodge Plan
International Confederation of Free
Trade Unions. *See* ICFTU
International Cooperation Adminis-
tration, U.S. *See* Foreign Opera-
tions Administration, U.S.
International Labor Organization
(ILO), 25, 63, 157
Iwai Akira, 84, 85

Japan Coal Miners Union. *See*
Miners
Japan Communist Party, 79n, 81n,
84n, 86, 97
Japan Congress of Trade Unions.
See Zenrō Kaigi
Japan Council of National and
Local Government Workers
Unions. *See Kankōrō*
Japan Express Company, 110
Japan Federation of Employers'
Associations. *See Nikkeiren*
Japan Federation of Iron and Steel
Industry Workers Unions. *See*
Steel workers
Japan Federation of Synthetic

Chemical Workers Union. *See*
Chemical workers
Japan General Federation of Pri-
vate Railway Workers Union.
See Railway workers
Japan ILO Association, 114
Japan Labor Federation. *See Sōdō-
mei*
Japan Teachers Union. *See* Teach-
ers
Japanese Chamber of Commerce
and Industry. *See* Employer
associations
Japanese Congress of Labor Unions
(*Nihon Rōdō Kumiai Kaigi*), 71
Japanese Council of Labor Unions
(*Nihon Rōdō Kumiai Hyōgikai*),
64, 65
Japanese Federation of Labor. *See
Sōdōmei*
Japanese Productivity Center, 115,
122
Japanese Seamen's Union. *See* Sea-
men
Japanese Trade Union Congress.
See Zenrō Kaigi
Jo Tsunetaro, 61
Joint consultation, 47, 49, 58, 62,
65, 111, 112, 115, 120, 121,
122, 126, 171, 181

Kankōrō (*Nihon Kankōchō Rōdō
Kumiai Kyōgikai*), 94. *See also*
Government employees
Kantō Employers Association. *See*
Employer associations
Katayama Sen, 61, 62
Keidanren (*Keiei Dantai Rengō-
kai*), 51-52, 115. *See also* Em-
ployer associations
Korean War, 11, 28, 76-77, 83,
116, 133
Kotoku Shusui, 62
Kyōchōkai. See Harmonization
Society

LRAL. *See* Labor Relations Adjustment Law